IF IGNORANCE IS BLISS, WHY AREN'T THERE MORE HAPPY PEOPLE?

JOHN LLOYD is the producer of the hit British comedy shows *Not the Nine O'Clock News*, *Blackadder*, and *Spitting Image*. He earned a lifetime achievement award from the British Academy of Film and Television Arts (BAFTA).

JOHN MITCHINSON is a former publisher and bookseller who now writes for the British television show *QI* (Quite Interesting).

Praise for previous QI books:

'Trivia buffs and know-it-alls alike will exult to find so much repeatable wisdom gathered in one place.' *New York Times*

'Eye-watering, eyebrow-raising, terrific . . . Such fine and creative research genuinely deserves to be captured in print.' *Daily Mail*

'Lloyd and Mitchinson dare to ask questions I stopped asking when I supposedly learned to know better.' *Associated Press*

A Quite Interesting Book

If Ignorance Is Bliss, Why Aren't There More Happy People?

QUOTES FOR INTERESTING TIMES

John Lloyd and John Mitchinson

faber and faber

First published as *Advanced Banter* in 2008
by Faber and Faber Ltd
Bloomsbury House
74–77 Great Russell Street
London WC1B 3DA
This export paperback edition first published in 2010

Typeset by Palindrome
Printed in England by CPI Bookmarque, Croydon
All rights reserved
© QI Ltd, 2008

Additional research by James Harkin, Molly Oldfield and Xander Cansell

The right of QI Ltd to be identified as author of this work
has been asserted in accordance with Section 77
of the Copyright, Designs and Patents Act 1988

A CIP record for this book
is available from the British Library

ISBN 978-0-571-25484-2

2 4 6 8 10 9 7 5 3 1

CONTENTS

*Composers Computers Consciousness Conversation
Cosmology Courage Cows Creation Creativity Crime
Criticism Crying Curiosity*

*Daffodils Dancing Danger Dating Daughters Death
Decisions Democracy Desire Desperation Destiny
Diamonds Diaries Dictators Dieting Differences Difficulty
Diplomacy Discoveries Divorce Doctors Dogs Doubt
Drawing Dreams Drink Drugs Drunks Duty*

*Ears Earth Economics Education Effort Eggs Ego
Electricity Encouragement Ends Enemies England
Enlightenment Enthusiasm Equality Events Evil
Evolution Excuses Exercise Experience Expressions Eyes*

*Faces Facts Failure Faith Fame Families Fashion Fathers
Fear Fish Flowers Food Football Forgetfulness Forgiveness
Freedom Free Speech Free Will Friendship Fun Future*

*Gardening Genius Geometry Giving God Gods Golf
Goodness Gossip Government Grass Gravity Greatness
Greeks*

*Habit Hands Happiness Hatred Heaven Hell Historians
History Honesty Hope Housework Human Beings
Human Body Human Nature Humility Humour*

*Ideas Idleness Ignorance Illness Imagination Impossibility
Insignificance Inspiration Integrity Intelligence
Interestingness Internet Intuition Inventions Investments*

PROLOGUE

Stephen Fry

They say that Samuel Taylor Coleridge was the last person to read everything. By the time he died there were now too many books, they suggest, for any one single brain to engage with. 'They', as usual, are wrong. There were already millions of books in Europe by the year 1500, just half a century after the first printed page flew from the first press. To read a million books in a lifetime you would have to read forty a day for seventy years. I couldn't even manage half that amount for half as long with cigarettes before giving up and it takes a lot longer to read a book than to smoke a cigarette, let me tell you.

Philosophers, wits, novelists, cooks, poets, essayists, herbalists, mathematicians, builders, poets and divines had poured out more thoughts in that first fifty years than had been committed to paper or vellum in the previous thousand. And the rate only continued to increase as it approached this century's dizzyingly insane levels of oversupply. With so much flowing from so many different human brains, who can be arsed to read it? Not I, sir and madam, not I. It's all I can do to peruse the side of a packet of breakfast cereal without distraction from radio, television and phone. I have no doubt you are in the same case. You would dearly like to suck intellectual and meta-physical juice from the fruity flesh of the world's best thinkers and writers but the treetops are all out of reach and it would be too much of a fag to go and fetch a ladder. If only someone would pick, pulp and squeeze that fruit for you, you have been thinking – not the usual anthologisers, but those splendid elves from the Quite Interesting team, the fruits of whose labours are offered with such satisfying and repetitive regularity on the BBC and channels Dave, Mike, Pete, Steve and Neville.

Your wish has been answered in the quote interesting volume even now stuffed up your pullover as you streak for the bookshop's security barrier. There has never been a collection like it. Look in vain for the obvious, the banal and the platitudinous. On every page you will marvel at 'what oft was thought but ne'er so well expressed'.

And you can quote me.

Biarritz, Dublin and Hell

PROVERB

Alan Davies

A small pie is soon eaten.

PREAMBLE

John Lloyd and John Mitchinson

Before you settle down, we have a confession to make. We love quotations. Not like, admire or retain a residual fondness for. We love them with a deep, never-to-be-fully-sated passion – the passion of men who spend too long cooped up indoors, burrowing through books and staring at screens. Quotations are our catnip. The more we have, the more we want.

There's an old craftsman's saw: 'If the other fellow can do it better, let him.' That's how we feel about quotations. They are the best bits of the best minds, the records of the funniest, truest, wisest and most memorable things anyone has ever said. A good quotation is a keyhole view of a boundless universe, like one of those windows called 'squints' in medieval cathedrals through which only the altar is visible.

Using quotations isn't a mark of cowardice, inarticulacy or false modesty. It's a demonstration of what sets us humans apart: our ability to learn from one another, to share, to talk and to remember. As you'll discover, there are people who exist only on the pages of quotation books, whose life and work has evaporated completely leaving behind just one or two tiny puddles of wisdom. Indeed, the strange and magical process by which we all seem to find the same things interesting also works for quotations. As Elias Canetti put it: 'The great writers of aphorisms read as if they had all known each other well.'

So, don't be expecting a reference book. It might look like one, but it's really a manifesto. It could have been ten times longer but we have forced ourselves to keep only the ones we couldn't live without, and then – painfully – to put them in some kind of order. Whether it's punch-the-air exactness of thought ('Erotica is using a feather, pornography is using the whole chicken,' Isabel Allende), subversive humour ('Everywhere I go I'm asked if I think the university stifles writers. My opinion is that they don't stifle enough of them,' Flannery O'Connor) or unexpected, disarming honesty ('I love those decadent wenches who do so trouble my dreams,' Rembrandt), every quote has fought to justify its inclusion here.

As for how you use it, all we'll say is that you can't have a conversation on your own. Banter is not a solitary activity. And quotations are the hard currency of banter. Whether you hoard them like shiny sovereigns in your pocket, or rub them like rabbits' feet in times of need, they are yours to do with what you will.

Time to let you judge for yourself. In the immortal words of Spike Milligan, 'We can't stand around here doing nothing, people will think we are workmen.'

Quotations will tell the full measure of meaning –
if you have enough of them.

JAMES MURRAY Editor of the *Oxford English Dictionary* 1879–1915

A

Acting

Man is a make-believe animal – he is never so truly himself as when he is acting a part.
WILLIAM HAZLITT

The question actors most often get asked is how they can bear saying the same things over and over again, night after night, but God knows the answer to that is, don't we all anyway; might as well get paid for it.
RICHARD BRINSLEY SHERIDAN 'Sherry' (as Byron called him) was at least as famous as an orator as a playwright. The poet would later recall how 'he talked and we listened, without one yawn, from six till one in the morning'.

Acting is not about dressing up. Acting is about stripping bare. The whole essence of learning lines is to forget them so you can make them sound like you thought of them that instant.
GLENDA JACKSON

It is not whether you really cry. It's whether the audience thinks you are crying.
INGRID BERGMAN

I made some mistakes in drama. I thought the drama was when the actors cried. But drama is when the audience cries.
FRANK CAPRA

When I played drunks I had to remain sober because I didn't know how to play them when I was drunk.
RICHARD BURTON

If you want to be an actor, my advice is to learn your lines and don't bump into the other actors.
CARY GRANT

I only have two acting styles: with and without a horse.
ROBERT MITCHUM

The part never calls for nudity, and I've never used that excuse. The box office calls for it.
HELEN MIRREN

I don't mind that I'm fat. You still get the same money.
MARLON BRANDO

Action

If we did all the things we are capable of doing, we would literally astonish ourselves.
THOMAS EDISON

The truth of the matter is, we always know the right thing to do. The hard part is doing it.
NORMAN SCHWARZKOPF

The great end of life is not knowledge but action.
T. H. HUXLEY

Never retreat. Never explain. Get it done and let them howl.
BENJAMIN JOWETT

I look for what needs to be done. After all, that's how the universe designs itself.
R. BUCKMINSTER FULLER

You must do the thing you think you cannot do.
ELEANOR ROOSEVELT

What we think, or what we know, or what we believe is, in the end, of little consequence. The only consequence is what we do.
JOHN RUSKIN

My personal philosophy is not to undertake a project unless it is manifestly important and nearly impossible.
EDWIN LAND Inventor of the Polaroid camera in 1947.

To get something done, a committee should consist of no more than three people, two of whom are absent.
ROBERT COPELAND

Regret for the things we did can be tempered by time; it is regret for the things we did not do that is inconsolable.
SYDNEY J. HARRIS Author of the 'Strictly Personal' column for the *Chicago Daily News*. Appeared on the infamous 1971 list of Nixon's enemies (along with Edwin Land, among many others).

Think like a man of action; act like a man of thought.
HENRI BERGSON

Adventure

In every man's heart there is anchored a little schooner.
HENRY MILLER

The distinguishing mark of true adventures, is that it is often no fun at all while they are actually happening.
KIM STANLEY ROBINSON

An inconvenience is only an adventure wrongly considered; an adventure is only an inconvenience rightly considered.
G. K. CHESTERTON

Adventure is just bad planning.
ROALD AMUNDSEN

Advertising

Advertisement is the rich asking for more money.
G. K. CHESTERTON

Many a small thing has been made large by the right kind of advertising.
MARK TWAIN

There will presently be no room in the world for things; it will be filled up with the advertisements of things.
WILLIAM DEAN HOWELLS

The superior man understands what is right; the inferior man understands what will sell.
CONFUCIUS He wrote nothing himself: like Socrates' dialogues, his *Analects* were gathered and retold by his disciples in the centuries following his death in 479 BC.

Introducing 'Lite' – The new way to spell 'Light', but with 20 per cent fewer letters.
JERRY SEINFELD

The only reason I made a commercial for American Express was to pay for my American Express bill.
PETER USTINOV

Let advertisers spend the same amount of money improving their product that they spend on advertising and they wouldn't have to advertise it.
WILL ROGERS

Doing business without advertising is like winking at a girl in the dark. You know what you are doing, but nobody else does.
STEUART HENDERSON BRITT One of the few ad men who was also a professor of psychology, author of the classic defence of consumer marketing, *The Spenders* (1960).

Advertising has annihilated the power of the most powerful adjectives.
PAUL VALÉRY

Advertising is the rattling of a stick inside a swill bucket.
GEORGE ORWELL

Historians and archaeologists will discover that the advertisements of our time are the richest and most faithful reflections that any society ever made of its entire range of activities.
MARSHALL McLUHAN

Advice

A word to the wise ain't necessary, it is the stupid ones who need all the advice.
BILL COSBY

Quit now, you'll never make it. If you disregard this advice, you'll be halfway there.
DAVID ZUCKER

Giving advice to a stupid man is like giving salt to a squirrel.
KASHMIRI PROVERB

No one wants advice – only corroboration.
JOHN STEINBECK

Advice is what we ask for when we already know the answer but wish we didn't.
ERICA JONG

Some people like my advice so much that they frame it upon the wall instead of using it.
GORDON R. DICKSON Canadian-born sci-fi writer who described his books as 'laboratory pieces'. Before he died in 2001, he had written eighty, selling more than ten million copies.

The only thing to do with good advice is to pass it on. It is never of any use to oneself.
OSCAR WILDE

Never believe in anything until it has been officially denied.
OTTO VON BISMARCK

Never play cards with a man called Doc. Never eat in a place called Mom's. Never sleep with a woman whose troubles are worse than your own.
NELSON ALGREN Quoted in *Newsweek* in July 1956 soon after the publication of the American translation of Simone de Beauvoir's novel *The Mandarins*, which revealed details of their torrid affair.

Never take the advice of someone who has not had your kind of trouble.
SYDNEY J. HARRIS

It is a little embarrassing that, after forty-five years of research and study, the best advice I can give to people is to be a little kinder to each other.
ALDOUS HUXLEY

Do not think of your faults, still less of other's faults; look for what is good and strong, and try to imitate it. Your faults will drop off, like dead leaves, when their time comes.
JOHN RUSKIN

Don't sweat the petty things and don't pet the sweaty things.
GEORGE CARLIN

Never look back unless you are planning to go that way.
HENRY DAVID THOREAU

Never read by candlelight anything smaller than the ace of clubs.
SIR HENRY HALFORD

Don't try to solve serious matters in the middle of the night.
PHILIP K. DICK

Always serve too much hot fudge sauce on hot fudge sundaes. It makes people overjoyed, and puts them in your debt.
JUDITH OLNEY

Never put anything on paper, my boy, and never trust a man with a small black moustache.
P. G. WODEHOUSE

Afterlife

Strange is it not? that of the myriads who
Before us pass'd the Door of darkness through,

Not one returns to tell us of the Road,
Which to discover, we must travel too.
OMAR KHAYYAM His *Rubaiyat* (about 1120) is heavily influenced by sentiments of
its Victorian translator, Edward FitzGerald. A shame, as Khayyam himself is also
credited with solving quadratic equations and suggesting the Earth revolved on its
axis while circling the sun.

We do not know what to do with this short life, yet we yearn for
another that will be eternal.
ANATOLE FRANCE

We have no reliable guarantee that the afterlife will be any less
exasperating than this one, have we?
NOËL COWARD

If there is a sin against life, it consists perhaps not so much in
despairing of life as in hoping for another life and in eluding the
implacable grandeur of this life.
ALBERT CAMUS

The yearning for an afterlife is the opposite of selfish: it is love and
praise for the world that we are privileged, in this complex interval of
light, to witness and experience.
JOHN UPDIKE

The primary question about life after death is not whether it is a fact,
but even if it is, what problems that really solves.
LUDWIG WITTGENSTEIN

Age

There is still no cure for the common birthday.
JOHN GLENN

Age is something that doesn't matter, unless you are a cheese.
LUIS BUÑUEL

When I turned two I was really anxious, because I'd doubled my age in
a year. I thought, if this keeps up, by the time I'm 6 I'll be 90.
STEVEN WRIGHT

When I grow up I want to be a little boy.
JOSEPH HELLER

When I was ten, I read fairy tales in secret. Now that I am 50 I read
them openly. When I became a man I put away childish things,

including the fear of childishness.
C. S. LEWIS

It is sobering to consider that when Mozart was my age he had already been dead for a year.
TOM LEHRER

Very few people do anything creative after the age of 35. The reason is that very few people do anything creative before the age of 35.
JOEL HILDEBRAND Pioneer chemist and centenarian who discovered that adding helium to oxygen could overcome the problem of the bends in divers.

She said she was approaching 40, and I couldn't help wondering from what direction.
BOB HOPE

When I was young, people used to say to me: Wait until you're 50, you'll see. I am 50. I haven't seen anything.
ERIC SATIE Dadaist and the father of ambient music, who lived until he was 59. Less well-known compositions include *Three Dried-Up Embryos* (1913) and *Flabby Preludes for a Dog* (1913).

You must not pity me because my sixtieth year finds me still astonished. To be astonished is one of the surest ways of not growing old too quickly.
COLETTE

One starts to get young at the age 60 and then it's too late.
PABLO PICASSO

The years between 50 and 70 are the hardest. You are always being asked to do things, and yet you are not decrepit enough to turn them down.
T. S. ELIOT

When you hit 70 you sleep sounder, you feel more alive than when you were 30. Obviously it's healthier to have women on your mind than on your knees.
MAURICE CHEVALIER

At 73 I learned a little about the real structure of animals, plants, birds, fishes and insects. Consequently when I am 80 I'll have made more progress. At 90 I'll have penetrated the mystery of things. At 100 I shall have reached something marvellous, but when I am 110 everything I do, the smallest dot, will be alive.
HOKUSAI The great Japanese artist died at 89 but didn't start work on his masterpiece, *Thirty-six Views of Mount Fuji*, until 1826, when he was in his late sixties.

If you can eat a boiled egg in England at 90, they think you deserve a Nobel Prize.
ALAN BENNETT

You can live to be 100 if you give up all the things that make you want to live to be 100.
WOODY ALLEN

If I'd known I was going to live this long, I'd have taken better care of myself.
EUBIE BLAKE Ragtime pianist and composer who died in 1983 aged 100, having made his first recording in 1917.

I've never known a person to live to 110 or more, and then die, to be remarkable for anything else.
JOSH BILLINGS

Growing old – it's not nice, but it's interesting.
AUGUST STRINDBERG

Old age isn't so bad when you consider the alternative.
MAURICE CHEVALIER

I don't feel old. I don't feel anything till noon. That's when it's time for my nap.
BOB HOPE

Inside every older woman is a young girl wondering what the hell happened.
CORA HARVEY ARMSTRONG

I'm at an age when my back goes out more than I do.
PHYLLIS DILLER

Old people shouldn't eat health foods. They need all the preservatives they can get.
ROBERT ORBEN

I do not ask to be young again; all I want is to go on getting older.
KONRAD ADENAUER

Aliens

To consider the Earth the only populated world in infinite space is as absurd as to assert that in an entire field sown with millet only one grain will grow.
METRODORUS OF CHIOS He believed, like his teacher Democritus, that

everything was made from atoms. He also thought stars were made fresh each morning from the action of the sun on moisture in the air.

Sometimes I think we're alone. Sometimes I think we're not. In either case, the thought is staggering.
R. BUCKMINSTER FULLER

Where is everybody?
ENRICO FERMI The Nobel Prize-winning inventor of the nuclear reactor in 1950 as he formulated what became known as the Fermi Paradox: if the universe is full of potentially inhabited planets, why haven't we heard from any of them?

Sometimes I think the surest sign that intelligent life exists elsewhere in the universe is that none of it has tried to contact us.
BILL WATTERSON Creator of the Calvin and Hobbes comic strip which ran from 1985 to 1995. The characters were named after the sixteenth-century theologian and seventeenth-century philosopher respectively.

If it's true that our species is alone in the universe, then I'd have to say the universe aimed rather low and settled for very little.
GEORGE CARLIN

UFOs are better explained in terms of the unknown irrationalities of terrestrial beings rather than by any unknown rationalities of extra-terrestrial beings.
RICHARD FEYNMAN

Ambition

Like dogs in a wheel, birds in a cage or squirrels in a chain, ambitious men still climb and climb, with great labour, and incessant anxiety, but never reach the top.
ROBERT BROWNING

I long to accomplish a great and noble task; but it is my chief duty to accomplish small tasks as if they were great and noble.
HELEN KELLER

All rising to great place is by a winding stair.
FRANCIS BACON

At the age of 6 I wanted to be a cook. At 7 I wanted to be Napoleon. And my ambition has been growing steadily ever since.
SALVADOR DALÍ

I hope that the ambitious realize they are more likely to succeed with success as opposed to failure.
GEORGE W. BUSH From an interview with Associated Press, 18 January 2001.

America

What would this country be, without this great land of ours?
RONALD REAGAN

America is a mistake, a giant mistake!
SIGMUND FREUD

The trouble with America is that there are far too many wide-open spaces surrounded by teeth.
CHARLES LUCKMAN Known as the 'Boy Wonder of American business' when he was appointed president of Pepsodent Toothpaste in 1939 at the age of 30. In 1950 he resigned to become an architect, designing the NASA space centre at Houston, Texas in 1965.

The United States is like the guy at the party who gives cocaine to everybody and still nobody likes him.
JIM SAMUELS

The three great American vices seem to be efficiency, punctuality, and the desire for achievement and success. They are the things that make the Americans so unhappy and so nervous.
LIN YUTANG He produced the first workable Chinese typewriter in 1946 and the landmark *Chinese-English Dictionary of Modern Usage* in 1972.

A citizen of America will cross the ocean to fight for democracy, but won't cross the street to vote in a national election.
BILL VAUGHAN Folksy columnist in the *Kansas City Star* for thirty-one years.

I have no further use for America. I wouldn't go back there if Jesus Christ was President.
CHARLIE CHAPLIN

What a pity, when Christopher Colombus discovered America, that he ever mentioned it.
MARGOT ASQUITH The outspoken, free-spirited aristocratic wife of Herbert Asquith, the Liberal Prime Minister of Britain from 1908 to 1916.

Of course, America had often been discovered before, but it had always been hushed up.
OSCAR WILDE

America is a large friendly dog in a small room. Every time it wags its tail it knocks over a chair.
ARNOLD TOYNBEE

American women expect to find in their husbands a perfection that English women only hope to find in their butlers.
W. SOMERSET MAUGHAM

America . . . just a nation of two hundred million used car salesmen with all the money we need to buy guns and no qualms about killing anybody else in the world who tries to make us uncomfortable.
HUNTER S. THOMPSON

I am America. I am the part you won't recognize, but get used to me. Black, confident, cocky – my name, not yours. My religion, not yours. My goals, my own. Get used to me.
MUHAMMAD ALI

There's nothing wrong with this country that we couldn't cure by turning it over to the police for a couple of weeks.
GEORGE WALLACE Segregationist Governor of Alabama speaking in 1967. In the late 1970s he became a born-again Christian and renounced his former racism.

Never criticise Americans. They have the best taste that money can buy.
MILES KINGTON

American Cities

I have just returned from Boston. It is the only sane thing to do if you find yourself up there.
FRED ALLEN

I'd move to Los Angeles if New Zealand and Australia were swallowed up by a tidal wave, if there was a bubonic plague in England and if the continent of Africa disappeared from some Martian attack.
RUSSELL CROWE

Miami Beach is where neon goes to die.
LENNY BRUCE

On my first day in New York a guy asked me if I knew where Central Park was. When I told him I didn't he said, 'Do you mind if I mug you here?'
PAUL MERTON

I once spent a year in Philadelphia. It think it was on a Sunday.
W. C. FIELDS

Washington is a city of southern efficiency and northern charm.
JOHN F. KENNEDY

Anger

Anger is a wind which blows out the lamp of the mind.
ROBERT GREEN INGERSOLL

It is a waste of energy to be angry with a man who behaves badly, just as it is to be angry with a car that won't go.
BERTRAND RUSSELL

Anger is the only thing to put off till tomorrow.
CZECH PROVERB

It's practically impossible to look at a penguin and feel angry.
JOE MOORE Main news anchorman on Hawaii's most popular television station KHON-TV since 1969. Has appeared in both *Hawaii Five-O* and *Magnum P.I.*

Count up the days in which you have not been angry. I used to get angry every day, then every other day, then every three or four days. If you manage not to be angry for as long as thirty days, offer a sacrifice of thanksgiving to God.
EPICTETUS

When angry, count ten before you speak; if very angry, an hundred.
THOMAS JEFFERSON

There is another man within me that is angry with me.
C. S. LEWIS

Holding on to anger is like grasping a hot coal with the intent of throwing it at someone else; you are the one who gets burned.
BUDDHA

How much more grievous are the consequences of anger than the causes of it.
MARCUS AURELIUS

Speak when you are angry and you will make the best speech you will ever regret.
AMBROSE BIERCE

Whatever is begun in anger ends in shame.
BENJAMIN FRANKLIN

Let us not look back in anger or forward in fear, but around in awareness.
JAMES THURBER

Animals

I think that I could turn and live with animals, they are so placid and
self-contain'd;
I stand and look at them long and long.
They do not sweat and whine about their condition;
They do not lie awake in the dark and weep for their sins;
They do not make me sick discussing their duty to God;
Not one is dissatisfied – not one is demented by the mania of owning
things;
Not one kneels to another, nor to his kind that lived thousands of years
ago;
Not one is respectable or industrious over the whole earth.
WALT WHITMAN

There is no beast without cruelty.
FRIEDRICH NIETZSCHE

Animals are not brethren, they are not underlings; they are other
nations, caught with ourselves in the net of life and time.
HENRY BESTON

Pigs are not corrupted by the Higher Imperialism. Tigers have no
spiritual pride. Whales never sneer. Crocodiles are not (despite a
pleasing legend) in the least hypocritical. On examining their exterior,
it is difficult to understand why anyone ever gave them credit for so
vivacious and ingenious a quality. The worst sins of all are the purely
human sins.
G. K. CHESTERTON

Man is the only animal that blushes. Or needs to.
MARK TWAIN

Man is the only animal that can remain on friendly terms with the
victims he intends to eat until he eats them.
SAMUEL BUTLER

Man is the only animal whose existence is a problem that he has to solve.
ERICH FROMM

Humans are the only animals that have children on purpose with the
exception of guppies, who like to eat theirs.
P. J. O'ROURKE

What differentiates man from other animals is perhaps feeling rather
than reason. I have seen a cat reason more often than laugh or weep.

Perhaps it laughs or reasons within itself – but then perhaps within itself a crab solves equations of the second degree.
MIGUEL DE UNAMUNO

I believe that animals have feelings and other states of consciousness but neither I nor anyone else has been able to prove it. We can't even prove that other people are conscious, much less other animals.
PROFESSOR JOSEPH LEDOUX Professor of Neuroscience at New York University and member of the science-rock band, The Amygdaloids.

All the ingenious men, and all the scientific men, and all the imaginative men in the world could never invent, if all their wits were boiled into one, anything so curious and so ridiculous as the lobster.
CHARLES KINGSLEY

Ants are so much like human beings as to be an embarrassment. They farm fungi, raise aphids as livestock, launch armies into war, use chemical sprays to alarm and confuse enemies, capture slaves, engage in child labour, exchange information ceaselessly. They do everything but watch television.
LEWIS THOMAS

How be it that I clean my mouth with salt every day, yet all the people living in the United Netherlands are not as many as the living animals I carry in my mouth?
ANTONIE VAN LEEUWENHOEK He kept his new technique for making lenses secret, thus ensuring his subsequent fame as the father of microbiology. His lenses revealed both bacteria and sperm for the first time.

The fox knows many things; the hedgehog, one big thing.
ERASMUS

A winkle is just a bogey with a crash helmet on.
MICK MILLER

If a swamp alligator could talk, it would sound like Tennessee Williams.
REX REED

I suppose nobody has ever been struck a direct blow by a rabbit. At least, not *deliberately.*
SIR WILLIAM CONNOR Left-wing journalist who wrote the Cassandra column in the *Daily Mirror* from 1935 until his death in 1967.

It is a ravening beast, feigning itself gentle and tame, but being touched it biteth deep, and poisoneth deadly. It beareth a cruel mind,

desiring to hurt anything, neither is there any creature it loveth.
EDWARD TOPSELL On the shrew in *A History of Four-Footed Beasts* (1607).

Did you know that squirrels are the Devil's oven mitts?
MISS PIGGY

Antarctica

First you fall in love with Antarctica, and then it breaks your heart.
KIM STANLEY ROBINSON

The land looks like a fairytale.
ROALD AMUNDSEN

Great God! This is an awful place.
CAPTAIN ROBERT FALCON SCOTT

In Antarctica you get to know people so well that in comparison you do not seem to know the people in civilisation at all.
APSLEY CHERRY-GARRARD The youngest member of Scott's ill-fated 1910–13 expedition to the Pole, he wrote the classic first-hand account, *The Worst Journey in the World* (1922), a title suggested by his friend and neighbour, George Bernard Shaw.

Anxiety

The most anxious man in the prison is the governor.
GEORGE BERNARD SHAW

Anxiety is fear of oneself.
WILHELM STEKEL

Anxiety is a thin stream of fear trickling through the mind. If encouraged, it cuts a channel into which all other thoughts are drained.
ARTHUR ROCHE

Anxiety is the handmaiden of creativity.
CHUCK JONES Legendary animator and director, responsible for many of Bugs Bunny and Daffy Duck's finest moments.

I have never known a man who died from overwork, but many who died from doubt.
DR CHARLES MAYO

I don't have big anxieties. I wish I did. I'd be much more interesting.
ROY LICHTENSTEIN

Apathy

Science may have found a cure for most evils; but it has found no remedy for the worst of them all – the apathy of human beings.
HELEN KELLER

Do not fear your enemies. The worst they can do is kill you. Do not fear friends. At worst, they may betray you. Fear those who do not care; they neither kill nor betray, but betrayal and murder exist because of their silent consent.
BRUNO JASIENSKI Polish Jew and author of the futurist anti-capitalist novel *I Burn Paris* (1929). He moved to Moscow in 1932 and supported the purges against fellow writers, only to fall victim to them himself in 1938.

The world is not dangerous because of those who do harm but because of those who look at it without doing anything.
ALBERT EINSTEIN

Apes

It is curious how there seems to be an instinctive disgust in Man for his nearest ancestors and relations. If only Darwin could conscientiously have traced man back to the Elephant or the Lion or the Antelope, how much ridicule and prejudice would have been spared to the doctrine of Evolution.
HENRY HAVELOCK ELLIS Wrote on sex, despite being a virgin until the age of 60, when he became aroused by watching a woman urinate. He was also a eugenicist, a pioneer of the 'open marriage', and coined the word 'homosexual'.

I would rather be the offspring of two apes than be a man and afraid to face the truth.
T. H. HUXLEY

Those who run to the apes to explain our behaviour are chuckle-heads too dumb to know their arse from a hole-in-the-ground.
W. H. AUDEN

It is even harder for the average ape to believe that he has descended from man.
H. L. MENCKEN

Apples

With an apple I will astonish Paris.
PAUL CÉZANNE

To me apples are fruit. To Cézanne they were mountains.
DAVID SMITH Abstract expressionist famous for his large steel installations.

An apple is an excellent thing – until you have tried a peach.
GEORGE DU MAURIER

Any fool can count the seeds in an apple. Only God can count all the apples in one seed.
ROBERT H. SCHULLER

The God of the Christians is a father who is a great deal more concerned about his apples than he is about his children.
DENIS DIDEROT

Architecture

A doctor can bury his mistakes but an architect can only advise his client to plant vines.
FRANK LLOYD WRIGHT

Don't look at buildings: watch them.
JOHN RUSKIN

Buildings are my dolls.
FREDERICK THE GREAT

Architecture is frozen music.
GANOPATI STHAPAT

Architecture is inhabited sculpture.
CONSTANTIN BRANCUSI

All architecture is great architecture after sunset; perhaps architecture is really a nocturnal art, like the art of fireworks.
G. K. CHESTERTON

A chair is a very difficult object. A skyscraper is almost easier. That is why Chippendale is famous.
LUDWIG MIES VAN DER ROHE

Everywhere in the world, music enhances a hall with one exception: Carnegie Hall enhances the music.
ISAAC STERN

A building has integrity just like a man. And just as seldom.
AYN RAND Controversial Russian-born US philosopher and novelist, whose books continue to sell in their hundreds of thousands and whose philosophical creed of

Objectivism has influenced people as diverse as Alan Greenspan, Hugh Hefner and Jimmy Wales, the founder of Wikipedia.

To you, to me, Stonehenge and Chartres Cathedral are works by the same Old Man under different names: we know what He did, what, even He thought He thought, but we don't see why.
W. H. AUDEN

The Parthenon is really only a farmyard over which someone put a roof; colonnades and sculptures were added because there were people in Athens who happened to be working and wanted to express themselves.
PABLO PICASSO

Ruins are the most persistent form of architecture.
JOSEPH BRODSKY

It looks like a typewriter full of oyster shells; like a broken Pyrex casserole dish in a brown cardboard box.
CLIVE JAMES

In my experience, if you have to keep the lavatory door shut by extending your leg, it's modern architecture.
NANCY BANKS-SMITH

I declare this thing open, whatever it is.
PRINCE PHILIP On opening the new east wing of Vancouver City Hall in 1970.

Arguments

Argument is the worst sort of conversation.
JONATHAN SWIFT

Discussion is an exchange of knowledge; argument an exchange of ignorance.
ROBERT QUILLEN He wrote droll pieces about his home town of Fountain Inn, South Carolina, that were syndicated all over America in the early decades of the twentieth century.

The aim of argument, or of discussion, should not be victory, but progress.
JOSEPH JOUBERT

In most instances, all an argument proves is that two people are present.
TONY PETITO Listed everywhere against this one quote, with no other details provided, he might be an Arts Administrator in New Jersey, the founding Artistic Director

of Singapore Repertory Theatre or a singer in an *a cappella* group on Long Island.

No matter what side of an argument you're on, you always find some people on your side that you wish were on the other side.
JASCHA HEIFETZ

Art

In art there is only one thing that counts: the bit that cannot be explained.
GEORGES BRAQUE

The purpose of art is to lay bare the questions which have been hidden by the answers.
JAMES BALDWIN

I shut my eyes in order to see.
PAUL GAUGUIN

I invent nothing. I rediscover.
AUGUSTE RODIN

A work of art is useless. So is a flower.
OSCAR WILDE

I am following Nature without being able to grasp her – I perhaps owe having become a painter to flowers.
CLAUDE MONET

The position of the artist is humble. He is essentially a channel.
PIET MONDRIAN

Art happens – no hovel is safe from it, no prince may depend upon it, the vastest intelligence cannot bring it about.
JAMES McNEILL WHISTLER

A painter who has the feel of breasts and buttocks is saved.
PIERRE-AUGUSTE RENOIR

Every child is an artist. The problem is how to remain an artist once he grows up.
PABLO PICASSO

Modern art is what happens when painters stop looking at girls and persuade themselves they have a better idea.
JOHN CIARDI Famous for his word histories on US National Public Radio's *Morning Edition*.

The aim of art is not to represent the outward appearance of things, but their inward significance.
ARISTOTLE

Art disturbs, science reassures.
GEORGES BRAQUE

Art is the only way to run away without leaving home.
TWYLA THARP

Art is a collaboration between God and the artist, and the less the artist does the better.
ANDRÉ GIDE

The naked truth about me is to the naked truth about Salvador Dalí as an old ukelele in an attic is to a piano in a tree, and I mean a piano with breasts.
JAMES THURBER

Art is not a mirror with which to reflect the world, but a hammer with which to shape it.
VLADIMIR MAYAKOVSKY

Impressionism is the newspaper of the soul.
HENRI MATISSE

There's not a different set of rules for the artists than for other people. Artists are shit compared to people. Art is the coward's way out, I think. If you put what you put into art into other people, you'd have a much fuller, more brilliant life.
DAMIEN HIRST

Art is whatever you can get away with.
JOHN CAGE

If that's art, I'm a Hottentot.
HARRY S. TRUMAN

Artichokes

One of the earth's monstrosities.
PLINY THE ELDER

Life is like eating artichokes; you have got to go through so much to get so little.
THOMAS ALOYSIUS DORGAN Better known as the cartoonist 'TAD' whose strip in

the *New York Journal* from 1905 to 1929 helped popularise a host of slang expressions including '23 skiddoo', 'hard-boiled', 'dumb-bell', 'drug-store cowboy' and 'yes, we have no bananas'.

These things are just plain annoying. After all the trouble you go to, you get about as much actual 'food' out of eating an artichoke as you would from licking thirty or forty postage stamps. Have the shrimp cocktail instead.
MISS PIGGY

Artists

An artist cannot fail; it is a success to be one.
CHARLES HORTON COOLEY Inventor of the idea of 'the looking-glass self', which remains a cornerstone of modern social psychology.

A man is born an artist as a hippopotamus is born a hippopotamus; and you can no more make yourself one than you can make yourself a giraffe.
JOHN RUSKIN

God is really only another artist. He invented the giraffe, the elephant, the ant. He has no style. He just goes on trying other things.
PABLO PICASSO

You can't write a chord ugly enough to say what you want sometimes, so you have to rely on a giraffe filled with whipped cream.
FRANK ZAPPA

A happy man may be a successful bishop, dog-catcher, movie actor or sausage-monger, but no happy man ever produced a first-rate piece of painting, sculpture, music or literature.
G. J. NATHAN

To be an artist at all is like living in Switzerland during a world war.
TOM STOPPARD

The artist should never try to be popular. Rather the public should be more artistic.
OSCAR WILDE

To send light into the darkness of men's hearts – such is the duty of the artist.
ROBERT SCHUMANN

Astrology

The stars, as I have already stated, are attached to the world and not, as the man in the street thinks, assigned to each of us, shining in proportion to our individual lot.
PLINY THE ELDER

Astrology is a disease, not a science.
MOSES MAIMONIDES Also known by a Hebrew acrostic as the Rambam, a Jewish philosopher born into twelfth-century Cordoba who attempted to reconcile the rationalism of Aristotle with Jewish theology and Muslim philosophy and science.

A physician without astrology is like a pudding without fat.
NICHOLAS CULPEPER

That we can think of no mechanism for astrology is relevant but unconvincing. No mechanism was known, for example, for continental drift when it was proposed by Wegener. Nevertheless, we see that Wegener was right, and those who objected on the grounds of unavailable mechanism were wrong.
CARL SAGAN

Astronomy

I'm not very interested in other planets. I like them where they are, in the sky.
W. H. AUDEN

There are countless suns and countless earths all rotating around their suns. The countless worlds in the universe are no worse and no less inhabited than our Earth.
GIORDANO BRUNO

Damn the solar system! Bad light – planets too distant – pestered with comets – feeble contrivance – could make a better with great ease!
SYDNEY SMITH In a letter of 1807 parodying the irritable scepticism of his friend Francis Jeffrey, editor of the *Edinburgh Review*.

That the world is spherical, in the form of a perfect orb, is shown in the first place from its name, i.e. that people all call it an orb, but also from the evidence of the facts.
PLINY THE ELDER

Astronomy is thus a four-legged animal standing on sound and false observations at the front and false observations at the rear. Amazingly,

the beast can limp forward, and sometimes even gallop, from one
discovery to the next.
STEPHEN JAY GOULD

Atheism

Among the repulsions of atheism for me has been its drastic uninterest-
ingness as an intellectual position. Where was the ingenuity, the
ambiguity, the humanity (in the Harvard sense) of saying that the
universe just happened to happen and that when we're dead we're dead?
JOHN UPDIKE

If there were no God, there would be no atheists.
G. K. CHESTERTON

I'm still an atheist, thank God.
LUIS BUÑUEL

We tell ourselves that God is dead, when what we mean is God is Dad,
and we wish him dead.
A. N. WILSON

He was an embittered atheist, the sort of atheist who does not so much
disbelieve in God as personally dislike Him.
GEORGE ORWELL

A little philosophy inclineth man's mind to atheism; but depth in
philosophy bringeth men's minds about to religion.
FRANCIS BACON From his essay *On Atheism* (1601).

Most physicists are not sufficiently interested in religion even to
qualify as practising atheists.
STEVEN WEINBERG

An atheist is a man who has no invisible means of support.
JOHN BUCHAN

The Glaswegian definition of an atheist: a bloke who goes to a
Rangers–Celtic match to watch the football.
SANDY STRANG

When I told the people of Northern Ireland that I was an atheist, a
woman in the audience stood up and said, 'Yes, but is it the God of the
Catholics or the God of the Protestants in whom you don't believe?'
QUENTIN CRISP

The equal toleration of all religions . . . is the same thing as atheism.
POPE LEO XIII

With most people unbelief in one thing is founded upon blind belief in another.
G. C. LICHTENBERG

Atoms

Nothing exists except atoms and empty space; everything else is opinion.
DEMOCRITUS OF ABDERA Also known as 'the Laughing Philosopher' because of his unfailingly cheerful outlook.

When it comes to atoms, language can only be used as in poetry.
NIELS BOHR

The atoms come together in different order and position, like the letters, which, though they are few, yet, by being placed together in different ways, produce innumerable words.
EPICURUS Atomist, like the earlier Democritus. He believed happiness was the highest good, better achieved by self-denial and the company of friends than through hedonistic self-indulgence.

Atoms cannot be proven to exist. They can never be seen or touched, and exist only in our imagination. They are things of thought.
ERNST MACH

The electron is not as simple as it looks.
SIR WILLIAM LAWRENCE BRAGG

It is probably as meaningless to discuss how much room an electron takes up as it is to discuss how much room a fear, an anxiety or an uncertainty takes up.
SIR JAMES JEANS

Attention

The capacity for delight is the gift of paying attention.
JULIA MARGARET CAMERON Pioneering Victorian photographer who set up the first 'celebrity portrait' studio on the Isle of Wight in 1863 after the chance gift of a camera when she was in her late forties.

Life is denied by lack of attention, whether it be to cleaning windows or trying to write a masterpiece.
NADIA BOULANGER

The moment one gives close attention to anything, even a blade of grass, it becomes a mysterious, awesome, indescribably magnificent world in itself.
HENRY MILLER

Tell me what you pay attention to and I will tell you who you are.
JOSÉ ORTEGA Y GASSET

Attitude

The greatest discovery of my generation is that a human being can alter his life by altering his attitudes of mind.
WILLIAM JAMES

I am more and more convinced that our happiness or unhappiness depends far more on the way we meet the events of life, than on the nature of those events themselves.
ALEXANDER VON HUMBOLD

Attitude is more important than the past, than education, than money, than circumstances, than what other people think or say or do. It is more important than appearance, giftedness, or skill. It will make or break a company, a church, a home. The remarkable thing is, we have a choice every day regarding the attitude we will embrace for that day. We cannot change the past. We cannot change the fact that people will act in a certain way. We cannot change the inevitable. The only thing we can do is play the one string we have, and that is our attitude.
CHUCK SWINDOLL

Consider that everything is opinion, and opinion is in thy power. Take away then, when thou choosest, thy opinion, and like a mariner who has doubled the promontory, thou wilt find calm, everything stable, and a waveless bay.
MARCUS AURELIUS

Autobiography

Only when one has lost all curiosity about the future has one reached the age to write an autobiography.
EVELYN WAUGH

Autobiography: an obituary in serial form with the last instalment missing.
QUENTIN CRISP

I don't think anybody should write his autobiography until after he is dead.
SAMUEL GOLDWYN

An autobiography usually reveals nothing bad about its writer except his memory.
FRANKLIN P. JONES

All art is autobiographical; the pearl is the oyster's autobiography.
FEDERICO FELLINI

Autobiography is an unrivalled vehicle for telling the truth about other people.
PHILIP GUEDALLA Referring to his unusual surname, the Englishman told the *Literary Digest* in 1936: 'My own pronunciation is gwuh-dal'lah. I have very little doubt that this is wholly incorrect.'

Awards

All anybody needs to know about prizes is that Mozart never won one.
HENRY MITCHELL

Every society honours its live conformists and its dead troublemakers.
MIGNON McLAUGHLIN A writer on *Vogue* and *Glamour* magazines whose two *Neurotic's Notebooks* became endlessly quoted bestsellers in the 1960s.

The only thing one can be proud of is having worked in such a way that an official reward for your labour cannot be envisaged by anyone.
JEAN COCTEAU

The Council of the Royal Society is a collection of men who elect each other to office and then dine together at the expense of this society to praise each other over wine and give each other medals.
CHARLES BABBAGE

I have always felt there is something degrading in offering rewards for intellectual exertion, and that societies or academies, or even kings and emperors should mingle in the matter does not remove the degradation.
MICHAEL FARADAY

The Nobel is a ticket to one's funeral. No one has ever done anything after he got it.
T. S. ELIOT

B

Banking

I believe that banking institutions are more dangerous to our liberties than standing armies.
THOMAS JEFFERSON

A banker is a person who is willing to make you a loan if you present sufficient evidence to show you don't need it.
HERBERT V. PROCHNOW Vice-President of the First National bank of Chicago and author of *The Toastmaster's Handbook* (1949).

A banker need not be popular. Indeed, a good banker in a healthy capitalist society should probably be much disliked.
J. K. GALBRAITH

If you would like to know the value of money, try to borrow some.
BENJAMIN FRANKLIN

I could never convince the financiers that Disneyland was feasible because dreams offer too little collateral.
WALT DISNEY

Drive-in banks were established so most of the cars today could see their real owner.
E. JOSEPH COSSMAN

Beauty

When the candles are out, all women are fair.
PLUTARCH

All God's children are not beautiful. Most of God's children are, in fact, barely presentable.
FRAN LEBOWITZ

Remember that the most beautiful things in the world are the most useless; peacocks and lilies, for example.
JOHN RUSKIN

The most beautiful thing in the world is, of course, the world itself.
WALLACE STEVENS

It is amazing how complete is the delusion that beauty is goodness.
LEO TOLSTOY

What makes the desert beautiful is that somewhere it hides a well.
ANTOINE DE SAINT-EXUPÉRY

Beauty, to me, is about being comfortable in your own skin. That, or a kick-ass red lipstick.
GWYNETH PALTROW

Where lipstick is concerned, the important thing is not the colour, but to accept God's final decision on where your lips end.
JERRY SEINFELD

There is no excellent beauty that hath not some strangeness in the proportion.
FRANCIS BACON

When I am working on a problem, I never think about beauty. I think only how to solve the problem. But when I have finished, if the solution is not beautiful, I know it is wrong.
R. BUCKMINSTER FULLER

Belief

I do not believe in ghosts, astrology, palmistry, John Cage, love, or God.
GORE VIDAL

I never believed in Santa Claus because I knew no white dude would come into my neighborhood after dark.
DICK GREGORY African American comedian and civil rights campaigner; his 1964 autobiography, *Nigger*, sold SEVEN million copies.

Maybe true. Maybe not true. Better you believe.
SHERPA SAYING

I do not believe in belief.
E. M. FORSTER

The average person today is about as credulous as was the average person in the Middle Ages.
GEORGE BERNARD SHAW

As I get older I seem to believe less and less and yet to believe what I do

believe more and more.
GERALD BRENAN

An idea isn't responsible for the people who believe in it.
DON MARQUIS

The dust of exploded beliefs may make a fine sunset.
GEOFFREY MADAN

There is a great difference between *still* believing something and
believing it *again*.
GEORG CHRISTOPH LICHTENBERG

There's nothing that can help you understand your own beliefs better
than trying to explain them to an inquisitive child.
FRANK CLARK Writer of the daily 'Country Parson' cartoon in the *Des Moines
Register & Tribune* from 1955 until his death in 1991. It was syndicated in more than
200 newspapers.

The fact that an opinion has been widely held is no evidence whatever
that it is not utterly absurd; indeed in view of the silliness of the majority
of mankind, a widespread belief is more likely to be foolish than sensible.
BERTRAND RUSSELL

Believe not because some old manuscripts are produced, believe not
because it is your national belief, believe not because you have been
made to believe from your childhood, but reason truth out, and after
you have analysed it, then if you find it will do good to one and all,
believe it, live up to it and help others live up to it.
BUDDHA

A man's got to believe in something. I believe I'll have another drink.
W. C .FIELDS

The Bible

Properly read, the Bible is the most potent force for atheism ever
conceived.
ISAAC ASIMOV

There are indeed secrets in the Bible, and some very subversive ones,
but they are so muffled up in complications, in archaic ways of
thinking, that Christianity has become incredibly difficult to explain to
a modern person.
ALAN WATTS

No man ever believes that the Bible means what it says; he is always convinced that it says what he means.
GEORGE BERNARD SHAW

The Bible is a wonderful source of inspiration for those who don't understand it.
GEORGE SANTAYANA

It ain't those parts of the Bible that I can't understand that bother me, it's the parts that I do understand.
MARK TWAIN

Whenever we read the obscene stories, the voluptuous debaucheries, the cruel and tortuous executions, the unrelenting vindictiveness with which more than half the Bible is filled, it would be more consistent that we call it the word of a demon than the word of God. It is a history of wickedness that has served to corrupt and brutalize mankind.
THOMAS PAINE

It's absolutely bloody amazing to think that anyone could have believed that – absolute balls.
PHILIP LARKIN

The total absence of humour from the Bible is one of the most singular things in all literature.
A. N. WHITEHEAD

Ye are the children of the Lord your God: ye shall not cut yourselves, nor make any baldness between the eyes for the dead.
DEUTERONOMY 14:1

A man shall not take his father's wife, nor discover his father's skirt.
DEUTERONOMY 22:30 This isn't an early prohibition against cross-dressing. Discover means 'uncover' and the skirt is the garment the bridegroom spreads over the bride as part of the ancient Jewish marriage ceremony. So, don't sleep with your father's wife.

Cursed be he that lieth with his mother in law.
DEUTERONOMY 27:23

The driving is like the driving of Jehu son of Nimshi; for he driveth furiously.
2 KINGS 9:20

Birds

If I were reincarnated, I'd want to come back a buzzard. Nothing hates him or envies him or wants him or needs him. He is never bothered or in danger, and he can eat anything.
WILLIAM FAULKNER

It is to be regretted that domestication has seriously deteriorated the moral character of the duck. In a wild state, he is a faithful husband, but no sooner is he domesticated than he becomes polygamous, and makes nothing of owning ten or a dozen wives at a time.
MRS BEETON

A sparrow fluttering about the church is an antagonist which the most profound theologian in Europe is wholly unable to overcome.
SYDNEY SMITH

Swallows certainly sleep all winter. A number of them conglobulate together, by flying round and round, and then all in a heap throw themselves under water, and lye in the bed of a river.
SAMUEL JOHNSON Quoted in Boswell's *Life of Samuel Johnson* (1791).

Swans have an air of being proud, stupid and mischievous – three qualities that go well together.
DENIS DIDEROT

If only I were a bird! Ah, but eating caterpillars?
PALESTINIAN PROVERB

The mosquito is the state bird of New Jersey.
ANDY WARHOL

Books

A book should serve as an axe for the frozen sea within us.
FRANZ KAFKA

There are more books on books than on any other subject.
MICHEL DE MONTAIGNE

Never lend books; no one ever returns them. The only books I have in my library are books other people have lent me.
ANATOLE FRANCE

Outside of a dog, a book is man's best friend. Inside of a dog, it's too dark to read.
GROUCHO MARX

To be well informed, one must read quickly a great number of merely instructive books. To be cultivated, one must read slowly and with a lingering appreciation the comparatively few books that have been written by men who lived, thought, and felt with style.
ALDOUS HUXLEY

The reason why so few good books are written is that so few people who can write know anything.
WALTER BAGEHOT

I don't think any good book is based on factual experience. Bad books are about things the writer already knew before he wrote them.
CARLOS FUENTES

How long most people would look at the best book before they would give the price of a large turbot for it?
JOHN RUSKIN

Some books are undeservedly forgotten, none are undeservedly remembered.
W. H. AUDEN

A classic is something that everybody wants to have read and nobody wants to read.
MARK TWAIN

The worst thing about new books is that they keep us from reading the old ones.
JOSEPH JOUBERT

All of the books in the world contain no more information than is broadcast as video in a single large American city in a single year. Not all bits have equal value.
CARL SAGAN

The most difficult book I have ever read was a manual on the use of iron mangles by A. J. Thompson.
SPIKE MILLIGAN

There are only two kinds of math books. Those you cannot read beyond the first sentence, and those you cannot read beyond the first page.
CHEN NING YANG The best attempt yet made to describe the interactions of the subatomic particles that make up matter.

One is never obliged to write a book.
HENRI BERGSON

Everyone has a book in them and that, in most cases, is where it should stay.
CHRISTOPHER HITCHENS

There are books in which the footnotes, or the comments scrawled by some reader's hand in the margin, are more interesting than the text. The world is one of those books.
GEORGE SANTAYANA

And there are also many other things which Jesus did, the which, if they should be written every one, I suppose that even the world itself could not contain the books that should be written.
JOHN 21:25 The last words.

A book worth reading is worth buying.
JOHN RUSKIN

The covers of this book are too far apart.
AMBROSE BIERCE

Big book, big bore.
CALLIMACHUS

Boredom

We have a world of pleasures to win, and nothing to lose but boredom.
RAOUL VANEIGEM Situationist sloganeer and author of *The Revolution of Everyday Life* (1967).

A tremendous number of people in America work very hard at something that bores them. Even a rich man thinks he has to go down to the office every day. Not because he likes it but because he can't think of anything else to do.
W. H. AUDEN

Boredom is the root of all evil.
SØREN KIERKEGAARD

Is not life a hundred times too short for us to bore ourselves?
FRIEDRICH NIETZSCHE

The cure for boredom is curiosity. There is no cure for curiosity.
DOROTHY PARKER

Boredom is a vital problem for the moralist since half the sins of humanity are caused by fear of it.
BERTRAND RUSSELL

Boredom is rage spread thin.
PAUL TILLICH

Entertainment is, in fact, the biggest cause of boredom in the modern world. The more man is entertained, the more bored he grows.
ANTHONY DANIELS

When I bore people at a party, they think it is their fault.
HENRY KISSINGER

In Zen they say: If it is boring after two minutes listen to it for four. If still boring, listen for eight or sixteen or thirty-two, and so on. Soon we discover that it is not boring at all but actually very interesting.
JOHN CAGE

Boxing

Boxing isn't a metaphor: it's the thing itself.
JOYCE CAROL OATES

To me, boxing is like a ballet, except there's no music, no choreography and the dancers hit each other.
JACK HANDY 'Deep Thoughts' were an integral part of the American comedy showcase *Saturday Night Live* in the 1990s. Handey would read the pieces off screen over soft music and gentle scenes of rural life.

It's just a job. Grass grows, birds fly, waves pound the sand. I beat people up.
MUHAMMAD ALI

This boxer is doing what is expected of him, bleeding from his nose.
HARRY CARPENTER

BARONESS EDITH SUMMERSKILL: Mr Cooper, have you looked in the mirror lately and seen the state of your nose?
HENRY COOPER: Well, madam, have you looked in the mirror and seen the state of *your* nose? Boxing is my excuse. What's yours?
LADY SUMMERSKILL The anti-boxing campaigner, doctor and socialist peer was questioning Henry Cooper about the brutalities of his sport.

Sure, there have been injuries and deaths in boxing – but none of them serious.
ALAN MINTER

Brain

The brain is a wonderful organ. It starts working the moment you get up in the morning, and does not stop until you get into the office.
ROBERT FROST

If the human brain were so simple that we could understand it, we would be so simple that we wouldn't.
EMERSON PUGH

The evolution of the brain not only overshot the needs of prehistoric man, it is the only example of evolution providing a species with an organ which it does not know how to use.
ARTHUR KOESTLER

Your brain, doctor, is a culture medium for question marks!
PAUL VALÉRY

If little else, the brain is an educational toy.
TOM ROBBINS

Bureaucracy

Every revolution evaporates and leaves behind only the slime of a new bureaucracy.
FRANZ KAFKA

Bureaucracy is a giant mechanism operated by pygmies.
HONORÉ DE BALZAC

Britain has invented a new missile. It's called the civil servant – it doesn't work and it can't be fired.
GENERAL SIR WALTER WALKER Senior British soldier who led a brilliant campaign in the Malayan Emergency in the 1950s using helicopters for the first time. He later became notorious for his extreme anti-Communist views, regularly expressed in letters to the *Daily Telegraph*.

Bureaucrats: they are dead at 30 and buried at 60. They are like custard pies; you can't nail them to a wall.
FRANK LLOYD WRIGHT

Business

Beware the barrenness of a busy life.
SOCRATES

It is not enough to stay busy. So, too, are the ants. The question is what you are busy about.
HENRY DAVID THOREAU

The law does not pretend to punish everything that is dishonest. That would seriously interfere with business.
CLARENCE S. DARROW

I found in running businesses that the best results come from letting high-grade people work unencumbered.
WARREN BUFFETT

The salary of the chief executive of the large corporation is not a market award for achievement. It is frequently in the nature of a warm personal gesture by the individual to himself.
J. K. GALBRAITH

Thought, not money, is the real business capital, and if you know absolutely that what you are doing is right, then you are bound to accomplish it in due season.
HARVEY FIRESTONE Established Firestone, now the world's largest tyre company, in 1900. With his close friends Henry Ford and Thomas Edison, Firestone is considered one of the three founding fathers of modern American business.

The successful man is the one who finds out what is the matter with his business before his competitors do.
ROY L. SMITH Inspirational Methodist pastor from Minneapolis, active from the 1920s and author of many books including the twelve-volume 'Know Your Bible' series.

A lasting relationship with a woman is only possible if you're a business failure.
JOHN PAUL GETTY

They intoxicate themselves with work so they won't see how they really are.
ALDOUS HUXLEY

I understand small business growth. I was one.
GEORGE W. BUSH

Butterflies

Butterflies are creatures of little importance and have never played much part in international commerce, either of goods or ideas.
Collins Field Guide to the Butterflies & Moths of Britain & Europe (1997)

What the caterpillar calls the end of the world, the master calls a butterfly.
RICHARD BACH Author of *Jonathan Livingstone Seagull* (1970).

The butterfly counts not months but moments, and has time enough.
RABINDRANATH TAGORE

The caterpillar does all the work but the butterfly gets all the publicity.
GEORGE CARLIN

The butterfly often forgets it once was a caterpillar.
SWEDISH PROVERB

C

Cabbage

Cabbage served twice is death.
GREEK PROVERB

Boiled cabbage à l'Anglaise is something compared with which steamed coarse newsprint bought from bankrupt Finnish salvage dealers and heated over smoky oil stoves is an exquisite delicacy.
WILLIAM CONNOR ('CASSANDRA')

A louse in the cabbage is better than no meat at all.
PENNSYLVANIA DUTCH PROVERB

Cauliflower is nothing but a cabbage with a college education.
MARK TWAIN

California

The State of California has no business subsidizing intellectual curiosity.
RONALD REAGAN As Governor of California, referring to student unrest on campuses in 1969.

California is a place where they shoot too many pictures and not enough actors.
WALTER WINCHELL

Hollywood is a place where people from Iowa mistake each other for stars.
FRED ALLEN One of the greats of radio comedy during the 30s and 40s, whose commentary on current events by using interviews with eccentric characters was hugely influential on the 'new comedy' of the 1960s.

I love California: I practically grew up in Phoenix.
DAN QUAYLE

There is science, logic, reason; there is thought verified by experience. And then there is California.
EDWARD ABBEY

California is a fine place to live – if you happen to be an orange.
FRED ALLEN

Nothing is wrong with California that a rise in the ocean level wouldn't cure.
ROSS MACDONALD

Canada

When I'm in Canada, I feel this is what the world should be like.
JANE FONDA

When Columbus made his well-remembered voyage to the Caribbean, Canada had been known to Europeans for more than 500 years.
R. A. J. PHILLIPS

Very little is known of the Canadian country since it is rarely visited by anyone but the Queen and illiterate sport fishermen.
P. J. O'ROURKE

It's going to be a great country when they finish unpacking it.
ANDREW H. MALCOLM

Canada is not so much a country as a clothesline nearly 4,000 miles long. St John's in Newfoundland is closer to Milan, Italy, than it is to Vancouver.
SIMON HOGGART

I don't even know what street Canada is on.
AL CAPONE

Canada is the essence of not being. Not English, not American, it is the mathematic of not being. And a subtle flavour – we're more like celery as a flavour.
MIKE MYERS

In any world menu, Canada must be considered the vichyssoise of nations – it's cold, half-French and difficult to stir.
STUART KEATE

We have never been a melting pot. The fact is we are more like a tossed salad. We are green, some of us are oily and there's a little vinegar injected when you get up to Ottawa.
ARNOLD EDINBOROUGH

The beaver, which has come to represent Canada as the eagle does the United States and the lion Britain, is a flat-tailed, slow-witted, toothy rodent known to bite off its own testicles or to stand under its own falling trees.
JUNE CALLWOOD

Canada was built on dead beavers.
MARGARET ATWOOD

When I was crossing the border into Canada, they asked if I had any firearms with me. I said, 'Well, what do you need?'
STEVEN WRIGHT

A Canadian is someone who knows how to make love in a canoe.
PIERRE BERTON A Canadian himself, author of more than fifty best-selling books of popular history, TV host and self-confessed marijuana user, he was the only man ever to secure a TV interview with martial arts legend Bruce Lee in 1971.

Candles

There is no better, there is no more open door by which you can enter into the study of natural philosophy, than by considering the physical phenomena of a candle.
MICHAEL FARADAY

Thousands of candles can be lighted from a single candle, and the life of the candle will not be shortened. Happiness never decreases by being shared.
BUDDHA

Man loves company – even if it is only that of a small burning candle.
G. C. LICHTENBERG

To light a candle is to cast a shadow.
URSULA LE GUIN

When your candle burns low, you've got to believe that the last light shows you something besides the progress of darkness.
TENNESSEE WILLIAMS Inscribed on a photo of his lover Frank Merlo.

It's better to light a candle than to curse the darkness.
ELEANOR ROOSEVELT

If Thomas Edison invented electric light today, Dan Rather would report it on CBS News as 'candle-making industry threatened'.
NEWT GINGRICH

Curiosity is the wick in the candle of learning.
WILLIAM A. WARD

Nirvana is not the blowing out of the candle. It is the extinguishing of the flame because day is come.
RABINDRANATH TAGORE

Careers

When I was four, I told my mother I wanted to be a rock star when I grow up. She said, 'You can't do both.'
STEVEN TYLER Lead singer with rock band Aerosmith and with guitarist Joe Perry one half of the 'Toxic Twins', whose drug excesses were the stuff of legend, even for the 1970s. Both men have remained clean for twenty years, although Tyler returned briefly to rehab in 2008 because of a 'foot problem'.

My mother has always been unhappy with what I do – she would rather I do something nice, like be a bricklayer.
MICK JAGGER

It's no good running a pig farm badly for thirty years while saying, 'Really I was meant to be a ballet dancer'. By that time, pigs will be your style.
QUENTIN CRISP

If I had only known, I would have been a locksmith.
ALBERT EINSTEIN

If a man is called to be a streetsweeper, he should sweep streets even as Michelangelo painted, or Beethoven composed music, or Shakespeare wrote poetry. He should sweep streets so well that all the hosts of heaven and earth will pause to say, here lived a great streetsweeper who did his job well.
MARTIN LUTHER KING

I don't know anything about music. In my line you don't have to.
ELVIS PRESLEY

If I had known my son was going to be president of Bolivia, I would have taught him to read and write.
ENRIQUE PEÑARANDA'S MOTHER

My choice early in life was either to be a piano player in a whorehouse or a politician. And to tell the truth, there's hardly any difference.
HARRY S. TRUMAN

When a man is determined, what can stop him? Cripple him and you have Sir Walter Scott. Put him in a prison cell and you have a John Bunyan. Bury him in the snows of Valley Forge and you have a George Washington. Have him born in abject poverty and you have a Lincoln. Put him in the grease pit of a locomotive roundhouse and you have a Walter P. Chrysler. Make him second fiddle in an obscure South African orchestra and you have a Toscanini. The hardships of life are sent not

to be an unkind destiny to crush, but to challenge.
SAM E. ROBERTS

The society which scorns excellence in plumbing as a humble activity and tolerates shoddiness in philosophy because it is an exalted activity will have neither good plumbing nor good philosophy . . . neither its pipes nor its theories will hold water.
JOHN W. GARDNER Secretary of Health, Education and Welfare under Lyndon Johnson, he was responsible in 1965 both for launching Medicare and introducing the landmark Elementary and Secondary Education Act which targeted the children of poor families.

One has to look out for engineers – they begin with sewing machines and end up with the atomic bomb.
MARCEL PAGNOL

I founded Wang Laboratories to show that Chinese could excel at things other than running laundries and restaurants.
A. N. WANG

Not 16 per cent of the human race is, or ever has been, engaged in any kinds of activity at which they excel.
PHILIP MAIRET One of those overlooked but influential operators of English letters: translator of Sartre, disciple of Adler, friend to T. S. Eliot, mentor to Orwell and through his editorship of *New English Weekly* one of the early promoters of organic agriculture.

We all live under the same sky, but we do not all have the same horizon.
KONRAD ADENAUER

The feeling of having taken a wrong turning in life was made worse by the fact that he could not, for the life of him, remember having taken any turnings at all.
CHARLES FERNYHOUGH From his story 'Fado' in *New Writing* 11 (2002).

If in one hundred years I am only known as the man who invented Sherlock Holmes, then I will have considered my life a failure.
SIR ARTHUR CONAN DOYLE

Cars

Have you ever noticed? Anybody going slower than you is an idiot, and anyone going faster than you is a moron.
GEORGE CARLIN

Why do they call it rush hour when nothing moves?
ROBIN WILLIAMS

In the history of the world, no one has ever washed a rented car.
LARRY SUMMERS Secretary of the Treasury under Bill Clinton and President of Harvard University from 2001 to 2006 when he resigned amid controversy about remarks he'd made concerning women's intelligence.

Onion rings in the car cushions do not improve with time.
ERMA BOMBECK

Catastrophes

Human history becomes more a race between education and catastrophe.
H. G. WELLS

We are dismayed when we find that even disaster cannot cure us of our faults.
LUC DE CLAPIERS, MARQUIS DE VAUVENARGUES

Gentlemen, in the little moment that remains to us between the crisis and the catastrophe, we may as well drink a glass of champagne.
PAUL CLAUDEL

If the English language made any sense, a catastrophe would be an apostrophe with fur.
DOUG LARSON Mysterious quote-maker listed variously as an English runner and gold medal winner at the 1924 Olympics, a racing car driver, a US cartoonist and the writer of the 'Senator Soaper' column, which ran in over 100 newspapers from the 1920s to 2003. This last seems the safest bet.

Cathedrals

I never weary of great churches. It is my favourite kind of mountain scenery. Mankind was never so happily inspired as when it made a cathedral.
ROBERT LOUIS STEVENSON

Regard it as just as desirable to build a chicken house as to build a cathedral.
FRANK LLOYD WRIGHT

Cathedrals cannot be built by those who are paralysed by doubt and cynicism.
HENRY KISSINGER

He who has seen one cathedral ten times has seen something; he who has seen ten cathedrals once has seen but little; and he who has spent half an hour in each of a hundred cathedrals has seen nothing at all.
SINCLAIR LEWIS

A cathedral, a wave of a storm, a dancer's leap, never turn out to be as high as we had hoped.
MARCEL PROUST

Cats

Cats are intended to teach us that not everything in nature has a function.
GARRISON KEILLOR

When I play with my cat, who knows if I am not more of a pastime to her than she is to me?
MICHEL DE MONTAIGNE

Do not meddle in the affairs of cats, for they are subtle and will piss on your computer.
BRUCE GRAHAM

They say the test of literary power is whether a man can write an inscription. I say, 'Can he name a kitten?'
SAMUEL BUTLER

If cats could talk, they wouldn't.
NAN PORTER Every quote book or site devoted to cats includes this one-liner but there's not one scrap of information about Nan Porter on any of them. And it's the only thing she's listed as saying. If you're still out there, Nan, get in touch and solve the mystery!

Cats and Dogs

If a dog jumps in your lap, it is because he is fond of you; but if a cat does the same thing, it is because your lap is warmer.
A. N. WHITEHEAD

Cats are smarter than dogs. You cannot get eight cats to pull a sled through snow.
JEFF VALDEZ

Cats are the ultimate narcissists. You can tell this because of all the time they spend on personal grooming. Dogs aren't like this. A dog's idea of personal grooming is to roll on a dead fish.
JAMES GORMAN

Celery

The thought of two thousand people crunching celery at the same time horrified me.
GEORGE BERNARD SHAW Shaw, a vegetarian, was explaining why he had turned down an invitation to a vegetarian gala dinner.

There ought t'be some way t'eat celery so it wouldn't sound like you wuz steppin' on a basket.
FRANK 'KIN' HUBBARD

I'm afraid of losing my obscurity. Genuineness only thrives in the dark, like celery.
ALDOUS HUXLEY

The Democrats seem to be basically nicer people, but they have demonstrated time and again that they have the management skills of celery.
DAVE BARRY

Certainty

I cannot help saying to myself, forty times a day: 'My God, how right I am!'
METTERNICH

It is not certain that everything is uncertain.
BLAISE PASCAL

If a man will begin with certainties, he shall end in doubts; but if he will be content to begin with doubt he shall end in certainties.
FRANCIS BACON

As far as the laws of mathematics refer to reality, they are not certain; and as far as they are certain, they do not refer to reality.
ALBERT EINSTEIN

Doubt is not a very agreeable status, but certainty is a ridiculous one.
VOLTAIRE

Inquiry is fatal to certainty.
WILL DURANT The doyen of American popular historians who, with his wife Ariel, won the Pulitzer Prize for their eleven-volume work *The Story of Civilization* (1935–75). They died within a few days of each other in 1981.

Chairs

If more designers had bad backs, we would have more good chairs.
RALPH CAPLAN

It isn't so much what's on the table that matters, as what's on the chairs.
W. S. GILBERT

The Prime Minister should be intimidating, there's not much point being a weak, floppy thing in a chair.
MARGARET THATCHER Quoted in John Birt's autobiography *The Harder Path* (2002).

All religions will pass, but this will remain: simply sitting in a chair and looking into the distance.
V. V. ROZANOV

I have discovered that all human evil comes from this, man's being unable to sit still in a room.
BLAISE PASCAL

Champagne

Come quickly, I am tasting the stars!
DOM PÉRIGNON Supposedly at the moment he invented champagne. In fact, he spent most of his time trying to remove the fizz from wine. These words first appeared in a Moët et Chandon advertisement for their luxury Dom Pérignon brand in the 1890s.

I'm only a beer teetotaller, not a champagne teetotaller.
GEORGE BERNARD SHAW

Champagne has the taste of an apple peeled with a steel knife.
ALDOUS HUXLEY

Champagne does have one regular drawback: swilled as a regular thing a certain sourness settles in the tummy, and the result is permanent bad breath. Really incurable.
TRUMAN CAPOTE

The House of Lords is like a glass of champagne that has stood for five days.
CLEMENT ATTLEE

No government could survive without champagne. Champagne in the throats of our diplomatic people is like oil in the wheels of an engine.
JOSEPH DARGENT Quoted in the *New York Herald Tribune*, 21 July 1955.

In victory, you deserve champagne, in defeat, you need it.
NAPOLEON BONAPARTE

My only regret in life is that I did not drink more champagne.
JOHN MAYNARD KEYNES

Chance

Everything existing in the universe is the fruit of chance.
DEMOCRITUS OF ABDERA

A general is a man who takes chances. Mostly he takes a fifty-fifty chance; if he happens to win three times in succession he is considered a great general.
ENRICO FERMI

We all know that chance, fortune, fate or destiny – call it what you will – has played a considerable part in many of the great discoveries in science. We do not know how many, for all scientists who have hit on something new have not disclosed exactly how it happened.
ALEXANDER FLEMING From his 1945 Nobel Prize speech, delivered seventeen years after his accidental discovery of the antibacterial properties of penicillin mould. He shared the prize with Howard Florey and Ernst Chain.

Men argue learnedly over whether life is chemical chance or antichance, but they seem to forget that the life *in* chemicals may be the greatest chance of all, the most mysterious and unexplainable property of matter.
LOREN EISELEY

The man who is not dead still has a chance.
LEBANESE PROVERB

Change

If you want to make enemies, try to change something.
WOODROW WILSON

Our wretched species is so made that those who walk on the well-trodden path always throw stones at those who are showing a new road.
VOLTAIRE

You can recognize a pioneer by the arrows in his back.
BEVERLY RUBIK Cutting-edge biophysicist and founder of the Insitutute for Frontier Science in Oakland, California, which is dedicated to understanding the human bioenergy field (the new name for the 'aura').

The one unchangeable certainty is that nothing is unchangeable or certain.
JOHN F. KENNEDY

I wanted to change the world. But I have found that the only thing one can be sure of changing is oneself.
ALDOUS HUXLEY

Never doubt that a small group of thoughtful, committed citizens can change the world. Indeed, it's the only thing that ever has.
MARGARET MEAD

To Change One's Life:
  1. Start immediately.
  2. Do it flamboyantly.
  3. No exceptions.
WILLIAM JAMES

It is in change that things find rest.
HERACLITUS The weeping philospher (often paired with Democritus, the 'laughing philosopher' and near contemporary). His work survives only as a sequence of profound allusive fragments and he ended his days depressed, in self-exile from people, living on grass and herbs.

Character

Character is destiny.
HERACLITUS

A man never discloses his own character so clearly as when he describes another's.
JEAN PAUL RICHTER

If you cannot mould yourself as you would wish, how can you expect other people to be entirely to your liking?
THOMAS À KEMPIS

Character is doing the right thing when nobody's looking.
J. C. WATTS From a speech at the 1996 Republican convention. Watts, a black congressman, former professional football player, successful businessman and regular TV pundit is touted as a future presidential candidate.

She was not quite what you would call refined. She was not quite what you would call unrefined. She was the kind of person who keeps a parrot.
MARK TWAIN

Cheerfulness

I feel an earnest and humble desire, and shall do till I die, to increase the stock of harmless cheerfulness.
CHARLES DICKENS

Start every day off with a smile and get it over with.
W. C. FIELDS

I have tried too, in my time, to be a philosopher; but I don't know how, cheerfulness was always breaking in.
OLIVER EDWARDS Old college friend of Dr Johnson reminiscing about their time spent drinking in alehouses as students. Both men were in their late sixties at the time. (Boswell's *Life*, 1791).

I got the blues thinking of the future, so I left off and made some marmalade. It's amazing how it cheers one up to shred oranges and scrub the floor.
D. H. LAWRENCE

Mirth is like a flash of lightning that breaks through a gloom of clouds and glitters for a moment; cheerfulness keeps up a kind of daylight in the mind and fills it with a steady and perpetual serenity.
BERTRAND RUSSELL

Gaiety is the most outstanding feature of the Soviet Union.
JOSEF STALIN

Cheese

Poets have hitherto been mysteriously silent on the subject of cheese.
G. K. CHESTERTON

Cheese is the biscuit of drunkards.
GRIMOD DE LA REYNIÈRE The first restaurant critic, whose eight-volume *Almanach des gourmands* (1803–12) was the original guide to eating out, and brought the words 'gourmet' and 'gourmand' into popular currency. Grimod also threw his own funeral banquet, just to see who would turn up.

A dinner which ends without cheese is like a beautiful woman with only one eye.
JEAN-ANTHELME BRILLAT-SAVARIN

A corpse is meat gone bad. Well and what's cheese? Corpse of milk.
JAMES JOYCE

I think I'm liquefying like an old Camembert.
GUSTAVE FLAUBERT

God's feet!
LÉON-PAUL FARGUE When presented with a particularly strong-smelling Camembert.

How can one govern a country which has 246 varieties of cheese?
CHARLES DE GAULLE

Mozzarella has to be perfect and impeccably sourced or it's like eating a blind whale's eyeball.
A. A. GILL

Chemistry

Organic chemistry is the chemistry of carbon compounds. Bio-chemistry is the study of carbon compounds that crawl.
MIKE ADAMS

Not all chemicals are bad. Without chemicals such as hydrogen and oxygen, for example, there would be no way to make water, a vital ingredient in beer.
DAVE BARRY

To most people solutions mean finding the answers. But to chemists solutions are things that are still all mixed up.
POLISH PROVERB

A chemist without a nose is in for trouble.
PRIMO LEVI

Chess

Victory goes to the player who makes the next-to-last mistake.
SAVIELLY TARTAKOWER

Regarded as a game, chess is more intellectual than life . . . or bridge.
THOMAS HARDY

A kind heart is of little value in chess.
NICOLAS CHAMFORT

Chess is as elaborate a waste of human intelligence as you can find outside of an advertising agency.
RAYMOND CHANDLER

Chickens

Stupidity is the devil. Look in the eye of a chicken and you'll know. It's the most horrifying, cannibalistic, and nightmarish creature in this world.
WERNER HERZOG The visionary German film-maker suffers from *alektorophobia*, a morbid fear of chickens. The bleak ending of *Stroszek* (1977) features a chicken dancing in an amusement arcade. This was the film playing when Ian Curtis of Joy Division committed suicide in 1981.

A hen is only an egg's way of making another egg.
SAMUEL BUTLER

You may observe mother instinct at its height in a fond hen sitting on china eggs – instinct but no brain.
CHARLOTTE GILMAN

We didn't starve, but we didn't eat chicken unless we were sick, or the chicken was.
BERNARD MALAMUD

Children

I don't dislike babies, though I think very young ones rather disgusting.
QUEEN VICTORIA

People who say they sleep like a baby usually don't have one.
LEO J. BURKE

Babies do not want to hear about babies; they like to be told of giants and castles.
SAMUEL JOHNSON From *Anecdotes of Samuel Johnson* (1786) by Mrs Piozzi (formerly Thrale). Mostly studied for her friendship with Johnson she was an accomplished travel writer and etymologist and her collected anecdotes and observations (known as 'Thraliana') initiated a new literary genre.

Children are travellers newly arrived in a strange country of which they know nothing.
JOHN LOCKE

To children, childhood holds no particular advantage.
KATHLEEN NORRIS

The events of childhood do not pass, but repeat themselves like seasons of the year.
ELEANOR FARJEON

Were we closer to the ground as children, or is the grass emptier now?
ALAN BENNETT

Even when freshly washed and relieved of all obvious confections, children tend to be sticky.
FRAN LEBOWITZ

Nothing is sweeter, nor more bitter, than one's own children.
MACEDONIAN PROVERB

Before I got married, I had six theories about bringing up children; now I have six children and no theories.
JOHN WILMOT, EARL OF ROCHESTER There are only records of Rochester having five children: Anne, Charles, Elizabeth and Mallet by his wife Anne; and a girl by his mistress Elizabeth Barry. Despite succumbing to pox and alcoholism at 33, he seems to have been a popular and attentive father.

I have found the best way to give advice to children is to find out what they want and then advise them to do it.
HARRY S. TRUMAN

He that will have his son have a respect for him and his orders, must himself have a great reverence for his son.
JOHN LOCKE

You can learn many things from children. How much patience you have, for instance.
FRANKLIN P. JONES

The children of other nations always seem precocious.
F. SCOTT FITZGERALD

There's no such thing as a tough child – if you parboil them for seven hours, they always come out tender.
W. C. FIELDS

Even very young children need to be informed about dying. Explain the concept of death very carefully to your child. This will make threatening him with it much more effective.
P. J. O'ROURKE

Advantages out of all proportion to the importance of the immediate aim in view are apt to accrue whenever an honest endeavour is made to find an answer to one of those awkward questions which are constantly arising from the natural workings of a child's mind.
W. H. MATTHEWS The first sentence of his classic archaeological book *Mazes and Labyrinths* (1922).

A child of five would understand this. Send somebody to fetch a child of five.
GROUCHO MARX

Children are a great comfort in your old age. And they help you reach it faster, too.
LIONEL KAUFMAN

Never raise your hand to your children – it leaves your mid-section unprotected.
ROBERT ORBEN His books of gags such as the *Encyclopedia of Patter* were used as source books by almost all stand-up comedians in the 1950s. In 1974 he became President Gerald Ford's chief speechwriter.

Chocolate

There are two kinds of people in the world. Those who love chocolate, and communists.
LESLIE MOAK MURRAY Chicago comic artist in her daily strip *Murray's Law*.

Research tells us fourteen out of any ten individuals like chocolate.
SANDRA BOYNTON

Strength is the capacity to break a chocolate bar into four pieces with your bare hands – and then eat just one of the pieces.
JUDITH VIORST

There's no metaphysics on earth like chocolates.
FERNANDO PESSOA The Portuguese poet wrote under seventy-two different personas. Each, including 'Fernando Pessoa', had their own distinct authorial styles, interests and attitudes as well as names: he called them heteronyms rather than pseudonyms.

What you see before you, my friend, is the result of a lifetime of chocolate.
KATHARINE HEPBURN

Christianity

I have recently been examining all the known superstitions of the world, and do not find in our particular superstition (Christianity) one redeeming feature. They are all alike founded on fables and mythology.
THOMAS JEFFERSON

Christ rode on an ass, but now asses ride on Christ.
HEINRICH HEINE

'The Christian ideal', it is said, 'has not been tried and found wanting: it has been found difficult and left untried.'
G. K. CHESTERTON

I have read in Plato and Cicero sayings that are wise and very beautiful; but I have never read in either of them: 'Come unto me all ye that labour and are heavy laden.'
SAINT AUGUSTINE

The last Christian died on the Cross.
FRIEDRICH NIETZSCHE

The good news is that Jesus is coming back. The bad news is that he's really pissed off.
BOB HOPE

Cigars

I have made it a rule never to smoke more than one cigar at a time.
MARK TWAIN

A woman is only a woman, but a good cigar is a smoke.
RUDYARD KIPLING

Sometimes a cigar is just a cigar.
SIGMUND FREUD

Civilisation

Civilisation is a movement, not a condition; a voyage, not a harbour.
ARNOLD TOYNBEE

Civilisation is a stream with banks. The stream is sometimes filled with blood from people killing, stealing, shouting and doing the things historians usually record, while on the banks, unnoticed, people build homes, make love, raise children, sing songs, write poetry and even whittle statues. The story of civilisation is what happened on the banks.
WILL DURANT

But look, suppose people could be in the country in five minutes' walk, and had few wants; almost no furniture for instance and no servants, and studied (the difficult) arts of enjoying life, and finding out what they really wanted: then I think one might hope civilisation had really begun.
WILLIAM MORRIS

A great city is one that handles art and garbage equally well.
BOB TALBERT South Carolina-born prolific columnist for the *Detroit Free Press*. He died in 1999 having written over 9,000 columns – an average of six a week.

We live in an age when pizza gets to your home before the police.
JEFF MARDER

If civilisation had been left in female hands, we would still be living in grass huts.
CAMILLE PAGLIA

Clarity

Everything that can be said, can be said clearly.
LUDWIG WITTGENSTEIN

All my efforts go into creating an art that can be understood by everyone.
HENRI MATISSE

Good prose is like a window pane.
GEORGE ORWELL

I don't know what directors do, if they don't make things *clear*.
ALAN BENNETT

Cleverness

Cleverness is serviceable for everything, sufficient for nothing.
HENRI FRÉDÉRIC AMIEL

A clever person solves a problem. A wise person avoids it.
ALBERT EINSTEIN

Patience and tenacity of purpose are worth more than twice their weight in cleverness.
THOMAS HUXLEY

The man who is clever and industrious is suited to high staff appointments; use can be made of a man who is stupid and lazy; the man who is clever and lazy is suited for the highest command, he has the nerve to deal with all situations; but the man who is stupid and industrious is a danger and must be dismissed immediately.
BARON VON HAMMERSTEIN-EQUORD The 'Red General', a left-leaning German aristocrat who opposed the rise of Nazism.

The desire to seem clever often keeps us from being so.
LA ROCHEFOUCAULD

A man thinks that by mouthing hard words he understands hard things.
HERMAN MELVILLE

Never stay up on the barren heights of cleverness, but come down into the green valleys of silliness.
LUDWIG WITTGENSTEIN

Clowns

The arrival in town of a good clown is of more benefit to the people than the arrival of twenty asses laden with medicine.
THOMAS SYDENHAM Often called the 'father of English medicine', famous for his no-nonsense diagnoses. He once cured a hypochondriac by sending him to see a non-existent specialist in Inverness, and recommended *Don Quixote* as the most useful of medical texts.

That's it! You people have stood in my way long enough. I'm going to clown college!
HOMER SIMPSON

The fact that some geniuses were laughed at does not imply that all who are laughed at are geniuses. They laughed at Columbus, they laughed at Fulton, they laughed at the Wright Brothers. But they also laughed at Bozo the Clown.
CARL SAGAN

To me, clowns aren't funny. In fact, they're kind of scary. I've wondered where this started and I think it goes back to the time I went to the circus, and a clown killed my dad.
JACK HANDEY

I once made love to a female clown. It was weird because she twisted my penis into a poodle.
DAN WHITNEY

Coffee

Coffee isn't my cup of tea.
SAMUEL GOLDWYN

Coffee falls into the stomach … ideas begin to move, things remembered arrive at full gallop . . . the shafts of wit start up like sharp-shooters, similes arise, the paper is covered with ink. Coffee is

your ally and writing ceases to be a struggle.
HONORÉ DE BALZAC

I never drink coffee at lunch. I find it keeps me awake for the afternoon.
RONALD REAGAN

I put instant coffee in a microwave and almost went back in time.
STEVEN WRIGHT

If this is coffee, please bring me some tea; if this is tea, please bring me some coffee.
ABRAHAM LINCOLN

If I can't drink my coffee three times a day, I shrivel up like a piece of roast goat.
J. S. BACH From his *Coffee Cantata* (BMV 221) of 1732, in which a father tries and fails to persuade his headstrong teenage daughter to give up coffee, the eighteenth-century equivalent of Red Bull. Bach's own ensemble often performed in Zimmerman's coffee house in Leipzig.

Colour

I want to know one thing. What is colour?
PABLO PICASSO

Colour is the place where our brain and the universe meet.
PAUL KLEE

The purest and most thoughtful minds are those which love colour the most.
JOHN RUSKIN

I have been forty years in the discovery that the queen of all colours is black.
AUGUSTE RENOIR

Green is like a fat, very healthy cow lying still and unmoving, only capable of chewing the cud, regarding the world with stupid dull eyes.
WASSILY KANDINSKY

Pink is the navy blue of India.
DIANA VREELAND

Picasso had his pink period and his blue period. I am in my blonde period right now.
HUGH HEFNER

My experience helped me to see how isolated and fragile the Earth really is. It was also beautiful. It was the only object in the entire universe that was neither black nor white.
FRANK BORMAN

Colours are the deeds and sufferings of light.
GOETHE

I want meadows red in tone and trees painted in blue. Nature has no imagination.
CHARLES BAUDELAIRE

Artists can colour the sky red because they know it's blue. Those of us who aren't artists must colour things the way they really are or people might think we're stupid.
JULES FEIFFER

Anyone who paints a sky green and fields blue ought to be sterilised.
ADOLF HITLER

Comedy

Not a shred of evidence exists in favour of the idea that life is serious.
BRENDAN GILL

Comedy is simply a funny way of being serious.
PETER USTINOV

The wit makes fun of other persons; the satirist makes fun of the world; the humorist makes fun of himself.
JAMES THURBER

The whole object of comedy is to be yourself, and the closer you get to that, the funnier you will be.
JERRY SEINFELD

It has always surprised me how little attention philosophers have paid to humour, since it is a more significant process of mind than reason. Reason can only sort out perceptions, but the humour process is involved in changing them.
EDWARD DE BONO

There is not one female comedian who was beautiful as a little girl.
JOAN RIVERS

My comedy is all born of tragedy. If there were no more anger and

despair in the world I'd be standing in the unemployment line – right next to J. Edgar Hoover.
LENNY BRUCE

When a thing is funny, search it for a hidden truth.
GEORGE BERNARD SHAW

Committees

God so loved the world that he didn't send a committee.
MERVYN STOCKWOOD The colourful and controversial bishop combined socialism with High Church piety. Despite championing radical theology and gay rights, he famously declared Monty Python's *The Life of Brian* blasphemous on television in 1979.

A committee is a group of people who individually can do nothing, but together can decide that nothing can be done.
FRED ALLEN

A committee is a cul-de-sac down which ideas are lured and then quietly strangled.
SIR BARNETT COCKS

Not even computers will replace committees, because committees buy computers.
SHEPHERD MEAD Former ad man and author of *How to Succeed in Business without Really Trying* (1952) which became a hit Broadway show. True to its own message, the book took him four days to write.

Communism

Communism is not love. Communism is a hammer which we use to crush the enemy.
MAO ZEDONG

How do you tell a communist? Well, it's someone who reads Marx and Lenin. And how do you tell an anti-communist? It's someone who understands Marx and Lenin.
RONALD REAGAN

The best way to make communists is to put Americans into a place where there were no communists before.
NORODOM SIHANOUK King of Cambodia on and off from 1953 until his abdication in 2004, he holds the world record for having held the highest number of political offices, as well as being a composer, film-maker and the only head of state to launch a genuinely popular personal website.

Composers

A composer is a guy who goes around forcing his will on unsuspecting air molecules, often with the assistance of unsuspecting musicians.
FRANK ZAPPA

In order to compose, all you need to do is remember a tune that no one else has thought of.
ROBERT SCHUMANN

Don't write music unless it is impossible for you not to write music.
DIMITRI SHOSTAKOVICH

Give me a laundry list and I will set it to music.
GIOACHINO ROSSINI

I write as a sow piddles.
WOLFGANG AMADEUS MOZART

Handel is the greatest composer who has ever lived. I would uncover my head and kneel at his grave.
LUDWIG VAN BEETHOVEN

I would vote for Bach, all of Bach, streamed out into space, over and over again. We would be bragging of course, but it is surely excusable to put the best possible face on at the beginning of such an acquaintance. We can tell the harder truths later.
LEWIS THOMAS On 1974's Communication with Extraterrestrial Intelligence (CETI) experiment led by Frank Drake and Carl Sagan.

There is one god – Bach – and Mendelssohn is his prophet.
HECTOR BERLIOZ

Berlioz is a regular freak, without a vestige of talent.
FELIX MENDELSSOHN

To me, Schumann's memory is holy. The noble, pure artist forever remains my ideal. I will hardly be privileged ever to love a better person.
JOHANNES BRAHMS

I have played over the music of that scoundrel Brahms. What a giftless bastard!
PYOTR TCHAIKOVSKY In his diary, 1886.

I hate Tchaikovsky and I will not conduct him.
PIERRE BOULEZ A radical modernist composer, but as a conductor not above turning in some lush accounts of Tchaikovsky's contemporaries Bruckner and Wagner.

Pretty monotonous and monotonously pretty.
IGOR STRAVINSKY On Pierre Boulez's *Pli Selon Pli* (1962).

One has in one's mouth the bizarre and charming taste of a pink sweet stuffed with snow.
CLAUDE DEBUSSY On the music of Edvard Grieg.

I am sure my music has a taste of codfish in it.
EDVARD GRIEG

New music? Hell, there's been no new music since Stravinsky.
DUKE ELLINGTON

Computers

Computers are stupid. They can only give you answers.
PABLO PICASSO

The question of whether computers can think is just like the question of whether submarines can swim.
EDGAR DIJKSTRA

Intelligence cannot be present without understanding. No computer has any awareness of what it does.
ROGER PENROSE

Computers make it easier to do a lot of things, but most of the things they make it easier to do don't need to be done.
ANDY ROONEY

Computers have enabled people to make more mistakes faster than almost any invention in history, with the possible exception of tequila and hand guns.
MITCH RATCLIFFE

Man is the best computer we can put aboard a spacecraft . . . and the only one that can be mass-produced by unskilled labour.
WERNHER VON BRAUN

Programming today is a race between software engineers striving to build bigger and better idiot-proof programs and the Universe trying to produce bigger and better idiots. So far, the Universe is winning.
RICH COOK

I think there is a world market for maybe five computers.
THOMAS WATSON Chairman of IBM, 1943. Except there is no evidence he ever said it. It first appeared in 1981 in *Facts and Fallacies: A Book of Definitive Mistakes and Misguided Predictions* by Chris Morgan and David Langford.

There is no reason for any individual to have a computer in his home.
KEN OLSEN President, Chairman, CEO and Founder of Digital Equipment Corporation, 1977. He didn't mean home PCs, however. He was referring to the widespread fear at the time that houses themselves and their waste, food preparation, heating and lighting systems would shortly become entirely computerised.

Consciousness

An enormous space whose boundaries, even by travelling along every path, cannot be found out.
HERACLITUS

Consciousness is a fascinating but elusive phenomenon: it is impossible to specify what it is, what it does, or why it evolved. Nothing worth reading has been written on it.
STUART SUTHERLAND A bracingly forthright assessment in his standard reference work, the Macmillan *Dictionary of Psychology* (1987).

Consciousness, or sentience, the raw sensation of toothaches and redness and saltiness and middle C, is still wrapped in a mystery inside an enigma.
STEVEN PINKER

How it is that anything so remarkable as consciousness comes about as a result of irritating nervous tissue, is just as unaccountable as the appearance of the Djin when Aladdin rubbed his lamp.
THOMAS HUXLEY

Somehow, we feel, the water of the physical brain is turned into the wine of consciousness, but we draw a total blank on the nature of this conversion.
COLIN McGINN

The intellectual life of man, his culture and history and religion and science, is different from anything else we know of in the Universe. That is fact. It is as if all life evolved to a certain point, and then ourselves turned at a right angle and simply exploded in a different direction.
JULIAN JAYNES

Our normal waking consciousness, rational consciousness as we call it, is but one special type of consciousness, whilst all about it, parted from it by the filmiest of screens, there lie potential forms of consciousness entirely different.
WILLIAM JAMES

Conversation

People say conversation is a lost art; how often I have wished it were.
EDWARD R. MURROW

No one really listens to anyone else, and if you try it for a while you'll see why.
MIGNON McLAUGHLIN

Talk to people about themselves and they will listen for hours.
BENJAMIN DISRAELI

There is no such thing as conversation. It is an illusion. There are intersecting monologues, that is all.
REBECCA WEST

The trouble with her is that she lacks the power of conversation but not the power of speech.
GEORGE BERNARD SHAW

If other people are going to talk, conversation becomes impossible.
JAMES McNEILL WHISTLER

John Wesley's conversation is good, but he is never at leisure. He is always obliged to go at a certain hour. This is very disagreeable to a man who loves to fold his legs and have out his talk, as I do.
SAMUEL JOHNSON

One way to prevent conversation from being boring is to say the wrong thing.
FRANK SHEED

Cosmology

There is speculation; there is wild speculation; and there is cosmology.
ANONYMOUS

Cosmology is still not a proper science, in the sense that as usually practised, it has no predictive power . . . To go further, and be a real science, cosmology would have to predict how the universe should be.
STEPHEN HAWKING

Ever since Newton, we've understood the 'clockwork' of planetary orbits; modern cosmologists make confident inferences about what happens billions of light years away. In contrast, scientists still can't agree on what food is good for us. There is a real sense in which dietetics is harder than cosmology.
SIR MARTIN REES

After a giving a lecture on the solar system, William James, the American psychologist and philosopher, was approached by an elderly lady. 'We don't live on a ball rotating around the sun,' she said, firmly. 'We live on a crust of earth on the back of a giant turtle.' James was a kindly man. 'If your theory is correct, madam, what does this turtle stand on?' he asked patiently. 'The first turtle stands on the back of a second, far larger turtle, of course!' she snorted. 'But what does this *second* turtle stand on?' pressed the philosopher. 'It's no use, Mr James,' crowed the old lady triumphantly, 'it's turtles all the way down!' **THIS APOCRYPHAL ENCOUNTER** has been attributed to a number of other famous thinkers including Bertrand Russell and Isaac Asimov. The earliest version is recounted by John Locke in 1690: 'But being again pressed to know what gave support to the broad-backed tortoise, replied – something, he knew not what.'

Courage

What is good, you ask. To be brave is good.
FRIEDRICH NIETZSCHE

Life shrinks or expands in proportion to one's courage.
ANAÏS NIN

Leap, and the net will appear.
JULIA MARGARET CAMERON

Living at risk is jumping off the cliff and building your wings on the way down.
RAY BRADBURY

Brave men are all vertebrates; they have their softness on the surface and their toughness in the middle.
LEWIS CARROLL

Facing it, always facing it, that's the way to get through. Face it.
JOSEPH CONRAD

To believe yourself to be brave is to be brave; it is the only essential thing.
MARK TWAIN

Bravery never goes out of style.
WILLIAM MAKEPEACE THACKERAY

Cows

To control your cow, give it a bigger pasture.
ROSHI SUZUKI

Some people want to see God with their eyes as they see a cow, and to love Him as they love their cow – for the milk and cheese and profit it brings them.
MEISTER ECKHART

A mind of the calibre of mine cannot derive its nutriment from cows.
GEORGE BERNARD SHAW

I could dance with you until the cows come home. On second thoughts I'd rather dance with the cows until you come home.
GROUCHO MARX

Who discovered we could get milk from cows, and what did he think he was doing at the time?
BILLY CONNOLLY

Parties who want milk should not seat themselves on a stool in the middle of the field in hope that the cow will back up to them.
ELBERT HUBBARD

Creation

The Lord created the universe in seven days but the Lord had the wonderful advantage of being able to work alone.
KOFI ANNAN

If there are any marks at all of special design in creation, one of the things most evidently designed is that a large proportion of all animals should pass their existence in tormenting and devouring other animals.
JOHN STUART MILL

I cannot persuade myself that a beneficent and omnipotent God would have designedly created the Ichneumonidae with the express intention of their feeding within the living bodies of caterpillars, or that a cat should play with mice.
CHARLES DARWIN

It is myth that creates the world. Without Neptune, the sea would be dead, and the waves owe half their of their fascination to the human invention of Venus.
FEDERICO GARCÍA LORCA

Creativity

Creativity is the defeat of habit by originality.
ARTHUR KOESTLER

Nothing great is created suddenly, any more than a bunch of grapes or a fig. If you tell me that you desire a fig, I answer you that there must be time. Let it first blossom, then bear fruit, then ripen.
EPICTETUS Influential Stoic and a disciple of Socrates, he believed it was our attitude to events, not the events themselves, that mattered. A friend to the emperor Hadrian, he was born a slave: his name means 'acquired' in Greek.

In dance, in composition, in sculpture, the experience is the same: we are more the conduit than the creator of what we express.
JULIA MARGARET CAMERON

I myself do nothing. The Holy Spirit accomplishes all through me.
WILLIAM BLAKE

Create like a god; command like a king; work like a slave.
CONSTANTIN BRANCUSI

Truth and reality in art do not arise until you no longer understand what you are doing.
HENRI MATISSE

You are lost the instant you know what the result will be.
JUAN GRIS

Crime

Crime leaves a trail like a water beetle; like a snail, it leaves its silver track; like a horse-mango, it leaves its smell.
MALAWIAN PROVERB

Always shoot to kill. Dead men cannot grass.
RONNIE KRAY

There's a difference between criminals and crooks. Crooks steal. Criminals blow some guy's brains out. I'm a crook.
RONALD BIGGS

The greatest crimes are caused by surfeit, not by want. Men do not become tyrants so as not to suffer cold.
ARISTOTLE

What a force was coiled up in the skull of Napoleon. Of the sixty thousand men making his army at Eylau, it seems some thirty thousand were thieves and burglars.

RALPH WALDO EMERSON He is probably overstating his case for effect here to show how powerful Napoleon's leadership skills were: he could even turn thieves into soldiers. But the *Grande Armée* did introduce mass conscription for the first time, and plenty of criminals did find their way in – most of the 1807 Neapolitan contingent were convicts.

A thief believes everybody steals.

E. W. HOWE Self-styled 'Sage of Potato Hill', Kansas, a curmudgeonly newspaper editor, novelist and master of the cynical one-liner. Admired by Mark Twain and a major influence on H. L. Mencken and Sinclair Lewis, Howe declared himself 'devoted to information and indignation'.

It is criminal to steal a purse, daring to steal a fortune, a mark of greatness to steal a crown. The blame diminishes as the guilt increases.
FRIEDRICH SCHILLER

If England treats her criminals the way she treated me, she doesn't deserve to have any.
OSCAR WILDE

Criticism

Honest criticism is hard to take – especially when it comes from a relative, a friend, an acquaintance, or a stranger.
FRANKLIN P. JONES

I didn't like the play. But I saw it under unfavorable circumstances – the curtains were up.
GROUCHO MARX

It had only one fault. It was kind of lousy.
JAMES THURBER

Pay no attention to what the critics say. A statue has never been erected in honour of a critic.
JEAN SIBELIUS

Critics can't even make music by rubbing their back legs together.
MEL BROOKS

Writing about music is like dancing about architecture – it's really a stupid thing to want to do.
ELVIS COSTELLO

Before you criticize someone, walk a mile in his shoes. That way, if he gets angry, he'll be a mile away – and barefoot.
SARAH JACKSON The original quote mentioned 'moccasins' not shoes and was first recorded in the *Lincoln Star* (Nebraska) in 1930 as an 'Indian Maxim'. Sarah Jackson may be a minor British comedian from the 1980s, a New York psychotherapist or one of the other 4,183 Sarah Jacksons estimated to live in the USA.

Coarse blotches, suggestive of putrescent flesh,
was how they described my '*impressions*'
in those early days. No wonder every so often,
Monet and I to escape would stuff ourselves
with larded turkey, washed down with Chambertin.
PIERRE AUGUSTE RENOIR

Some critics are like chimneysweepers; they put out the fire below, and frighten the swallows from the nests above; they scrape a long time in the chimney, cover themselves with soot, and bring nothing away but a bag of cinders, and then sing out from the top of the house, as if they had built it.
HENRY WADSWORTH LONGFELLOW

Critics have their purposes, and they're supposed to do what they do, but sometimes they get a little carried away with what they think someone should have done, rather than concerning themselves with what they did.
DUKE ELLINGTON

Critics may well be like eunuchs in a harem who know how it's done, having seen it done every day, they just don't fancy having it done to them.
A. A. GILL

Crying

Only man is cast forth on the day of his birth naked on the bare earth, to the accompaniment of crying and whimpering. No other creature is more given to tears – and that right at the beginning of life. The well-known first smile occurs, at the earliest, only after 40 days in any child.
PLINY THE ELDER

I came into this world and everyone was laughing as I was crying. I leave the world and everyone is crying and I am laughing.
KABIR A weaver by profession he refused all organised religions for a vision of

oneness written in simple Hindi vernacular. As a result, he is acclaimed by Hindus, Sikhs and Muslims, particularly Sufis, and is probably still India's most quoted poet.

Ready tears are a sign of treachery, not of grief.
PUBLILIUS SYRUS

You can recognise a cruel man: he cries in the cinema.
GRAHAM GREENE

Curiosity

The greatest virtue of man is perhaps curiosity.
ANATOLE FRANCE

The important thing is not to stop questioning.
ALBERT EINSTEIN

Pigs eat acorns, but neither consider the sun that gives them life, nor the influence of the heavens by which they were nourished, nor the very root of the tree from whence they came.
THOMAS TRAHERNE

All human beings, by nature, desire to know.
ARISTOTLE

Curiosity killed the cat, but for a while, I was a suspect.
STEVEN WRIGHT

I hold every day lost, when I do not acquire some new knowledge of man and nature.
SIR WILLIAM 'ORIENTAL' JONES

Be not curious in unnecessary matters; for more things are shewed unto thee than men understand.
ECCLESIASTICUS 3:23 Also known as *Sirach* (The Wisdom of Ben Sira), it was written in Hebrew about 180 BC by a Jew called Ben Sira, probably based in Alexandria. It is included in the Apocrypha of the King James Bible and is part of the biblical canon for Catholic and Orthodox Christians but not Protestants.

Be less curious about people and more curious about ideas.
MARIE CURIE

Desire to know why, and how, curiosity; such as is in no living creature but man: so that man is distinguished, not only by his reason, but also by this singular passion from other animals; in whom the appetite of food, and other pleasures of sense, by predominance, take away the

care of knowing causes; which is a lust of the mind, that by a perseverance of delight in the continual and indefatigable generation of knowledge, exceedeth the short vehemence of any carnal pleasure.
THOMAS HOBBES

There always comes a time when curiosity becomes a sin.
ANATOLE FRANCE

I loathe that low vice, curiosity.
LORD BYRON

Curiosity is one of the lowest of the human faculties. You will have noticed in daily life that when people are inquisitive they nearly always have bad memories and are usually stupid at bottom.
E. M. FORSTER

People die when curiosity goes.
GRAHAM SWIFT

D

Daffodils

Consider the daffodil. And while you're doing that, I'll be over here,
looking through your stuff.
JACK HANDEY

Deprivation is for me what daffodils were for Wordsworth.
PHILIP LARKIN

He that has two cakes of bread, let him sell one of them for some
flowers of the Narcissus, for bread is food for the body, but Narcissus is
food of the soul.
MUHAMMAD

Fallen leaves lying on the grass in the November sun bring more
happiness than the daffodils.
CYRIL CONNOLLY

The chaplet of the infernal gods.
SOPHOCLES This unidentified translation of lines 681–2 from *Oedipus at Colonus*
has had a curious history. It appeared in a herbal by Dr W. T. Fernie in 1895 and
perhaps because of the connection between the narcotic properties of narcissi and
the deadliness of hemlock, he misattributed it to Socrates, who has taken the credit
in all subsequent anthologies until now.

Dancing

Let us read and let us dance – two amusements that will never do any
harm to the world.
VOLTAIRE

All the ills of mankind, all the tragic misfortunes that fill the history
books, all the political blunders, all the failures of the great leaders
have arisen merely from a lack of skill at dancing.
MOLIÈRE

Everything in the universe has rhythm. Everything dances.
MAYA ANGELOU

People who dance are considered insane by those who can't hear the music.
GEORGE CARLIN

No sane man will dance.
CICERO

Mind you, Hugh Gaitskell was a very good dancer. And to me, that is more important than politics in a man.
BARBARA CASTLE

Nobody cares if you can't dance well. Just get up and dance. Great dancers are not great because of their technique, they are great because of their passion.
MARTHA GRAHAM

I have no desire to prove anything by dancing. I have never used it as an outlet or a means of expressing myself. I just dance. I just put my feet in the air and move them around.
FRED ASTAIRE

I do not try to dance better than anyone else. I try to dance better than myself.
MIKHAIL BARYSHNIKOV

Dancing is a perpendicular expression of a horizontal desire.
GEORGE BERNARD SHAW

Dancing begets warmth, which is the parent of wantonness. It is, Sir, the great grandfather of cuckoldom.
HENRY FIELDING

Dancing is a sweat job.
FRED ASTAIRE

Danger

The chief danger in life is that you may take too many precautions.
ALFRED ADLER

There's more danger in the violence you don't face.
MICHAEL ONDAATJE

People who make no noise are dangerous.
JEAN DE LA FONTAINE

If you meet it promptly and without flinching – you will reduce the danger by half. Never run away from anything. Never!
WINSTON CHURCHILL

When danger or pain press too nearly, they are incapable of giving any delight and are simply terrible; but at certain distances, and with certain modifications, they may be, and they are, delightful, as we every day experience.
EDMUND BURKE

Life is either a daring adventure or nothing. Security does not exist in nature, nor do the children of men as a whole experience it. Avoiding danger is no safer in the long run than outright exposure. The fearful are caught as often as the bold.
HELEN KELLER

Dating

I'm dating a homeless woman. It was easier talking her into staying over.
GARRY SHANDLING

Whenever I date a guy, I think, is this the man I want my children to spend their weekends with?
RITA RUDNER

Let's face it: a date is a job-interview that lasts all night. The only difference between a date and a job-interview is: not many job-interviews is there a chance you'll end up naked at the end of it.
JERRY SEINFELD

Employees make the best dates. You don't have to pick them up and they're always tax-deductible.
ANDY WARHOL

I can't go on any more bad dates. I would rather be home alone than out with some guy who sells socks on the internet.
CYNTHIA NIXON Actor from *Sex in the City*.

Watching your daughter being collected by her date feels like handing over a million-dollar Stradivarius to a gorilla.
JIM BISHOP Once touted as 'America's hottest writer', he invented 'The Day' style of narrative history. His 1957 account of Christ's last twenty-two hours, *The Day Christ Died*, remains a strong seller.

Daughters

You teach your daughters the diameters of the planets, and wonder when you have done that they do not delight in your company?
SAMUEL JOHNSON

I will not allow my daughters to learn foreign languages because one tongue is sufficient for a woman.
JOHN MILTON

My unhealthy affection for my second daughter has waned. Now I despise all my seven children equally.
EVELYN WAUGH

To my daughter Leonora without whose never-failing sympathy and encouragement this book would have been finished in half the time.
P. G. WODEHOUSE

Any astronomer can predict with absolute accuracy just where every star in the universe will be at 11.30 tonight. He can make no such prediction about his teenage daughter.
JAMES T. ADAMS

Don't tell your kids you had an easy birth or they won't respect you. For years I used to wake up my daughter and say, 'Melissa you ripped me to shreds. Now go back to sleep.'
JOAN RIVERS

Art is the daughter of freedom.
FRIEDRICH SCHILLER

Admiration is the daughter of ignorance.
BENJAMIN FRANKLIN

Death

Death is a very dull, dreary affair, and my advice to you is to have nothing whatsoever to do with it.
W. SOMERSET MAUGHAM

For three days after death, hair and fingernails continue to grow but phone calls taper off.
JOHNNY CARSON

Perhaps the whole root of our trouble, the human trouble, is that we will sacrifice all the beauty of our lives, will imprison ourselves in totems, taboos, crosses, blood sacrifices, steeples, mosques, races, armies, flags, nations, in order to deny the fact of death, which is the only fact we have.
JAMES BALDWIN

Death is like the rumble of distant thunder at a picnic.
W. H. AUDEN

If Shaw and Einstein couldn't cheat death, what chance have I got?
Practically none.
MEL BROOKS

Once you're dead, you're made for life.
JIMI HENDRIX

What is philosophy but the study of death?
SOCRATES

Death is the dark backing a mirror needs if we are to see anything.
SAUL BELLOW

Where does the soul go when the body dies? There is no necessity for it
to go anywhere.
JAKOB BÖHME A Lutheran mystic whose vision of the oneness of man, God and
the universe came in 1600 while staring at the light reflected in a pewter dish. His
work had a profound influence on the Quakers and the work of William Blake.

All say: 'How hard it is that we have to die' – a strange complaint to
come from the mouths of people who have had to live.
MARK TWAIN

Everybody has got to die, but I've always believed an exception would
be made in my case.
WILLIAM SAROYAN

Life is a great surprise. I do not see why death should not be an even
greater one.
VLADIMIR NABOKOV

Decisions

Be willing to make decisions. That's the most important quality in a
good leader. Don't fall victim to what I call the 'ready-aim-aim-aim-
aim syndrome.' You must be willing to fire.
GEORGE S. PATTON

Nothing is more difficult, and therefore more precious, than to be able
to decide.
NAPOLEON BONAPARTE

Decide promptly, but never give your reasons. Your decisions may be right, but your reasons are sure to be wrong.
LORD MANSFIELD

If someone tells you he is going to make 'a realistic decision', you immediately understand that he is going to do something bad.
MARY McCARTHY

Ever notice that 'what the hell' is always the right decision?
MARILYN MONROE

Democracy

The people are that part of the state that does not know what it wants.
G. W. F. HEGEL

For a state in which the law is respected, democracy is the worst form of government, but if the law is not respected, it is the best.
PLATO

Democracy is government by explanation.
A. J. BALFOUR

Those who cast the votes decide nothing. Those who count the votes decide everything.
JOSEF STALIN

Democracy consists of choosing your dictators after they've told you what you think it is you want to hear.
ALAN COREN

Democracy is a device that insures we shall be governed no better than we deserve.
GEORGE BERNARD SHAW

The more I see of democracy the more I dislike it. It just brings everything down to the mere vulgar level of wages and prices, electric light and water closets, and nothing else.
D. H. LAWRENCE

Under democracy, one party always devotes its chief energies to trying to prove that the other party is unfit to rule – and both commonly succeed, and are right.
H. L. MENCKEN

Democracy is the worst form of government except for all those other forms which have been tried from time to time.
WINSTON CHURCHILL

Democracy is two wolves and a lamb voting on what to have for lunch. Liberty is a well-armed lamb contesting the vote.
BENJAMIN FRANKLIN

If pigs could vote, the man with the slop bucket would be elected swineherd every time, no matter how much slaughtering he did on the side.
ORSON SCOTT CARD

It is almost universally felt that when we call a country democratic we are praising it; consequently, the defenders of every kind of regime claim that it is a democracy, and fear that they might have to stop using the word if it were tied down to any one meaning.
GEORGE ORWELL

Democracy means that anyone can grow up to be president, and anyone who doesn't grow up can be vice president.
JOHNNY CARSON

All through history, mankind has been bullied by scum. Each government is a parliament of whores. The trouble is, in a democracy, the whores are us.
P. J. O'ROURKE

Win or lose, we go shopping after the election.
IMELDA MARCOS Never one to hide her light under a bushel, Mrs Marcos herself suggested the adjective 'imeldific' to describe ostentatious extravagance, although she also claimed she never shopped for herself and all her possessions were, in fact, gifts from her husband, children and pets.

Desire

Desire is the very essence of man.
BARUCH SPINOZA

The desires of the heart are as crooked as corkscrews.
W. H. AUDEN

Suffering is caused by desire.
BUDDHA

Man is the only animal whose desires increase as they are fed; the only animal that is never satisfied.
HENRY GEORGE American economist and founder of 'Georgism' which proposed that rent for land should be shared equally across the community. This has only really been implemented on a large scale in Hong Kong, where a third of government revenues come directly from land tax.

The desire engendered in the male glands is a hundred times more difficult to control than the desire bred in the female glands. All girls who limit their actions to arousing desire and then defending their honour should be horsewhipped.
MARLENE DIETRICH

If men could regard the events of their own lives with more open minds they would frequently discover that they did not really desire the things they failed to obtain.
ANDRÉ MAUROIS

If you don't get what you want, it's a sign either that you did not seriously want it, or that you tried to bargain over the price.
RUDYARD KIPLING

There is nothing like desire for preventing the thing one says from bearing any resemblance to what one has in mind.
MARCEL PROUST

Desperation

The mass of men lead lives of quiet desperation.
HENRY DAVID THOREAU

Nowadays men lead lives of noisy desperation.
JAMES THURBER

You may not know it, but at the far end of despair, there is a white clearing where one is almost happy.
JOAN BAEZ

Desperation is like stealing from the Mafia: you stand a good chance of attracting the wrong attention.
DOUG HORTON

Destiny

What people commonly call fate is mostly their own stupidity.
ARTHUR SCHOPENHAUER

Lots of folks confuse bad management with destiny.
FRANK 'KIN' HUBBARD One of the first and best of the syndicated cartoon/aphorists, his 'Abe Martin of Brown County' appeared on the back of the *Indianapolis News* every day from 1905 to 1930. As a comic writer, Will Rogers thought 'no man in our generation was within a mile of him'.

Anatomy is destiny.
SIGMUND FREUD This appeared in *The Dissolution of the Oedipus Complex* (1924) and is adapted from Napoleon. Not many people remember what comes next: 'The little girl's clitoris behaves just like a penis to begin with; but, when she makes a comparison with a playfellow of the other sex, she perceives that she has 'come off badly'. . . The rest is history.

Whom the gods wish to destroy they first call promising.
CYRIL CONNOLLY

No trumpets sound when the important decisions of our life are made. Destiny is made known silently.
AGNES DE MILLE

Everything that happens, happens as it should, and if you observe carefully, you will find this to be so.
MARCUS AURELIUS

I do not believe in a fate that falls on men however they act; but I do believe in a fate that falls on them unless they act.
G. K. CHESTERTON

Failure or success seem to have been allotted to men by their stars. But they retain the power of wriggling, of fighting with their star or against it, and in the whole universe the only really interesting movement is this wriggle.
E. M. FORSTER

Destiny has two ways of crushing us – by refusing our wishes and by fulfilling them.
HENRI FRÉDÉRIC AMIEL

But the power of destiny is something awesome; neither wealth, nor Ares, nor a tower, nor dark-hulled ships might escape it.
SOPHOCLES

We are not permitted to choose the frame of our destiny. But what we put into it is ours.
DAG HAMMARSKJÖLD

Diamonds

Diamonds are sublimely useless. You cannot eat them or drive them home.
MATTHEW HART

Diamonds are nothing more than chunks of coal that stuck to their jobs.
MALCOLM S. FORBES

I never hated a man enough to give him his diamonds back.
ZSA ZSA GABOR

Big girls need big diamonds.
ELIZABETH TAYLOR

No pressure, no diamonds.
MARY CASE

Diaries

It's the good girls who keep diaries; the bad girls never have the time.
TALULLAH BANKHEAD If claims that the actress slept with '40 per cent of the British aristocracy' during her eight-year stay in 1920s London are overblown, her reckless exhibitionism is well attested. When crew complained of her lack of underwear on the set of *Lifeboat* in 1944, Hitchcock's laconic reply was: 'I don't know whether that's a concern for wardrobe or hairdressing.'

Keep a diary and one day it'll keep you.
MAE WEST

I never travel without my diary. One should always have something sensational to read in the train.
OSCAR WILDE

Diary, n. A daily record of that part of one's life, which he can relate to himself without blushing.
AMBROSE BIERCE

What is a diary as a rule? A document useful to the person who keeps it, dull to the contemporary who reads it, invaluable to the student, centuries afterwards, who treasures it!
ELLEN TERRY

Dictators

I like old Joe Stalin.
HARRY TRUMAN

Herr Hitler has one of the endearing characteristics of Ferdinand the Bull. Just when the crowds expect him to be most violent, he stops and smells the flowers.
BEVERLEY NICHOLS *Ferdinand the Bull* was an illustrated book by American

children's author Munro Leaf published in 1936. Nichols is best remembered for the perennial best-seller *Down the Garden Path*, a classic in the 'garden makeover' genre.

I can't help but think some people admire totalitarian regimes not because they want to live in one, but because they want to be in charge of one.
MICHAEL TOTTEN

I have never bothered with politics.
GENERAL FRANCO

Power does not interest me. After victory I want to go back to my village and just be a lawyer again.
FIDEL CASTRO Quoted in the *New York Times* in 1957 – two years before he started his forty-nine-year rule in Cuba.

I give Castro a year. No longer.
FULGENCIO BATISTA Former dictator of Cuba, speaking from exile in Madeira in 1959.

Europe is nothing but a collection of unjust dictatorships. All of humanity must strike these trouble-makers with an iron hand if it wishes to regain its tranquillity.
AYATOLLAH KHOMEINI

He is one of the best Prime Ministers. He is like Hitler – really tough – I admire him.
IDI AMIN On Edward Heath during his state visit to London in July 1971.

He's just a goddamn cannibal asshole. He'd eat his own mother. Christ! He'd eat his own grandmother!
RICHARD NIXON Describing Idi Amin in 1976.

I came to carry out a struggle, not to kill people. Even now, and you can look at me, am I a savage person? My conscience is clear.
POL POT

Dictators always look good until the last minutes.
TOMÁ? G. MASARYK

Dieting

'How long does getting thin take?' asked Pooh, anxiously.
A. A. MILNE

The one way to get thin is to re-establish a purpose in life.
CYRIL CONNOLLY

Part of the secret of success in life is to eat what you like and let the food fight it out inside.
MARK TWAIN

No diet will remove all the fat from your body because the brain is entirely fat. Without a brain, you might look good, but all you could do is run for public office.
GEORGE BERNARD SHAW

Those magazine dieting stories always have the testimonial of a woman who wore a dress that could slipcover New Jersey in one photo and thirty days later looked like a well-dressed thermometer.
ERMA BOMBECK

The second day of a diet is always easier than the first. By the second day you're off it.
JACKIE GLEASON

Differences

I learned very early the difference between knowing the name of something and knowing something.
RICHARD FEYNMANN

The difference between art and science is that science is what we understand well enough to explain to a computer. Art is everything else.
DONALD KNUTH

The difference between stupidity and genius is that genius has its limits.
ALBERT EINSTEIN

The difference between a misfortune and a calamity is this: If Gladstone fell into the Thames, it would be a misfortune. But if someone dragged him out again, that would be a calamity.
BENJAMIN DISRAELI

The difference between fiction and reality? Fiction has to make sense.
TOM CLANCY

The difference between sex and death is that with death you can do it alone and no one is going to make fun of you.
WOODY ALLEN

The difference between men and women is that, if given the choice between saving the life of an infant or catching a fly ball, a woman will

automatically choose to save the infant, without even considering if there's a man on base.
DAVE BARRY

The only difference between suicide and martyrdom is press coverage.
CHUCK PALAHNIUK

The only difference between me and a madman is that I'm not mad.
SALVADOR DALÍ

The big difference between sex for money and sex for free is that sex for money usually costs a lot less.
BRENDAN BEHAN

The only difference between doctors and lawyers is that lawyers merely rob you, whereas doctors rob you and kill you, too.
ANTON CHEKHOV

The only difference between a rut and a grave is their dimensions.
ELLEN GLASGOW A pessimist but she rescued Southern literature from cosiness and nostalgia, paving the way for Eudora Welty and William Faulkner. She won the Pulitzer Prize in 1942 for *In This Our Life*, the last of her nineteen novels. Dogs feature prominently in almost all of them.

The difference between tragedy and comedy: tragedy is something awful happening to somebody else, while comedy is something awful happening to somebody else.
AARON ALLSTON

Difficulty

All excellent things are as difficult as they are rare.
BARUCH SPINOZA

Clever people master life; the wise illuminate it and create fresh difficulties.
EMIL NOLDE

Man needs difficulties; they are necessary for health.
CARL JUNG

It is not because things are difficult that we do not dare; it is because we do not dare that they are difficult.
SENECA

I've learned that you can tell a lot about a person by the way he/she handles these three things: a rainy day, lost luggage, and tangled Christmas tree lights.
MAYA ANGELOU

The most difficult thing in the world is to know how to do a thing and to watch someone else do it wrong without comment.
T. H. WHITE Multi-talented English schoolteacher, storyteller and countryman who was also a sado-masochist, homosexual and alcoholic. J. K. Rowling claims him as a key influence on the Harry Potter books.

A difficulty is a light. An insurmountable difficulty is a sun.
PAUL VALÉRY

Out of difficulties grow miracles.
JEAN DE LA BRUYÈRE

A fool often fails because he thinks what is difficult is easy.
JOHN CHURTON COLLINS

The crisis is not out there in the world; it is in our own consciousness.
J. KRISHNAMURTI

Diplomacy

A diplomat is a man who always remembers a woman's birthday but never remembers her age.
ROBERT FROST

To say nothing, especially when speaking, is half the art of diplomacy.
WILL DURANT

Diplomacy is the art of saying 'Nice doggie' until you can find a rock.
WILL ROGERS

There are few ironclad rules of diplomacy but to one there is no exception. When an official reports that talks were useful, it can safely be concluded that nothing was accomplished.
J. K. GALBRAITH

Sincere diplomacy is no more possible than dry water or wooden iron.
JOSEF STALIN

Discoveries

The more original the discovery, the more obvious it seems afterwards.
ARTHUR KOESTLER

The most important of my discoveries have been suggested to me by my failures.
HUMPHREY DAVY

There's two possible outcomes: if the result confirms the hypothesis, then you've made a discovery. If the result is contrary to the hypothesis, then you've made a discovery.
ENRICO FERMI

One doesn't discover new lands without consenting to lose sight of the shore for a very long time.
ANDRÉ GIDE

Discovery consists of seeing what everybody has seen and thinking what nobody has thought.
ALBERT SZENT-GYSRGYI Winner of the 1937 Nobel prize for his discovery of vitamin C. He finally isolated it using the red peppers that Hungarians used to make paprika, their national spice, which contain six times as much as an orange or lemon.

The intellect has little to do on the road to discovery. There comes a leap in consciousness, call it intuition or what you will, and the solution comes to you and you don't know how or why.
ALBERT EINSTEIN

You must be satisfied with making discoveries. Take care never to offer explanations.
GEORGES BRAQUE

Divorce

You never really know a man until you have divorced him.
ZSA ZSA GABOR

Ah, yes, divorce, from the Latin word meaning to rip out a man's genitals through his wallet.
ROBIN WILLIAMS

My divorce came to me as a complete surprise. That's what happens when you haven't been home in eighteen years.
LEE TREVINO

When two people decide to get a divorce, it isn't a sign that they 'don't understand' one another, but a sign that they have, at last, begun to.
HELEN ROWLAND

The possibility of divorce renders both marriage partners stricter in their observance of the duties they owe to each other. Divorces help to improve morals and to increase the population.
DENIS DIDEROT

In Hollywood, an equitable divorce settlement means each party getting fifty percent of publicity.
LAUREN BACALL

A divorce is like an amputation; you survive, but there's less of you.
MARGARET ATWOOD

Doctors

The great secret of doctors, known only to their wives, but still hidden from the public, is that most things get better by themselves; most things, in fact, are better in the morning.
LEWIS THOMAS

Never go to a doctor whose office plants have died.
ERMA BOMBECK

The witch doctor succeeds for the same reason all the rest of us succeed. Each patient carries his own doctor inside him. They come to us not knowing the truth. We are best when we give the doctor who resides within each patient a chance to go to work.
ALBERT SCHWEITZER

The good physician treats the disease; the great physician treats the patient who has the disease.
WILLIAM OSLER

The best doctors in the world are Doctor Diet, Doctor Quiet, and Doctor Merryman.
JONATHAN SWIFT

To do the sort of things to a dog that one does to the average medical student requires a licence signed in triplicate by two archbishops.
J. B. S. HALDANE Pioneer geneticist and passionate Communist, he was a friend of Aldous Huxley and his work helped inspire *Brave New World*. Such was his commitment to experimentation he once ruptured his eardrums in a decompression chamber. This left him slightly deaf but able to blow tobacco smoke out of one ear, 'which was a social accomplishment'.

My doctor is wonderful. Once, in 1955, when I couldn't afford an operation, he touched up the X-rays.
JOEY BISHOP

My doctor gave me six months to live but when I couldn't pay the bill, he gave me six months more.
WALTER MATTHAU

Doctors are men who prescribe medicine of which they know little to cure diseases of which they know less in human beings of which they know nothing.
VOLTAIRE

A medical maxim – when you hear hoofbeats, think of horses before zebras.
HARLEY SMITH

Physicians think they do a lot for a patient when they give his disease a name.
IMMANUEL KANT

First the doctor told me the good news: I was going to have a disease named after me.
STEVE MARTIN

My doctor told me that jogging could add years to my life. I think he was right. I feel ten years older already.
MILTON BERLE

Specialist: A doctor who has a smaller practice, but a larger house.
RON DENTINGER

Doctors will have more lives to answer for in the next world than even we generals.
NAPOLEON BONAPARTE

As she lay there dozing next to me, one voice inside my head kept saying, 'Relax . . . you are not the first doctor to sleep with one of his patients,' but another kept reminding me, 'Howard, you are a veterinarian.'
DICK WILSON Born Riccardo DiGuglielmo, he was most famous for playing Mr Whipple, a fussy shop manager in 500 ads for Charmin toilet paper in the US. He got a lifetime supply of the product for his trouble. The attribution of this quote seems dubious, at best.

Dogs

From a dog's point of view his master is an elongated and abnormally cunning dog.
MABEL L. ROBINSON

To his dog, every man is Napoleon; hence the constant popularity of dogs.
ALDOUS HUXLEY

I loathe people who keep dogs. They are cowards who haven't got the guts to bite people themselves.
AUGUST STRINDBERG

A Canadian psychologist is selling a video that teaches you how to test your dog's IQ. Here's how it works: if you spend $12.99 for the video, your dog is smarter than you.
JAY LENO

Did you ever walk in a room and forget why you walked in? I think that's how dogs spend their lives.
SUE MURPHY

I've seen a look in dogs' eyes, a quickly vanishing look of amazed contempt, and I am convinced that basically dogs think humans are nuts.
JOHN STEINBECK

I wonder if other dogs think poodles are members of a weird religious cult?
RITA RUDNER

Doubt

Doubt grows with knowledge.
GOETHE

The press and the public like certainty and affirmation of popular biases. But real science thrives on the capacity for doubt.
WENDY KAMINER

Doubt is part of all religion. All the religious thinkers were doubters.
ISAAC BASHEVIS SINGER

If you can doubt at points where other people find no impulse to doubt, you are making progress.
ZHUANGZI (CHUANG TZU) His basic beliefs ('there is no good or bad, only thinking makes it so') combine elements of scepticism and libertarianism. He has been called the 'the world's first anarchist'.

True science teaches, above all, to doubt and to be ignorant.
MIGUEL DE UNAMUNO

Belief in truth begins with doubts of all truths in which one has previously believed.
FRIEDRICH NIETZSCHE

The great civilizer on earth seems to have been doubt. Doubt, the constantly debated and flexible inner condition of theological uncertainty, seems to have held people in thrall to ethical behaviour, while the true believers of whatever stamp, religious or religious-statist, have done the murdering.
E. L. DOCTOROW

A doubt that doubted everything would not be a doubt.
LUDWIG WITTGENSTEIN

Drawing

You can never do too much drawing.
TINTORETTO

One must keep right on drawing; draw with your eyes when you cannot draw with a pencil.
JEAN-AUGUSTE-DOMINIQUE INGRES

Drawing is not the same as form, it is a way of seeing form.
EDGAR DEGAS

The most accomplished monkey cannot draw a monkey, this too only man can do; just as it is only man who regards his ability to do this as a distinct merit.
G. C. LICHTENBERG

People who see a drawing in the *New Yorker* will think automatically that it's funny because it is a cartoon. If they see it in a museum, they think it is artistic; and if they find it in a fortune cookie they think it is a prediction.
SAUL STEINBERG He produced 1,200 illustrations and 85 covers for the *New Yorker*, including the classic, much copied 'View of the world from 9th Avenue' in 1976.

Drawing is the honesty of the art. There is no possibility of cheating. It is either good or bad.
SALVADOR DALÍ

Practise by drawing things large, as if equal in representation and reality. In small drawings every large weakness is easily hidden; in the large, the smallest weakness is easily seen.
LEON BATTISTA ALBERTI

All good and genuine draftsmen draw according to the picture inscribed in their minds, and not according to nature.
BAUDELAIRE

We should talk less and draw more. Personally, I would like to renounce speech altogether and, like organic nature, communicate everything I have to say in sketches.
GOETHE

Dreams

All that we see or seem is but a dream within a dream.
EDGAR ALLAN POE

Anyone can escape into sleep, we are all geniuses when we dream, the butcher's the poet's equal there.
E. M. CIORAN Profoundly pessimistic, he was friend to Eugene Ionesco and Samuel Beckett. His mother once remarked that if she'd known he was going to be so miserable she would have had him aborted.

Dreaming is an act of pure imagination, attesting in all men a creative power, which, if it were available in waking, would make every man a Dante or a Shakespeare.
F. H. HEDGE

I dream my painting and then paint my dream.
VINCENT VAN GOGH

Dreaming permits each and every one of us to be quietly and safely insane every night of our lives.
CHARLES WILLIAM DEMENT Author of the 1992 *Wake Up America* report which revealed that sleep deprivation reduced US economic productivity by $100 million dollars a year.

I have dreamed in my life, dreams that have stayed with me ever after, and changed my ideas; they have gone through and through me, like wine through water, and altered the colour of my mind.
EMILY BRONTË

He dreamed he was eating Shredded Wheat and woke up to find the mattress half gone.
FRED ALLEN

All men dream, but not equally. Those who dream by night in the dusty recesses of their minds, wake in the day to find that it was vanity: but the dreamers of the day are dangerous men, for they may act their dream with open eyes, to make it possible.
T. E. LAWRENCE

Only in our dreams are we free. The rest of the time we need wages.
TERRY PRATCHETT

Drink

Once, during Prohibition, I was forced to live for days on nothing but food and water.
W. C. FIELDS

The sway of alcohol over mankind is unquestionably due to its power to stimulate the mystical faculties of human nature, usually crushed to earth by the cold facts and dry criticisms of the sober hour. Sobriety diminishes, discriminates, and says no; drunkenness expands, unites, and says yes. Not through mere perversity do men run after it.
WILLIAM JAMES

One reason I don't drink is that I want to know when I am having a good time.
NANCY ASTOR

There is nothing wrong with sobriety in moderation.
JOHN CIARDI

As I don't drink alcohol, and giving up smoking would be far too serious a matter, I propose to stand in with Edward Lyttelton and give up Gibraltar: it's not such a habit with me.
RONALD KNOX Prominent Roman Catholic prelate and wit, who also wrote classic detective novels. Originally ordained an Anglican, his conversion came as result of his friendship with G. K. Chesterton. Evelyn Waugh was his literary executor and wrote the definitive biography in 1959.

Drugs

I don't do drugs. I am drugs.
SALVADOR DALÍ

I'm in favor of legalizing drugs. According to my values system, if people want to kill themselves, they have every right to do so. Most of the harm that comes from drugs is because they are illegal.
MILTON FRIEDMAN

Any musician who says he is playing better either on tea, the needle, or when he is juiced, is a plain straight liar.
CHARLIE PARKER

I hate to advocate drugs, alcohol, violence, or insanity to anyone, but they've always worked for me.
HUNTER S. THOMPSON

Don't do speed. Speed turns you into your parents.
FRANK ZAPPA

I don't like people who take drugs. Customs men, for example.
MICK MILLER

Cocaine isn't habit-forming. I should know, I've been using it for years.
TALULLAH BANKHEAD

Researchers have discovered that chocolate produces some of the same reactions in the brain as marijuana. The researchers also discovered other similarities between the two but can't remember what they are.
MATT LAUER American host of *The Today Show* on NBC since 1994, he was famously accused of being glib by Tom Cruise during a discussion on scientology and has confessed to a morbid fear of being struck by lightning.

A drug is a substance that, when injected into a rat, produces a scientific paper.
EGERTON Y. DAVIS JR

Words are, of course, the most powerful drug used by mankind.
RUDYARD KIPLING

Drunks

I drink too much. The last time I gave a urine sample it had an olive in it.
RODNEY DANGERFIELD

I drink no more than a sponge.
FRANÇOIS RABELAIS

I saw a notice which said 'Drink Canada Dry' and I've just started.
BRENDAN BEHAN

Actually, it only takes one drink to get me loaded. Trouble is, I can't remember if it's the thirteenth or fourteenth.
GEORGE BURNS

You're not drunk if you can lie on the floor without holding on.
DEAN MARTIN

I once shook hands with Pat Boone and my whole right side sobered up.
DEAN MARTIN

If you drink, don't drive. Don't even putt.
DEAN MARTIN

Always do sober what you said you'd do drunk. That will teach you to keep your mouth shut.
ERNEST HEMINGWAY

What is said when drunk has been thought out beforehand.
FLEMISH PROVERB

Duty

Duty is the most sublime word in our language. Do your duty in all things. You cannot do more. You should never wish to do less.
ROBERT E. LEE

I think a man's duty is to find out where the truth is, or if he cannot, at least to take the best possible human doctrine and the hardest to disprove, and to ride on this like a raft over the waters of life.
PLATO

Do something every day that you don't want to do; this is the golden rule for acquiring the habit of doing your duty without pain.
MARK TWAIN

It is better to do one's own duty, however defective it may be, than to follow the duty of another, however well one may perform it. He who does his duty as his own nature reveals it, never sins.
THE BHAGAVAD GITA

Conscientious people are apt to see their duty in that which is the most painful course.
GEORGE ELIOT

E

Ears

We have two ears and one mouth so that we can listen twice as much as we speak.
EPICTETUS

Students of evolution in the animal world tell us that the ear was the last of the sense organs to arrive; it is beyond question the most intricate and the most beautiful.
SIR JAMES JEANS

It is all very well to be able to write books, but can you waggle your ears?
J. M. BARRIE

Among the mammals
only man has ears
that can display no emotion.
W. H. AUDEN

Men love with their eyes; women love with their ears.
ZSA ZSA GABOR

For women the best aphrodisiacs are words. The G-spot is in the ears. He who looks for it below there is wasting his time.
ISABEL ALLENDE

Earth

God's golf ball.
CAPTAIN BEEFHEART

The world, when viewed from above, resembles a ball sewn from twelve pieces of skin.
SOCRATES

How inappropriate to call this planet Earth when clearly it is Ocean.
ARTHUR C. CLARKE

The Earth was small, light blue, and so touchingly alone, our home that must be defended like a holy relic. The Earth was absolutely round. I believe I never knew what the word round meant until I saw Earth from space.
ALEKSEI LEONOV

The colours were so vivid and the snow and the clouds were the whitest white. The land was brown in stark contrast to the crystal blue of the oceans. It was breathtaking. None of the pictures we took capture the emotion we had looking at the Earth.
CHARLIE DUKE

What is the Earth most like? It is most like a single cell.
LEWIS THOMAS

Look again at that dot. That's here. That's home. That's us. On it everyone you love, everyone you know, everyone you ever heard of, every human being who ever was, lived out their lives. The aggregate of our joy and suffering, thousands of confident religions, ideologies, and economic doctrines, every hunter and forager, every hero and coward, every creator and destroyer of civilization, every king and peasant, every young couple in love, every mother and father, hopeful child, inventor and explorer, every teacher of morals, every corrupt politician, every 'superstar,' every 'supreme leader,' every saint and sinner in the history of our species lived there – on a mote of dust suspended in a sunbeam.
CARL SAGAN In *Pale Blue Dot* (1994) a book inspired by Voyager I's photograph of the Earth from four billion miles' distance, against the vastness of space.

What is the good of having a nice house without a decent planet to put it on?
HENRY DAVID THOREAU

Economics

Economics is extremely useful as a form of employment for economists.
J. K. GALBRAITH

There are three kinds of economists. Those that can add, and those that can't.
HAMISH McCRAE

I want a one-armed economist so that the guy could never make a statement and then say 'on the other hand . . .'
HARRY S. TRUMAN

An economist is someone who will know tomorrow why the things he predicted yesterday didn't happen today.
LAWRENCE J. PETER Inventor of the Peter Principle, in which each employee in a hierarchy tends to rise to the level of his incompetence and stay there.

Making a speech on economics is a bit like pissing down your leg. It seems hot to you but never to anyone else.
LYNDON B. JOHNSON

The worse the economy, the better the economists.
ALFRED ZAUBERMAN Coined this in 1983 – it's now known as Zauberman's Law.

All the great economic ills the world has known this century can be directly traced back to the London School of Economics.
N. M. PERERA

Wall Street indices predicted nine out of the last five recessions.
PAUL SAMUELSON

In all recorded history there has not been one economist who has had to worry about where the next meal would come from.
PETER DRUCKER

Education

We spend the first twelve months of our children's lives teaching them to walk and talk and the next twelve years telling them to sit down and shut up.
PHYLLIS DILLER

All you have to do to educate a child is leave them alone and teach them to read. The rest is brainwashing.
ELLEN GILCRIST

I pity unlearned gentlemen on a rainy day.
LUCIUS CARY, VISCOUNT FALKLAND Secretary of State under Charles I, he gathered an extraordinary group of scholars, philosophers and poets to his country estate at Great Tew in Oxfordshire, including Ben Jonson, Lord Clarendon and Thomas Hobbes. Depressed by the onset of civil war he effectively committed suicide by riding unarmed into battle at Newbury in 1643.

Learning is the only thing the mind never exhausts, never fears, and never regrets.
LEONARDO DA VINCI

To teach is to learn.
JAPANESE PROVERB

Let early education be a sort of amusement. You will then be better able to discover the natural bent.
PLATO

A teacher is one who makes himself progressively unnecessary.
THOMAS CARRUTHERS

My education was interrupted only by my schooling.
WINSTON CHURCHILL

Sixty years ago I knew everything; now I know nothing; education is a progressive discovery of our own ignorance.
WILL DURANT

Children are educated by what the grown-up is and not by his talk.
CARL JUNG

Men are born ignorant, not stupid; they are made stupid by education.
BERTRAND RUSSELL

A child educated only at school is an uneducated child.
GEORGE SANTAYANA

Education . . . has produced a vast population able to read but unable to distinguish what is worth reading.
G. M. TREVELYAN

Education is the ability to listen to almost anything without losing your temper.
ROBERT FROST

When a subject becomes totally obsolete we make it a required course.
PETER DRUCKER

In the first place, God made idiots. That was for practice. Then he made school boards.
MARK TWAIN

Genius is a nuisance, and it is the duty of schools and colleges to abate it by setting genius-traps in its way.
SAMUEL BUTLER

College isn't the place to go for ideas.
HELEN KELLER

The fighting in academia is so vicious because the stakes are so low.
HENRY KISSINGER

The trouble with most men of learning is that their learning goes to their heads.
ISAAC GOLDBERG

You cannot teach a man anything, you can only help him find it within himself.
GALILEO GALILEI

Education is not the filling of a bucket, but the lighting of a fire.
W. B. YEATS

It is important that students bring a certain ragamuffin, barefoot irreverence to their studies; they are not here to worship what is known, but to question it.
JACOB BRONOWSKI

If one cannot state a matter clearly enough so that even an intelligent twelve-year-old can understand it, one should remain within the cloistered walls of the university and laboratory until one gets a better grasp of one's subject matter.
MARGARET MEAD

Anyone who tries to make a distinction between education and entertainment doesn't know the first thing about either.
MARSHALL McLUHAN

Effort

About the only thing that comes to us without effort is old age.
GLORIA PITZER

Nobody ever drowned in his own sweat.
ANN LANDERS 'Ann Landers' was one of the first and most infuential newspaper advice columns, running from 1942 to 2002, for most of that time produced by Chicago journalist Eppie Lederer. Her identical twin sister wrote a rival advice column, 'Dear Abby', under the name Abigail Van Buren. The two remained implacable enemies throughout their professional lives.

It is the greatest of all mistakes to do nothing because you can only do a little. *Do what you can.*
SYDNEY SMITH

You don't drown by falling in the water. You drown by staying in there.
EDWIN LOUIS COLE

God doesn't require us to succeed; he only requires that you try.
MOTHER TERESA

I have always tried to hide my own efforts and wished my works to have the lightness and joyousness of a springtime which never lets anyone suspect the labours it cost.
HENRI MATISSE

Eggs

Put all your eggs in one basket and then Watch That Basket.
ANDREW CARNEGIE From a speech in 1885 and 'borrowed' by Mark Twain.

Do you see this egg? With it you can overthrow all the schools of theology, all the churches of the earth.
DENIS DIDEROT

It is computed that eleven thousand persons have at several times suffered death rather than submit to break their eggs at the smaller end.
JONATHAN SWIFT

Ego

Whenever I climb I am followed by a dog called 'Ego'.
FRIEDRICH NIETZSCHE

When they discover the centre of the universe, a lot of people will be disappointed to discover they are not it.
BERNARD BAILEY A single quote with no obvious provenance, the best fit is probably Bernard C. Bailey, a long-time IBM executive and former CEO of Viisage, part of the world's biggest biometric security company and specialists in facial recognition software.

Egotism is the anaesthetic given by a kindly Nature to relieve the pain of being a damned fool.
BELLAMY BROOKS

You can't act with your ego, you have to search deeper. Ego is something that stops you telling the truth.
JAMES COBURN

If some really acute observer made as much of egotism as Freud has made of sex, people would forget a good deal about sex and find the explanation for everything in egotism.
WALLACE STEVENS

The nice thing about egotists is that they don't talk about other people.
LUCILLE S. HARPER

A human being is a part of this whole, called by us 'Universe', a part limited in time and space. He experiences himself, his thoughts and feelings as something separated from the rest – a kind of optical delusion of consciousness. This delusion is a kind of prison for us, restricting us to our personal desires and to apportion for a few persons nearest to us. Our task must be to free ourselves from this prison.
ALBERT EINSTEIN

Our real nature is not our imaginary, limited ego. Our true nature is vast, all-comprehensive, and intangible as empty space.
LAMA GOVINDA Born in Germany as Ernst Hoffman, he fought in World War I before visiting Tibet in 1931 and converting to Buddhism. *The Way of the White Clouds* (1966) is one of the great modern spiritual autobiographies. Before his death in 1985 he lived on the philosopher Alan Watts's houseboat in San Francisco.

Electricity

Electricity is the soul of the universe.
JOHN WESLEY

Electricity is actually made up of extremely tiny particles called electrons, that you cannot see with the naked eye unless you have been drinking.
DAVE BARRY

If it weren't for electricity, we'd all be watching television by candlelight.
GEORGE GOBEL

Her own mother lived the latter years of her life in the horrible suspicion that electricity was dripping invisibly all over the house.
JAMES THURBER

Encouragement

The finest gift you can give anyone is encouragement. Yet, almost no one gets the encouragement they need to grow to their full potential. If everyone received the encouragement they need to grow, the genius in most everyone would blossom and the world would produce abundance beyond our wildest dreams.
SIDNEY MADWED

There is no such whetstone, to sharpen a good wit and encourage a will to learning, as is praise.
ROGER ASCHAM Scholar, humanist, master archer, he wrote *The Scholemaster*

(1570), one of the first educational textbooks written in English rather than Latin, which set itself against the 'beat it into them' school of teaching.

Most children are given far too much praise for their early drawings, so much so that they rarely learn the ability to refine their first crude efforts the way their early attempts at language are corrected.
CHARLES DE LINT

Ends

About the time we think we can make ends meet, somebody moves the ends.
HERBERT HOOVER

From time to time, as we all know, a sect appears in our midst announcing that the world will very soon come to an end. Generally, by some slight confusion or miscalculation, it is the sect that comes to an end.
G. K. CHESTERTON

It is difficult beyond description to conceive that space can have no end; but it is more difficult to conceive an end. It is difficult beyond the power of man to conceive an eternal duration of what we call time; but it is more impossible to conceive when there shall be no time.
THOMAS PAINE

Great art picks up where nature ends.
MARC CHAGALL

Enemies

Books have the same enemies as people: fire, humidity, animals, weather, and their own content.
PAUL VALÉRY

An enemy can partly ruin a man, but it takes a good-natured injudicious friend to complete the thing and make it perfect.
MARK TWAIN

Friend is sometimes a word devoid of meaning; enemy never.
VICTOR HUGO

Never interrupt your enemy when he is making a mistake.
NAPOLEON BONAPARTE

If we could read the secret history of our enemies, we should find in each man's life sorrow and suffering enough to disarm all hostility.
HENRY WADSWORTH LONGFELLOW

For a person who cherishes compassion and love, the practice of tolerance is essential; and for that, an enemy is indispensable.
THE DALAI LAMA

As well as loving your enemies, treat your friends a little better.
MILTON FRIEDMAN

If you can't beat them, arrange to have them beaten.
GEORGE CARLIN

England

There are many things in life more worthwhile than money. One is to be brought up in this our England which is still the envy of less happy lands.
LORD DENNING

The air is soft and delicious. The men are sensible and intelligent. Many of them are learned. They know their classics, and so accurately that I have lost little in not going to Italy. The English girls are divinely pretty and they have one custom which cannot be too much admired. When you go anywhere on a visit, the girls kiss you. They kiss you when you arrive. They kiss you when you go away. They kiss you when you return. Once you have tasted how soft and fragrant those lips are, you could spend your life there.
ERASMUS

Living in England, provincial England, must be like being married to a stupid but exquisitely beautiful wife.
MARGARET HALSEY Writer in the Dorothy Parker mould whose acerbic observations of the English in *With Malice Toward Some* (1938) sold over 600,000 copies (in America).

It will be said of this generation that it found England a land of beauty and left it a land of beauty spots.
PROFESSOR CYRIL JOAD

One Englishman, an idiot; two Englishmen, a sporting event; three Englishmen, an empire.
GEORGE SANTAYANA

They have too many centuries of fog in their throats. They are naturally lazy, and spend half their time in taking tobacco.
SAMUEL DE SORBIÈRE An admirer and translator of Hobbes, he was inducted into the Royal Society in 1663 and then proceeded to scandalise his English colleagues by publishing a satirical account of his visit.

No people have true common sense but those who are born in England.
CHARLES DE MONTESQUIEU

Remember that you are an Englishman, and have consequently won first prize in the lottery of life.
CECIL RHODES

An Englishman, even if he is alone, forms an orderly queue of one.
GEORGE MIKES

The Englishman has all the qualities of a poker except its occasional warmth.
DANIEL O'CONNELL

You can trust all Englishmen except those who talk French.
OTTO VON BISMARCK

Every collection of five Englishmen needs a foreigner to stop it becoming a social health hazard.
A. A. GILL

Enlightenment

I gained nothing at all from supreme enlightenment, and for that very reason it is called supreme enlightenment.
BUDDHA

Enlightened people can still remember their phone numbers.
GARY ZUKAV A Green Beret in Vietnam who won the 1979 American Science Book of the Year for his overview of the new physics, *The Dancing Wu Li Masters*. His fluency in discussing connections between science and spirituality have earned him a regular place on Oprah Winfrey's couch.

If anybody finds enlightenment up on a mountain, he'd be selfish if he didn't come down and start talking about it.
YUSUF ISLAM (CAT STEVENS)

Enthusiasm

Nothing great was ever achieved without enthusiasm.
SAMUEL TAYLOR COLERIDGE

Enthusiasm is not contrary to reason. It is reason – on fire.
PETER MARSHALL

In the realm of ideas, everything depends on enthusiasm. In the real world all rests on perseverance.
GOETHE

The world belongs to the enthusiast who keeps cool.
WILLIAM McFEE

Equality

That all men are equal is a proposition which, at ordinary times, no sane individual has ever given his assent.
ALDOUS HUXLEY

No advance in wealth, no softening of manners, no reform or revolution has ever brought human equality a millimetre nearer.
GEORGE ORWELL

In our infinite ignorance, we are all equal.
KARL POPPER Of Austrian-Jewish extraction, he believed that all knowledge was conjectural and that propositions had to be 'testable' and repeatable to qualify as scientific truth, thereby ruling out disciplines like psychology and sociology as 'sciences'.

Events

An earthquake, a toothache, a mad dog, a telephone message – and all our house of peace falls like a pack of cards.
REGINALD H. BLYTH

Bad things are not the worst things that can happen to us. Nothing is the worst thing that can happen to us.
RICHARD BACH

An event is such a little piece of time-and-space you can mail it through the slotted eye of a cat.
DIANE ACKERMAN

When anyone asks me how I can best describe my experience in nearly forty years at sea, I merely say, uneventful. Of course there have been winter gales, and storms and fog and the like. But in all my experience, I have never been in any accident . . . or any sort worth speaking about. I have seen but one vessel in distress in all my years at sea. I never saw a wreck and never have been wrecked nor was I ever in any predicament that threatened to end in disaster of any sort.
EDWARD J. SMITH Captain of RMS *Titanic* in 1907. He was planning to retire after the maiden (and only) voyage in 1911.

Evil

There is no possible source of evil except good.
SAINT AUGUSTINE

The wicked are always surprised to find that the good can be clever.
MARQUIS DE VAUVENARGUES

No man knows how bad he is until he has tried to be good. There is a silly idea about that good people don't know what temptation means.
C. S. LEWIS

People are not evil; they are *schlemiels*.
ABRAHAM MASLOW *Schlemiel* is a difficult word to find an exact translation for: it carries connotations of clumsiness and awkwardness. New Yorker and former Congressman Stephen J. Solarz described a *schlemiel* as 'the fellow who climbs to the top of a ladder with a bucket of paint and then drops it. A *shimazl* is the fellow on whose head the bucket falls.'

There are two types of people in this world: good and bad. The good sleep better, but the bad seem to enjoy the waking hours much more.
WOODY ALLEN

Imaginary evil is romantic and varied; real evil is gloomy, monotonous, barren, boring. Imaginary good is boring; real good is always new, marvellous, intoxicating. 'Imaginative literature', therefore, is either boring or immoral or a mixture of both.
SIMONE WEIL

If only there were evil people somewhere insidiously committing evil deeds and it were necessary only to separate them from the rest of us and destroy them. But the line dividing good and evil cuts through the heart of every human being. And who is willing to destroy a piece of his own heart?
ALEKSANDR SOLZHENITSYN

The contrary to the good has no reality.
EUCLEIDES OF MEGARA

There is no explanation for evil. It must be looked upon as a necessary part of the order of the universe. To ignore it is childish, to bewail it senseless.
W. SOMERSET MAUGHAM

I've never been in a room with so many evil people in my life.
MATTHEW PARRIS On the tenth anniversary party of *Breakfast With Frost* (guests included Sheila Hancock, Edward Heath and Alastair Campbell).

The only thing that stops God sending a second Flood is that the first one was useless.
NICOLAS CHAMFORT

Evolution

The missing link between animals and the real human being is most likely ourselves.
KONRAD LORENZ

I am almost convinced (quite contrary to the opinion I started with) that species are not (it is like confessing a murder) immutable. I think I have found out (here's presumption!) the simple way by which species become exquisitely adapted to various ends.
CHARLES DARWIN

No other explanation has even been given of the marvellous fact that the embryos of a man, dog, seal, bat, reptile, etc., can at first hardly be distinguished from each other.
CHARLES DARWIN

I see no good reasons why the views given in this volume should shock the religious feelings of anyone.
CHARLES DARWIN

It is absurd for the Evolutionist to complain that it is unthinkable for an admittedly unthinkable God to make everything out of nothing, and then pretend that it is more thinkable that nothing should turn itself into everything.
G. K. CHESTERTON

It's hard to imagine that human engineers could be any clumsier or messier than that old slattern Dame Nature. The 'normal' processes of evolution are wasteful and cruel in stupefying degree. Dame Nature considers every species and every individual to be expendable, and has indeed expended them in horrifying numbers. Even an occasional calamitous error in planned development could scarcely match the slaughter, millennium in, millennium out, of fumble-fingered nature.
BOB ETTINGER Founder of the Cryonics Institute and author of the controversial *The Prospect of Immortality* in 1962. The bodies of both his wives and his mother have been cryo-preserved, awaiting future technology to revive them.

The essence of life is statistical improbability on a colossal scale.
RICHARD DAWKINS

If evolution really works, how come mothers only have two hands?
MILTON BERLE

Excuses

Never ruin an apology with an excuse.
KIMBERLY JOHNSON

The longer the excuse, the less likely it's the truth.
ROBERT HALF

Give me six lines written by the most honourable man, and I will find an excuse to hang him.
CARDINAL RICHELIEU Or at least words he is believed to have co-written with his protégé Jean Desmarets in the 1641 tragedy *Mirame*.

An excuse is worse and more terrible than a lie, for an excuse is a lie guarded.
POPE JOHN PAUL II

I attribute my success to this – that I never gave or took any excuse.
FLORENCE NIGHTINGALE

Ninety-nine percent of failures come from people who have the habit of making excuses.
GEORGE WASHINGTON CARVER

Exercise

The need for exercise is a modern superstition invented by people who ate too much, and had nothing to think about.
GEORGE SANTAYANA

I believe that the Good Lord gave us a finite number of heartbeats and I'm damned if I'm going to use up mine running up and down a street.
NEIL ARMSTRONG

My idea of exercise is a good, brisk sit.
PHYLLIS DILLER

The sum of the whole is this: walk and be happy; walk and be healthy.
CHARLES DICKENS

A vigorous five-mile walk will do more good for an unhappy but otherwise healthy adult than all the medicine and psychology in the world.
DUDLEY WHITE

Walking is the best possible exercise.
THOMAS JEFFERSON

Solvitur ambulando. It is solved by walking.
LATIN PROVERB

Strolling is the gastronomy of the eye. To walk is to vegetate, to stroll is to live.
HONORÉ DE BALZAC

Experience

Human beings, who are almost unique in having the ability to learn from the experience of others, are also remarkable for their apparent disinclination to do so.
DOUGLAS ADAMS

Experience is that marvelous thing that enables you to recognize a mistake when you make it again.
FRANKLIN P. JONES

Experience is the worst teacher. It always gives the test first and the instruction afterward.
BENJAMIN FRANKLIN

There are many truths of which the full meaning cannot be realised until personal experience has brought it home.
JOHN STUART MILL

To most men, experience is like the stern lights on a ship which illumine only the track it has passed.
SAMUEL TAYLOR COLERIDGE

Expressions

I loathe the expression 'What makes him tick.' It is the American mind, looking for simple and singular solution, that uses the foolish expression. A person not only ticks, he also chimes and strikes the hour, falls and breaks and has to be put together again, and sometimes stops like an electric clock in a thunderstorm.
JAMES THURBER

I must take issue with the term 'a mere child,' for it has been my invariable experience that the company of a mere child is infinitely preferable to that of a mere adult.
FRAN LEBOWITZ

'No comment' is a splendid expression. I am using it again and again.
WINSTON CHURCHILL

Eyes

What is a man's eye, but a machine for the little creature that sits behind his brain to look through.
SAMUEL BUTLER His time running a sheep farm in New Zealand and interest in Darwin were combined in his masterpiece, *Erewhon* (1872), a satirical novel in the tradition of *Gulliver's Travels*. George Bernard Shaw and E. M. Forster were fans and Huxley claimed it was a major inspiration for *Brave New World*.

The eyes are the spoons of speech.
ARABIC PROVERB

The eye of a human being is a microscope, which makes the world seem bigger than it really is.
KAHLIL GIBRAN

To suppose that the eye with all its inimitable contrivances for adjusting the focus to different distances, for admitting different amounts of light, and for the correction of spherical and chromatic aberration, could have been formed by natural selection, seems, I confess, absurd in the highest degree.
CHARLES DARWIN

I saw Napoleon at Elba. He had a dusky grey eye – what would be called a vicious eye in a horse.
LORD JOHN RUSSELL

Most of her strength seemed to go into the raising and lowering of her eye-lashes. No wonder. They were at least an inch long.
QUENTIN CRISP On Marlene Dietrich in *How to Have a Lifestyle* (1975).

One's eyes are what one is; one's mouth what one becomes.
JOHN GALSWORTHY

F

Faces

The serial number of the human specimen is the face, that accidental and unrepeatable combination of features. It reflects neither character nor soul nor what we call the self.
MILAN KUNDERA

The human face is really like one of those Oriental gods: a whole group of faces juxtaposed on different planes. It is impossible to see them all simultaneously.
MARCEL PROUST

A man's face is his autobiography. A woman's face is her work of fiction.
OSCAR WILDE

Our notion of symmetry is derived from the human face. Hence we demand symmetry horizontally and in breadth, not vertically nor in depth.
BLAISE PASCAL

Every European visitor to the United States is struck by the comparative rarity of what he would call a face, by the frequency of men and women who look like elderly babies.
W. H. AUDEN

My face looks like a wedding cake left out in the rain.
W. H. AUDEN

I have a face that is a cross between two pounds of halibut and an explosion in an old clothes closet.
DAVID NIVEN

I have a face like the behind of an elephant.
CHARLES LAUGHTON

No man, for any considerable period, can wear one face to himself, and another to the multitude, without finally getting bewildered as to which may be true.
NATHANIEL HAWTHORNE

A man determines upon the task of portraying the world. As the years pass he peoples a space with pictures of provinces, kingdoms, mountains, bays, ships, islands, fishes, dwellings, instruments, stars, horses and people. Shortly before he dies he discovers that the patient labyrinth of lines traces the image of his own face.
JORGE LUIS BORGES

For God's sake! What is that?
HAROLD ROSS Editor of the *New Yorker* on seeing Truman Capote for the first time in 1945.

Facts

The truth is more important than the facts.
FRANK LLOYD WRIGHT

In the spider-web of facts, many a truth is strangled.
PAUL ELDRIDGE

Facts are the enemy of truth.
MIGUEL CERVANTES

Do not become a mere recorder of facts, but try to penetrate the mystery of their origin.
IVAN PETROVICH PAVLOV Most famous for his investigation into the gastric function of dogs – he called the saliva produced before a food was tasted a 'psychic secretion'.

Facts are ventriloquist's dummies. Sitting on a wise man's knee they may be made to utter words of wisdom; elsewhere, they say nothing, or talk nonsense.
ALDOUS HUXLEY

I am no poet, but if you think for yourselves as I proceed, the facts will form a poem in your minds.
MICHAEL FARADAY

Anyone who is practically acquainted with scientific work is aware that those who refuse to go beyond fact rarely get as far as fact.
T. H. HUXLEY

There's nothing as deceptive as an obvious fact.
SIR ARTHUR CONAN DOYLE

There are no facts, only interpretations.
FRIEDRICH NIETZSCHE

Facts are what pedantic dull people have instead of opinions. Opinions
are always interesting. Facts are only the scaffolding, the trellis up
which bright opinions grow.
A. A. GILL

Failure

Everything I touch seems destined to turn into something mean and
farcical.
HENRIK IBSEN

When I was a young man I observed that nine out of ten things I did
were failures. I didn't want to be a failure, so I did ten times more work.
GEORGE BERNARD SHAW

Failure is the condiment that gives success its flavor.
TRUMAN CAPOTE

I don't know the key to success, but the key to failure is trying to please
everybody.
BILL COSBY

If at first you don't succeed, failure may be your style.
QUENTIN CRISP

Good people are good because they have come to wisdom through
failure. We get very little wisdom from success, you know.
WILLIAM SAROYAN

Failure is the key to success. Each mistake teaches us something.
MORIHEI UESHIBA Japanese martial artist who founded aikido, in which you
tune into an opponent's movements and disable him without causing injury. He
claimed the inspiration was watching his father being beaten by political rivals
when he was a small child.

It is only possible to succeed at second-rate pursuits – like becoming a
millionaire or a prime minister, winning a war, seducing beautiful
women, flying through the stratosphere or landing on the moon. First-
rate pursuits – involving, as they must, trying to understand what life is
about and trying to convey that understanding – inevitably result in a
sense of failure. A Napoleon, a Churchill, a Roosevelt can feel themselves
to be successful, but never a Socrates, a Pascal, a Blake. Understanding is
for ever unattainable. Therein lies the inevitability of failure in
embarking upon its quest, which is none the less the only one worthy of
serious attention.
MALCOLM MUGGERIDGE

Dealing with failure is easy: Work hard to improve. Success is also easy to handle: You've solved the wrong problem. Work hard to improve.
ALAN J. PERLIS

Every failure to cope with a life situation must be laid, in the end, to a restriction of consciousness. Wars and temper tantrums are the makeshifts of ignorance; regrets are illuminations come too late.
JOSEPH CAMPBELL

Faith

My faith is the grand drama of my life. I'm a believer, so I sing words of God to those who have no faith. I give bird songs to those who dwell in cities and have never heard them, make rhythms for those who know only military marches or jazz, and paint colours for those who see none.
OLIVIER MESSIAEN

To me faith means not worrying.
JOHN DEWEY

My faith is that the only soul a man must save is his own.
WILLIAM DOUGLAS

Faith is much better than belief. Belief is when someone else does the thinking.
R. BUCKMINSTER FULLER

Faith is under the left nipple.
MARTIN LUTHER

The opposite of faith isn't doubt, it's certainty.
ANONYMOUS No one knows who originally coined this pithy apophthegm, although the German/American existential theologian Paul Tillich comes closest with 'Doubt is not the opposite of faith; it is one element of faith.'

Fame

Glory is fleeting, but obscurity is forever.
NAPOLEON BONAPARTE

Being famous has its benefits, but fame isn't one of them.
LARRY WALL

Fame is the noise of madmen.
DIOGENES

Fame is a figment of everyone else's imagination.
VAN MORRISON

It's like having Alzheimer's disease. You don't know anybody, but they all know you.
TONY CURTIS

If I spit, they will take my spit and frame it as great art.
PABLO PICASSO

Just because you like my stuff, doesn't mean I owe you anything.
BOB DYLAN

A man who is being delivered from the danger of a fierce lion does not object whether this service is performed by an unknown or an illustrious individual. Why therefore do we seek knowledge from the famous?
EL-GHAZALI Author of *The Book of Knowledge*, his scepticism anticipates the work of Descartes and Hume – he believed that the confusion of knowledge and opinion was the source of most of the world's unhappiness.

A celebrity is a person who works hard all his life to become known, then wears dark glasses to avoid being recognised.
FRED ALLEN

Being a star has made it possible for me to get insulted in places where the average Negro could never hope to get insulted.
SAMMY DAVIS JR

Everyone wants to be Cary Grant. Even I want to be Cary Grant.
CARY GRANT

Those who are very beautiful, very good and very powerful scarcely ever learn the truth about anything. In their presence we involuntarily lie.
FRIEDRICH NIETZSCHE In *Dawn of Day* (1881), a collection of meditations and aphorisms on 575 different subjects.

The easiest kind of relationship for me is with ten thousand people. The hardest is with one.
JOAN BAEZ

With fame I become more and more stupid, which, of course, is a very common phenomenon.
ALBERT EINSTEIN

Glory: to become a literary theme, or a common noun, or an epithet.
PAUL VALÉRY

I'm never going to be famous. My name will never be writ large on the roster of Those Who Do Things. I don't do any thing. Not one single thing. I used to bite my nails, but I don't even do that any more.
DOROTHY PARKER

It's wonderful to be famous as long as you remain unknown.
EDGAR DEGAS

Families

The family you come from isn't as important as the family you're going to have.
RING LARDNER

Personal hatred and family affection are not incompatible; they often flourish and grow strong together.
WILLA CATHER

There is no such thing as fun for the whole family.
JERRY SEINFELD

If Mr Vincent Price were to be co-starred with Miss Bette Davis in a story by Mr Edgar Allan Poe directed by Mr Roger Corman, it would not fully express the pent-up violence and depravity of a single day in the life of the average family.
QUENTIN CRISP

Happiness is having a large, loving, caring, close-knit family in another city.
GEORGE BURNS

Fashion

Fashion is a form of ugliness so intolerable that we have to alter it every six months.
OSCAR WILDE

Oh, never mind the fashion. When one has a style of one's own, it is always twenty times better.
MARGARET OLIPHANT Prolific writer of over 120 books, few of which are still read. Born Margaret Oliphant Wilson, she married a cousin in 1852 and became Margaret Oliphant Oliphant.

I have heard with admiring submission the experience of the lady who declared that the sense of being well-dressed gives a feeling of inward tranquillity which religion is powerless to bestow.
RALPH WALDO EMERSON

Fashion is what goes out of fashion.
JEAN COCTEAU

Beware of any enterprise that requires new clothes.
HENRY DAVID THOREAU

When Spring comes around, I merely write my tailor, send him a small sample of dandruff, and tell him to match it exactly.
OLIVER HEREFORD

Once you can accept the universe as being something expanding into an infinite nothing which is something, wearing stripes with plaid is easy.
ALBERT EINSTEIN

Every generation laughs at the old fashions, but follows religiously the new.
HENRY DAVID THOREAU

Wee goe brave in apparell that we be taken for better men than wee bee; we use much bombastings and quiltings to seem better formed, better showldered, smaller wassted and fuller thyght than wee are; wee barbe and shave ofte, to seem yownger than we are; we use perfumes both inward and outward to seeme sweeter then wee bee; corkt shooes to seeme taller than wee bee; we use cowrtuows salutations to seem kinder than wee bee; lowly obaysances to seeme humbler then wee bee; and sometyme grave and godly communication, to seem wyser or devowter then wee bee.
SIR JOHN HARINGTON From his *Treatise on Playe* (1597), a defence of those activities which bring the mind or spirit pleasure. Harington is best remembered for inventing the 'Ajax', a flushing water closet which, after initial scepticism, Elizabeth I installed at court. Some claim the US slang term 'john' derives from Harington, but as it first appeared in the 1930s, this seems unlikely.

Dressing with style is akin to issuing a manifesto; dressing fashionably is like signing a petition.
JANI ALLAN

Fathers

It is easy to become a father, but very difficult to be a father.
WILHELM BUSCH

My father had a profound influence on me, he was a lunatic.
SPIKE MILLIGAN

I did not become a father because I am fond of children.
THALES OF MILETUS Often referred to as the father of science or the first philosopher, Thales was active at the end of the sixth century BC and is variously recorded as either having had one son, Cybisthon, or no children at all.

The time not to become a father is eighteen years before a war.
E. B. WHITE

Whoever has not got a good father should procure one.
FRIEDRICH NIETZSCHE

It doesn't matter who my father was; it matters who I remember he was.
ANNE SEXTON

You care for nothing but shooting, dogs, and rat-catching and you will be a disgrace to yourself and your family.
DR ROBERT DARWIN From a letter to his son Charles while he was meant to be studying for the priesthood at Cambridge.

I have done everything possible to please you. I am the most famous artist in the world. I have worked day and night and undergone hardships of every description, but I still do not know what you want of me . . .
MICHELANGELO BUONAROTTI To his father Lodovico.

There are fathers who do not love their children; there is no grandfather who does not adore his grandson.
VICTOR HUGO

Fear

Nothing in life is to be feared. It is only to be understood.
MARIE CURIE

Fear is that little darkroom where negatives are developed.
MICHAEL PRITCHARD

Anything I've ever done that ultimately was worthwhile initially scared me to death.
BETTY BENDER

It was high counsel that I once heard given to a young person, 'Always do what you are afraid to do'.
RALPH WALDO EMERSON

I prefer my people to be loyal out of fear rather than conviction. Convictions can change but fear remains.
JOSEF STALIN

The first duty of man is that of subduing fear. We must get rid of fear; we cannot act at all till then. A man's acts are slavish, not true but specious; his very thoughts are false, he thinks too as a slave and coward, till he have got fear under his feet.
THOMAS CARLYLE

Death is not the biggest fear we have; our biggest fear is taking the risk to be alive – the risk to be alive and express what we really are.
DON MIGUEL RUIZ

Yeah, though I walk through the valley of death I will fear no evil, for I am the meanest son of a bitch in the valley.
JOEL ROSENBERG

If a man harbors any sort of fear, it makes him landlord to a ghost.
LLOYD DOUGLAS

I'm not afraid of storms, for I'm learning how to sail my ship.
LOUISA MAY ALCOTT

Writing is a form of therapy; sometimes I wonder how all those who do not write, compose or paint can manage to escape the madness, the melancholia, the panic fear which is inherent in a human situation.
GRAHAM GREENE

Without fear and illness, I could never have accomplished all I have.
EDVARD MUNCH

You can discover what your enemy fears most by observing the means he uses to frighten you.
ERIC HOFFER He battled childhood blindness and poverty to become a truly original thinker (although he always referred to himself as a longshoreman). His 1951 classic, *The True Believer*, is one of the best books ever written on mass psychology and fanaticism.

There are only two forces that unite men – fear and interest.
NAPOLEON BONAPARTE

The only thing we have to fear is fear itself.
FRANKLIN D. ROOSEVELT

The only thing I am afraid of is fear.
ARTHUR WELLESLEY, DUKE OF WELLINGTON

Only when we are no longer afraid do we begin to live.
DOROTHY THOMPSON

Fear cannot be without hope, nor hope without fear.
BARUCH SPINOZA

A life lived in fear is a life half-lived.
SPANISH PROVERB

Needless fear and panic over disease and misfortune that seldom materialise are simply bad habits. By proper ventilation and illumination of the mind it is possible to cultivate tolerance, poise and real courage.
ELIE METCHNIKOFF Winner of the Nobel Prize for Medicine in 1908 for his work on microbes. He drank a glass of sour milk a day to keep his gut healthy.

People living deeply have no fear of death.
ANAÏS NIN

Fish

I know that the human being and the fish can co-exist peacefully.
GEORGE W. BUSH Using the language of the Cold War while campaigning in Saginaw, Michigan in 2000 – he was attempting to reassure the business community that he wasn't going to pull down any dams to protect threatened fish stocks.

There is no such thing as a fish.
THE ENCYLOPAEDIA OF UNDERWATER LIFE Edited by Andrew Campbell and John Dawes, published by Oxford University Press in 2005.

The Bible clearly states that God brought before Adam all the beasts of the field and all the fowl of the air. What about the fish? Did Adam name the fish?
UMBERTO ECO

Carp may be said to be water-sheep: herbivorous, gregarious, of a contented mind.
FRANK BUCKLAND

The catfish is a plenty good enough fish for anyone.
MARK TWAIN

A chub is the worst fish that swims.
IZAAK WALTON

Looking for fish? Don't climb a tree.
CHINESE PROVERB

The gods do not deduct from a man's allotted span the time he spends in fishing.
BABYLONIAN PROVERB

There's a fine line between fishing and standing on the shore looking like an idiot.
STEVEN WRIGHT

Flowers

People from a planet without flowers would think we must be mad with joy the whole time to have the things about us.
IRIS MURDOCH

The flower has no weekday self, dressed as it always is in Sunday clothes.
MALCOLM DE CHAZAL Divided his time between work as an agronomist on a sugar-cane plantation, painting primitive, colourful canvasses and penning philosophical one-liners (such as this one) which were all the rage in the Paris of the early 1950s.

Flowers in a city are like lipstick on a woman – it just makes you look better to have a little color.
LADY BIRD JOHNSON

The flower that follows the sun does so even on cloudy days.
ROBERT LEIGHTON

Perfumes are the feelings of flowers.
HEINRICH HEINE

The crown of petals is the flower's panties. Rip them off and you will have public indecency.
MALCOLM DE CHAZAL

All flowers are flirtatious – particularly if they carry hyphenated names. The more hyphens in the name, the flirtier the flower. The one-hyphen flowers – black-eyed Susan; lady-smock; musk-rose – may give you

only a shy glance and then drop their eyes; the two-hyphen flowers –
forget-me-not; flower-de-luce – keep glancing. Flowers with three or
more hyphens flirt all over the garden and continue even when they
are cut and arranged in vases. John-go-to-bed-at-noon does not go
there simply to sleep.
WILLARD R. ESPY

Our national flower is the concrete clover leaf.
LEWIS MUMFORD Author of *The City in History* (1961), Mumford believed the
medieval city to be the ideal and the invention of the clock more damaging than
that of the steam engine. His ideas on architecture and urban planning helped
inspire the US environmental movement.

Advice on dandelions: If you can't beat them, eat them.
JAMES DUKE

If dandelions were hard to grow, they would be most welcome on any
lawn.
ANDREW MASON

Science, or para-science, tells us that geraniums bloom better if they
are spoken to. But a kind word every now and then is really quite
enough. Too much attention, like too much feeding, and weeding and
hoeing, inhibits and embarrasses them.
VICTORIA GLENDINNING

The lily was created on the third day, early in the morning when the
Almighty was especially full of good ideas.
MICHAEL JEFFERSON-BROWN

A morning-glory at my window satisfies me more than the
metaphysics of books.
WALT WHITMAN

Some people are always grumbling that roses have thorns. I am
thankful that thorns have roses.
ALPHONSE KARR

The violets in the mountains have broken the rocks.
TENNESSEE WILLIAMS

Food

Food is an important part of a balanced diet.
FRAN LEBOWITZ

I eat at this German-Chinese restaurant and the food is delicious. The only problem is that an hour later you're hungry for power.
DICK CAVETT

You first parents of the human race, who ruined yourself for an apple, what might you not have done for a truffled turkey?
JEAN-ANTHELME BRILLAT-SAVARIN

Man cannot live by bread alone; he must have peanut butter.
JAMES A. GARFIELD

A gourmet who thinks of calories is like a tart who looks at her watch.
JAMES BEARD

Nobody really likes capers, no matter what you do with them. Some people pretend to like capers, but the truth is that any dish that tastes good with capers in it tastes even better with capers not in it.
NORA EPHRON

The capon is a cockerel made as it were female by carving away of his gendering stones.
BARTHOLOMEUS

There is more simplicity in the man who eats caviar on impulse than in the man who eats grape-nuts on principle.
G. K. CHESTERTON

The trouble with eating Italian food is that five or six days later you're hungry again.
GEORGE MILLER

There are two things I like stiff and one of them's jelly.
DAME NELLIE MELBA Born Helen Porter Mitchell, her stage name was an Italianised version of her native city, Melbourne. She was one of the first international superstars with an ego and appetites to match, and Escoffier invented Peach Melba and Melba toast in her honour.

There is no such thing as a pretty good omelette.
FRENCH PROVERB

He was a bold man who first swallowed an oyster.
KING JAMES I

'I wonder why they call this porridge,' he observed with mild interest. 'It would be far more manly and straightforward of them to give it its real name.'
P. G. WODEHOUSE

I believe that if ever I had to practise cannibalism, I might manage if there were enough tarragon around.

JAMES BEARD Food writer, often called the 'father of American gastronomy', he was the original TV chef in the 1950s. The awards named in his honour are known as the 'Oscars of Food'.

I think somebody should come up with a way to breed a very large shrimp. That way, you could ride him, then, after you camped at night, you could eat him. How about it, science?

JACK HANDEY

Football

All I know most surely about morality and obligations, I owe to football.

ALBERT CAMUS

Other countries have their history. Uruguay has its football.

ONDINO VIERA

In Latin America the border between soccer and politics is vague. There is a long list of governments that have fallen or been overthrown after the defeat of the national team.

LUIS SUÁREZ

The natural state of the football fan is bitter disappointment, no matter what the score.

NICK HORNBY

Some people think football is a matter of life and death. I assure you, it's much more important than that.

BILL SHANKLY Legendary Liverpool manager in a famous misquote. He was being interviewed on a Granada TV show called *Live from Two* hosted by Shelley Rohde, shortly before his death in 1981. What he said was: 'Someone said, "Football is more important than life and death to you," and I said, "Listen, it's more important than that." '

There is only one word to describe football and that is 'if only'.

BOBBY ROBSON

The reason women don't play football is because eleven of them would never wear the same outfit in public.

PHYLLIS DILLER

Football is a fertility festival. Eleven sperm trying to get into the egg. I feel sorry for the goalkeeper.

BJÖRK

Forgetfulness

There are three things I always forget. Names, faces, and the third I can't remember.
ITALO SVEVO

If a man can remember what he worried about last week, he has a very good memory.
WOODY ALLEN

How is it that we remember the least triviality that happens to us, and yet not remember how often we have recounted it to the same person.
DUC DE LA ROCHEFOUCAULD

When my daughter was about seven years old, she asked me one day what I did at work. I told her I worked at the college – that my job was to teach people how to draw. She stared back at me, incredulous, and said, 'You mean they forget?'
HOWARD IKEMOTO

Whenever you go out to paint, try to forget what objects you have in front of you – a tree, a house, a field or whatever. Merely think, here is a little squeeze of blue, here an oblong of pink, here a streak of yellow, and paint it just as it looks to you, until it gives your own naive impression of the scene in front of you.
CLAUDE MONET

There is nothing more difficult for a truly creative painter than to paint a rose, because before he can do so he has first to forget all the roses that were ever painted.
HENRI MATISSE

Forgiveness

There is no forgiveness in nature.
UGO BETTI

Without forgiveness life is governed by an endless cycle of resentment and retaliation.
ROBERTO ASSAGIOLI

I can forgive, but I cannot forget, is only another way of saying, I will not forgive. Forgiveness ought to be like a cancelled note, torn in two, and burned up, so that it never can be shown against one.
HENRY WARD BEECHER

You know you have forgiven someone when he or she has harmless passage through your mind.
KARYL HUNTLEY

Only the brave know how to forgive. A coward never forgives; it is not in his nature.
LAURENCE STERNE

He who cannot forgive others destroys the bridge over which he himself must pass.
GEORGE HERBERT

He who has not forgiven an enemy has not yet tasted one of the most sublime enjoyments of life.
JOHANN LAVATER

Many promising reconciliations have broken down because, while both parties came prepared to forgive, neither party came prepared to be forgiven.
CHARLES WILLIAMS English novelist and Anglican theologian admired by T. S. Eliot and W. H. Auden and a close friend and mentor to C. S. Lewis and J. R. R. Tolkien. He also produced the first English edition of the work of Danish existential philosopher Kierkegaard.

Always forgive your enemies; nothing annoys them so much.
OSCAR WILDE

Forgive your enemies, but never forget their names.
JOHN F. KENNEDY

Freedom

Freedom is when one hears the bell at seven o'clock in the morning and knows it is the milkman and not the Gestapo.
GEORGES BIDAULT

Freedom is the right to be wrong, not the right to do wrong.
JOHN DIEFENBAKER Popular criminal lawyer turned politician, known as 'Dief the Chief'. He was Prime Minister of Canada from 1957 to 1963 and brought in the Bill of Rights which guaranteed the vote for all Canada's aboriginal peoples.

All mankind is divided as it always has been into slaves and freemen. Whoever has less than two-thirds of his day for himself is a slave, be he a statesman, a merchant, an official or a scholar.
FRIEDRICH NIETZSCHE

It is true that liberty is precious; so precious that it must be carefully rationed.
LENIN

Everyone appears to be noticing only the statue's torch and not the manacles on her ankles.
ROGER L. GREEN Afro-American Democrat politician from Brooklyn on the Statue of Liberty.

A man's worst difficulties begin when he is able to do as he likes.
T. H. HUXLEY

If crime fighters fight crime and fire fighters fight fire, what do freedom fighters fight? They never mention that part to us, do they?
GEORGE CARLIN

I'm no linguist, but I have been told that in the Russian language there isn't even a word for freedom.
RONALD REAGAN In 1985. He was told wrong. The Russian word for freedom is *svoboda*.

Be a lamp unto yourself and seek your own liberation with diligence.
BUDDHA

Free Speech

People hardly ever make use of the freedom they have, for example, freedom of thought; instead they demand freedom of speech as compensation.
SØREN KIERKEGAARD

The right to be heard does not automatically include the right to be taken seriously.
HUBERT H. HUMPHREY

If we don't believe in freedom of expression for people we despise, we don't believe in it at all.
NOAM CHOMSKY

If liberty means anything at all, it means the right to tell people what they do not want to hear.
GEORGE ORWELL

Free Will

Everything is determined, the beginning as well as the end, by forces over which we have no control. It is determined for the insect as well as

the star. Human beings, vegetables, or cosmic dust, we all dance to a mysterious tune, intoned in the distance by an invisible piper.
ALBERT EINSTEIN

No one knows anything about will, what it is, how to make it, or how it works, or why it works as it does.
PEARL S. BUCK

A man can surely do what he wills to do, but cannot determine what he wills.
ARTHUR SCHOPENHAUER

Nothing which is independent of the will can hinder or damage it; the will can only hinder or damage itself.
EPICTETUS

You will say that I feel free. This is an illusion, which may be compared to that of the fly in the fable, who, upon the pole of a heavy carriage, applauded himself for directing its course.
BARON D'HOLBACH

The enormous value of the concept of free will in relieving parental shame and guilt is the only and overriding reason, in our opinion, that the lie of free will is well nigh universally taught to all children. If and when we can convince parents of total determinism, so they are freed from their own shame and guilt, they will no longer need to teach the vicious lie of free will to the world's children. A new world will be born.
DR PETER GILL Controversial psychotherapist who in 1985 founded the Society of Natural Science in Cambridge, Massachusetts.

Free will is probably located in the pre-frontal cortex, and we may even be able to narrow it down to the ventromedial pre-frontal cortex.
STEPHEN PINKER

This free will business is a bit terrifying anyway. It's almost pleasanter to obey, and make the most of it.
UGO BETTI

All theory is against the freedom of the will; all experience for it… Sir, we know our will is free, and there's an end on it.
SAMUEL JOHNSON

Friendship

Money can't buy friends, but you can get a better class of enemy.
SPIKE MILLIGAN

Your friend is the man who knows all about you and still likes you.
ELBERT HUBBARD

A true friend is one who likes you despite your achievements.
ARNOLD BENNETT

When I was a kid, I had two friends, and they were imaginary and they would only play with each other.
RITA RUDNER

We're born alone, we live alone, we die alone. Only through our love and friendship can we create the illusion for the moment that we're not alone.
ORSON WELLES

When one is trying to do something beyond his known powers it is useless to seek the approval of friends. Friends are at their best in moments of defeat.
HENRY MILLER

Adversity is the only balance to weigh friends.
PLUTARCH

The only reward of virtue is virtue: the only way to have a friend is to be one.
RALPH WALDO EMERSON

I lay it down as a fact that if all men knew what others say of them, there would not be four friends in the world.
BLAISE PASCAL

Each friend represents a world in us, a world possibly not born until they arrive, and it is only by this meeting that a new world is born.
ANAÏS NIN

My mother used to say that there are no strangers, only friends you haven't met yet. She's now in a maximum security twilight home in Australia.
DAME EDNA EVERAGE Barry Humphries's brilliant comic creation first appeared in 1955. An early outing in London at Peter Cook's Establishment Club was given a drubbing by Bamber Gascoigne in the *Spectator*, but Edna went on to conquer the world. She even has a street named after her in Melbourne.

Fun

When you have confidence, you can have a lot of fun. And when you have fun, you can do amazing things.
JOE NAMATH

People rarely succeed unless they have fun in what they are doing.
DALE CARNEGIE

I love fun, but too much is abominable.
WILLIAM BLAKE

Fun I love, but too much fun is of all things the most loathsome. Mirth is better than fun, and happiness is better than mirth.
THOMAS CARLYLE

Just to paint is great fun. The colours are lovely to look at and delicious to squeeze out. Matching them, however crudely, with what you see is fascinating and absolutely absorbing.
WINSTON CHURCHILL

People must not do things for fun. We are not here for fun. There is no reference to fun in any Act of Parliament.
A. P. HERBERT

Is ditchwater dull? Naturalists with microscopes have told me that it teems with quiet fun.
G. K. CHESTERTON

Just give me a comfortable couch, a dog, a good book, and a woman. Then if you can get the dog to go somewhere and read the book, I might have a little fun!
GROUCHO MARX

You've made your bed, now go bounce on it.
PETER SCOTT

Future

The future is like heaven, everyone exalts it, but no one wants to go there now.
JAMES BALDWIN

The best way to predict the future is to invent it.
ALAN KAY

I don't try to describe the future. I try to prevent it.
RAY BRADBURY

I never think of the future – it comes soon enough.
ALBERT EINSTEIN

The trouble with our times is that the future is not what it used to be.
PAUL VALÉRY

The future is made of the same stuff as the present.
SIMONE WEIL

The future will one day be the present and will seem as unimportant as the present does now.
W. SOMERSET MAUGHAM

G

Gardening

Won't you come into the garden? I would like my roses to see you.
RICHARD BRINSLEY SHERIDAN

I don't know whether nice people tend to grow roses or growing roses makes people nice.
ROLAND A. BROWNE Author of *The Rose Lover's Guide* in 1974, was once misspelt as Roland A. Beowne.

Gardening requires lots of water – most of it in the form of perspiration.
LOU ERICKSON

Of all the wonderful things in the wonderful universe of God, nothing seems to me more surprising than the planting of a seed in the blank earth and the result thereof.
CELIA THAXTER

The garden is so ferociously sexy at night, it's almost lurid.
ANNE RAVER

Garden writing is often very tame, a real waste when you think how opinionated, inquisitive, irreverent and lascivious gardeners themselves tend to be. Nobody talks much about the muscular limbs, dark,swollen buds, strip-tease trees and unholy beauty that have made us all slaves of the Goddess Flora.
KETZEL LEVINE

Anyone who has a library and a garden wants for nothing.
CICERO

To the makying of bookes of gardenyng there is noe ende.
THOMAS HYLL From *The Profitable Arte of Gardening* in 1563, the first gardening book published in English. If only he'd realised what he'd started . . .

Gardening is an active participation in the deepest mysteries of the universe.
THOMAS BERRY

Compared to gardeners, I think it is generally agreed that others understand very little about anything of consequence.
HENRY MITCHELL

In successive censuses gardeners are continuously found at the head of the tables of longevity.
WILLIAM BEACH THOMAS

A garden is always a series of losses set against a few triumphs, like life itself.
MAY SARTON

A man should never plant a garden larger than his wife can take care of.
T. H. EVERETT

My green thumb only came as a result of mistakes I made while learning to see things from the plant's point of view.
H. FRED ALE

There is no gardening without humility. Nature is constantly sending even its oldest scholars to the bottom of the class for some egregious blunder.
ALFRED AUSTIN Appointed Poet Laureate after Tennyson died and William Morris had turned the post down. The fact that he was a prominent Tory journalist and leader writer for the *Standard* probably got him the job: his rather dull poetry is barely read at all now.

A garden without a fence is like a dog without a tail.
MOROCCAN PROVERB

Botany is a sequel of murder and a chronicle of the dead.
JULIAN HAWTHORNE

Genius

Hats off, gentlemen, a genius!
ROBERT SCHUMANN

Genius is an African who dreams up snow.
VLADIMIR NABOKOV

Since the death of Einstein in 1955, there hasn't been a single living genius. From Michelangelo, through Shakespeare, Newton, Beethoven, Darwin, Freud and Einstein, there's always been a living genius. Now, for the first time in 500 years, we are on our own.
J. G. BALLARD

A genius is someone who has *two* great ideas.
JACOB BRONOWSKI

Everyone is born a genius, but the process of living de-geniuses them.
R. BUCKMINSTER FULLER

Everyone is a genius at least once a year. A real genius has his original ideas closer together.
G. C. LICHTENBERG Germany's first professor of physics who had laid the theoretical groundwork for the Xerox machine by the mid-eighteenth century. Severely hunchbacked, he nevertheless became one of the great aphorists of the age, recording his thoughts and observations in a series of alphabetical 'waste books' (he'd reached volume 'L' by the time he died in 1799).

With the stones we cast at them, geniuses build new roads for us.
PAUL ELDRIDGE

When a true genius appears in this world, you may know him by this sign: that the dunces are all in confederacy against him.
JONATHAN SWIFT

Genius is childhood recovered at will.
CHARLES BAUDELAIRE

The first and last thing required of genius is the love of truth.
GOETHE

What moves men of genius, or rather what inspires their work, is not new ideas, but their obsession with the idea that what has already been said is still not enough.
EUGÈNE DELACROIX

The function of genius is not to give new answers, but to pose new questions – which time and mediocrity can solve.
HUGH TREVOR-ROPER

The greatest thing by far is to be a master of metaphor; it is the one thing that cannot be learnt from others; and it is also a sign of genius, since a good metaphor implies an intuitive perception of the similarity in the dissimilar.
ARISTOTLE

Neither a lofty degree of intelligence, nor imagination, nor both together go to the making of genius. Love, love, love: that is the soul of genius.
WOLFGANG AMADEUS MOZART

Brain researchers estimate that your unconscious database outweighs the conscious on an order exceeding ten million to one. This database is the source of your hidden, natural genius. In other words, a part of you is much smarter than you are. The wise people regularly consult that smarter part.
MICHAEL J. GELB

Nothing has been more difficult than to be curious about an object or a person, without being obstructed by preconceived ideas. Occasionally the veil is lifted, and the one who lifts it is called a genius.
THEODORE ZELDIN

Men of genius are often dull and inert in society, as a blazing meteor when it descends to earth, is only a stone.
HENRY WADSWORTH LONGFELLOW

Genius and stupidity never stray from their paths: talent wanders after every light.
GEORGE MOORE

Nobody in football should be called a genius. A genius is a guy like Norman Einstein.
JOE THEISMANN

Geometry

Geometry is not true, it is advantageous.
HENRI POINCARÉ

A line is a dot that went for a walk.
PAUL KLEE

The cowboys have a way of trussing up a steer or a pugnacious bronco which fixes the brute so that it can neither move nor think. This is the hog-tie, and it is what Euclid did to geometry.
ERIC TEMPLE BELL

At the age of 11, I began Euclid, with my brother as my tutor. This was one of the great events of my life, as dazzling as first love. I had not imagined there was anything so delicious in the world.
BERTRAND RUSSELL

Giving

We should give as we would receive, cheerfully, quickly, and without

hesitation; for there is no grace in a benefit that sticks to the fingers.
SENECA

Blessed are those who can give without remembering, and take without forgetting.
PRINCESS ELIZABETH BIBESCO

Rich gifts wax poor when givers prove unkind.
WILLIAM SHAKESPEARE

Every man according as he purposeth in his heart, so let him give; not grudgingly, or of necessity: for God loveth a cheerful giver.
2 CORINTHIANS 9:7

The Lord loveth a cheerful giver. He also accepteth from a grouch.
CATHERINE HALL

There is a wonderful mythical law of nature that the three things we crave most in life – happiness, freedom, and peace of mind – are always attained by giving them to someone else.
PEYTON CONWAY MARCH US Army Chief of Staff during World War I. His father Francis Andrew March was an Anglo-Saxon scholar and the first American to work on the *Oxford English Dictionary*.

No one has ever become poor by giving.
ANNE FRANK

You have not lived until you have done something for someone who can never repay you.
JOHN BUNYAN

God

A gaseous vertebrate.
ERNEST HAECKEL German biologist, free thinker and illustrator whose drawings of the human embryo created the now discredited idea that humans pass through the history of evolution, from fish to mammals, in the womb. He coined the words 'phylum' and 'ecology' and was the first person recorded using the term 'First World War', as early as 1914.

God has no religion.
MAHATMA GANDHI

You must believe in God, despite what the clergy tell you.
BENJAMIN JOWETT

I believe in God. If you were me, and had my life, you would believe in God too.

MICHAEL CAINE Interview with Gyles Brandreth in the *Sunday Times* (23 December 2001). Caine's charlady mother was descended from Roma gypsies and his father was a fish-market porter. Born Maurice Micklewhite, he chose his stage name in 1954 while standing in a phone booth in Leicester Square when *The Caine Mutiny* was being shown at the Odeon.

In the absence of any other proof, the thumb alone would convince me of God's existence.

ISAAC NEWTON

I think it is a sign of human weakness to try to find out the shape and form of God.

PLINY THE ELDER

How can I believe in God when just last week I got my tongue caught in the roller of an electric typewriter?

WOODY ALLEN

When his life was ruined, his family killed, his farm destroyed, Job knelt down on the ground and yelled up to the heavens, 'Why God? Why me?' and the thundering voice of God answered: 'There's just something about you that pisses me off.'

STEPHEN KING

Had I been present at the creation, I would have given some useful hints for the better ordering of the universe.

ALFONSO THE WISE

Why attack God? He may be as miserable as we are.

ERIK SATIE

I have never understood why it should be considered derogatory to the Creator to suppose that he has a sense of humour.

WILLIAM RALPH INGE

If God were to appear in my room, obviously I would be in awe, but I don't think I would be humble. I might cry, but I think he would dig me like crazy.

MARC BOLAN

If God lived on earth, people would break his windows.

JEWISH PROVERB

If God was a woman, she would have made sperm taste like chocolate.

CARRIE SNOW

I would believe only in a God who could dance.
FRIEDRICH NIETZSCHE

That deeply emotional conviction of the presence of a superior reasoning power, which is revealed in the incomprehensible universe, forms my idea of God.
ALBERT EINSTEIN

Each attempt at defining God is like placing a pebble on Brighton beach: some are a few feet nearer the water than others, but that doesn't mean much when the place one is trying to approach is North Africa.
PAUL HANDLEY

My Me is God, nor do I recognise any other Me except my God Himself.
SAINT CATHERINE OF GENOA

The nature of God is a circle of which the centre is everywhere and the circumference is nowhere.
EMPEDOCLES

God is a verb, not a noun proper or improper.
R. BUCKMINSTER FULLER

God is beauty.
SAINT FRANCIS OF ASSISI

God speaks to us every day, but we don't know how to listen.
MAHATMA GHANDI

Remember me. I will remember you.
THE QUR'AN 2:152

I do not feel obliged to believe that the same God who has endowed us with sense, reason and intellect has intended us to forgo their use.
GALILEO GALILEI

The sun, with all those planets revolving round it and depending on it, can still ripen a bunch of grapes as if it had nothing else in the universe to do.
GALILEO GALILEI

One argument against God is how can he have the time to be interested in and care for everyone. This quote goes some way to solving this. The sun knows how a bunch of grapes is to be ripened. God stands in the same relationship to us. Be who you are, you are designed to work to live, as a pair of skis is designed to carve the turn. Stop fighting the mountain.

You see many stars in the sky at night, but not when the sun rises. Can you therefore say that there are no stars in the heavens during the day? Because you cannot find God in the days of your ignorance, say not that there is no God.
SRI RAMAKRISHNA

There is in God, some say,
A deep but dazzling darkness.
HENRY VAUGHAN

Why dost thou prate of God? Whatever thou sayest of Him is untrue.
MEISTER ECKHART

Gods

Kill one man and you are a murderer. Kill millions and you are a conqueror. Kill all and you are a God.
JEAN ROSTAND

Man is certainly stark raving mad. He cannot make a worm, yet he makes gods by the dozens.
MICHEL DE MONTAIGNE

If oxen and horses or lions had hands, and could paint with their hands, and produce works of art as men do, horses would paint the forms of gods like horses, and oxen like oxen, and make their bodies in the image of their several kinds.
XENOPHANES

Golf

Golf is a good walk spoiled.
MARK TWAIN Although it appears in none of his written works, and there are no records of him ever having said it.

Don't play too much golf. Two rounds a day are plenty.
HARRY VARDON

Although golf was originally restricted to wealthy, overweight Protestants, today it's open to anybody who owns hideous clothing.
DAVE BARRY

Rugger forwards can lose their temper and play the game of their lives; so, I believe, can bowlers. Golfers, never. Lose your temper and you are

done. Or, more insidious, get into a mood of self-pity and you are worse done.
PATRICK DICKINSON

I could never believe in a game where the one who hits the ball least wins.
WINSTON CHURCHILL

Goodness

There is no reason why good cannot triumph as often as evil. The triumph of anything is a matter of organisation. If there are such things as angels, I hope that they are organised along the lines of the Mafia.
KURT VONNEGUT

Unfortunately, goodness and honour are rather the exception than the rule among exceptional men, not to speak of geniuses.
CESARE LOMBROSO

On the whole, human beings want to be good, but not too good, and not quite all the time.
GEORGE ORWELL

Waste no more time arguing what a good man should be. Be one.
MARCUS AURELIUS

A good action is never lost; it is a treasure laid up and guarded for the doer's need.
PEDRO CALDERÓN DE LA BARCA

The Good is one, though it is called by many names, sometimes wisdom, sometimes God, and sometimes reason.
EUCLEIDES OF MEGARA He was so devoted to his teacher Socrates that when the Megarians were banned from Athens he dressed up as woman to visit him.

Gossip

Gossip needn't be false to be evil – there's a lot of truth that shouldn't be passed around.
FRANK CLARK

No one gossips about other people's secret virtues.
BERTRAND RUSSELL

I don't care what anybody says about me as long as it isn't true.
TRUMAN CAPOTE

If you haven't got anything nice to say about anybody, come sit next to me.
ALICE ROOSEVELT LONGWORTH Teddy Roosevelt's unconventional, hedonistic daughter became Mrs L. or 'the other Washington Monument': a formidable political institution in her own right for almost a century. She liked this quote so much she had it embroidered on a pillow for her couch.

Government

It may be true that you can't fool all the people all the time, but you can fool enough of them to rule a large country.
WILL DURANT

I believe that all government is evil, and that trying to improve it is largely a waste of time.
H. L. MENCKEN

Let the people think they govern, and they will be governed.
WILLIAM PENN

The punishment which wise men who refuse to take part in government suffer is to live under the government of worse men.
PLATO

The ideal form of government is democracy tempered by assassination.
VOLTAIRE

Grass

There is not a sprig of grass that shoots uninteresting to me.
THOMAS JEFFERSON

To me a lush carpet of pine needles or spongy grass is more welcome than the most luxurious Persian rug.
HELEN KELLER

Nothing is more pleasant to the eye than green grass, finely shorn.
FRANCIS BACON

Sitting quietly, doing nothing, spring comes, and the grass grows by itself.
ZEN SAYING

Grass is the cheapest plant to install and the most expensive to maintain.
PAT HOWELL

Gravity

Why is thought, being a secretion of the brain, more wonderful than gravity – a property of matter?
CHARLES DARWIN

It's a good thing we have gravity, or else when birds died they'd just stay right up there. Hunters would be all confused.
STEVEN WRIGHT

It is a mathematical fact that the casting of this pebble from my hand alters the centre of gravity of the universe.
THOMAS CARLYLE

We can lick gravity, but sometimes the paperwork is overwhelming.
WERNHER VON BRAUN

Greatness

The price of greatness is responsibility.
WINSTON CHURCHILL

Keep away from people who try to belittle your ambitions. Small people always do that, but the really great make you feel that you, too, can become great.
MARK TWAIN

No truly great man ever thought himself so.
WILLIAM HAZLITT

The essence of greatness is neglect of the self.
JAMES ANTHONY FROUDE

A great man's failures to understand define him.
ANDRÉ GIDE

Distance makes the mountain blue, and the man great.
ICELANDIC PROVERB

The three signs of great men are – generosity in the design, humanity in the execution, moderation in success.
OTTO VON BISMARCK

What makes a nation great is not primarily its great men, but the stature of its innumerable mediocre ones.
JOSÉ ORTEGA Y GASSET

Greeks

Except the blind forces of Nature, nothing moves in this world which is not Greek in its origin.
HENRY MAINE

The best chance of reproducing the ancient Greek temperament would be to cross the Scots with the Chinese.
HUGH MACDIARMID

Almost all of the hypotheses that have dominated modern philosophy were first thought of by the Greeks.
BERTRAND RUSSELL

After shaking hands with a Greek, count your fingers.
ALBANIAN PROVERB

H

Habit

Habit is a cable; we weave a thread of it every day, and at last we cannot break it.
HORACE MANN

Habits are worse than rabies.
TURKISH PROVERB

Habit with its iron sinews, clasps us and leads us day by day.
ALPHONSE DE LAMARTINE

Rigid, the skeleton of habit alone upholds the human frame.
VIRGINIA WOOLF

I hate to be near the sea, and to hear it raging and roaring like a wild beast in his den. It puts me in mind of the everlasting efforts of the human mind, struggling to be free and ending just where it began.
WILLIAM HAZLITT

The fixity of a habit is generally in direct proportion to its absurdity.
MARCEL PROUST

Habit is the ballast that chains the dog to his vomit. Breathing is habit. Life is habit.
SAMUEL BECKETT From his 1930 essay on Proust. An early statement of Beckett's famous pessimism, the only relief from the bonds of habit were moments of suffering.

We are what we repeatedly do. Excellence, then, is not an act, but a habit.
ARISTOTLE

Habit is overcome by habit.
THOMAS À KEMPIS

To change one's habits has a smell of death about it.
PORTUGUESE PROVERB

Hands

The hand is the cutting edge of the mind.
JACOB BRONOWSKI

Doodling is the brooding of the hand.
SAUL STEINBERG

On the other hand, you have different fingers.
STEVEN WRIGHT

Happiness

If only we'd stop trying to be happy we'd have a pretty good time.
EDITH WHARTON

Happy is the man that findeth wisdom and getteth understanding.
PROVERBS 3:13

Happiness in intelligent people is the rarest thing I know.
ERNEST HEMINGWAY

To make a goal of comfort or happiness has never appealed to me; a system of ethics built on this basis would be sufficient only for a herd of cattle.
ALBERT EINSTEIN

Very little is needed to make a happy life. It is all within yourself, in your way of thinking.
MARCUS AURELIUS

What's the secret to a long and happy life? Young women's saliva!
TONY CURTIS

Happiness: An agreeable sensation arising from contemplating the misery of another.
AMBROSE BIERCE

Some cause happiness wherever they go; others, whenever they go.
OSCAR WILDE

Happiness is a way of travel, not a destination.
ROY GOODMAN

It is neither wealth nor splendour, but tranquillity and occupation, which give happiness.
THOMAS JEFFERSON

The secret of happiness is freedom, and the secret of freedom, courage.
THUCYDIDES

Happiness is seldom found by those who seek it, and never by those who seek it for themselves.
F. EMERSON ANDREWS The historian of modern American philanthropy and author of *Corporation Giving* (1952), which set the template for the huge increase in US corporate giving over the next few decades.

I have no money, no resources, no hopes. I am the happiest man alive.
HENRY MILLER

If I could drop dead right now, I'd be the happiest man alive!
SAMUEL GOLDWYN

There are shortcuts to happiness, and dancing is one of them.
VICKI BAUM

For peace of mind, resign as general manager of the universe.
LARRY EISENBERG

To fill the hour – that is happiness.
RALPH WALDO EMERSON

In order to be utterly happy, the only thing necessary is to refrain from comparing this moment with other moments in the past.
ANDRÉ GIDE

Happiness is good health and a bad memory.
INGRID BERGMAN

If you observe a really happy man, you will find him building a boat, writing a symphony, educating his son, growing double dahlias in his garden, or looking for dinosaur eggs in the Gobi desert. He will not be searching for happiness as if it were a collar button that has rolled under a radiator.
W. BERAN WOLFE Although he only survives for most people through this quote, Walter Beran Wolfe was a real person, an Austrian-born American psychiatrist and student/translator of Alfred Adler. It comes from his masterpiece, *How to Be Happy Though Human* (1931), which was one of the first self-help bestsellers. Wolfe died in an accident at the age of 35.

The happiest person is the person who thinks the most interesting thoughts.
TIMOTHY DWIGHT

If only we wanted to be happy, it would be easy; but we want to be happier than other people, which is difficult, since we think them happier than they are.
CHARLES DE MONTESQUIEU

We act as though comfort and luxury were the chief requirements of life, when all that we need to make us happy is something to be enthusiastic about.
CHARLES KINGSLEY

Three grand essentials to happiness in this life are something to do, something to love and something to hope for.
JOSEPH ADDISON

I have now reigned about fifty years in victory and peace, beloved by my subjects, dreaded by my enemies, and respected by my allies. Riches and honours, power and pleasure, have waited on my call, nor does any earthly blessing appear to have been wanting to my felicity. In this situation I have diligently numbered the days of pure and genuine happiness which have fallen to my lot: they amount to fourteen.
ABD-AR-RAHMAN III The Caliph of Cordoba who presided over the golden age of Al-Andalus, the Moorish kingdom in southern Spain, famed for its art, religious tolerance and scientific prowess. According to some chroniclers he 'sunk in his later years into the self-indulgent habits of the harem'.

Happiness is a butterfly which, when pursued, is always beyond our grasp, but which, if you will sit down quietly, may alight upon you.
NATHANIEL HAWTHORNE

Happiness is when what you think, what you say, and what you do are in harmony.
MAHATMA GANDHI

Happiness consists in finding out precisely what 'the one thing necessary' may be in our lives, and in gladly relinquishing all the rest. For then, by a divine paradox, we find that everything else is given us together with the one thing we needed.
THOMAS MERTON

What do you take me for, an idiot?
GENERAL DE GAULLE On being asked by a journalist if he was happy.

Hatred

Clinical observation shows not only that love is with unexpected regularity accompanied by hate, and not only that in human relationships hate is frequently a forerunner of love, but also that in many circumstances hate changes into love and love into hate.
SIGMUND FREUD

Hatred is the coward's revenge for being intimidated.
GEORGE BERNARD SHAW

Like the greatest virtue and the worst dogs, the fiercest hatred is silent.
JEAN PAUL RICHTER

It is human nature to hate the one whom you have hurt.
TACITUS

Impotent hatred is the most horrible of all emotions; one should hate nobody whom one cannot destroy.
GOETHE

Heaven

In heaven all the interesting people are missing.
FRIEDRICH NIETZSCHE

Of the delights of this world, man cares most for sexual intercourse, yet he has left it out of his heaven.
MARK TWAIN

If there is a Heaven for homosexuals, it will be very poorly lit and full of people they can be pretty confident they'll never have to meet again.
QUENTIN CRISP

No man can enter Heaven until he is first convinced he deserves Hell.
JOHN W. EVERETT

Heaven is too much like Earth to be spoken of as it really is, lest the generality should think it like their Earth, which is Hell.
COVENTRY PATMORE

It is here, where we stand, that we should try to make shine the light of the hidden divine life.
MARTIN BUBER Existential philosopher and theologian whose most famous book, *I and Thou* (1923), made a noble attempt to combine the rigour of academic philosophy with religious mysticism.

Hell

Hell hath no limits, nor is circumscribed
In one self place, but where we are is Hell,
And where hell is there must we ever be.
CHRISTOPHER MARLOWE

I'm not concerned about all hell breaking loose, but that a *part* of hell
will break loose... it'll be much harder to detect.
GEORGE CARLIN Legendary American stand-up whose most famous routine –
Seven Words You Can Never Say on Television – led to his arrest for obscenity in
Milwaukee in 1972.

What is hell?
Hell is oneself,
Hell is alone, the other figures in it
Merely projections. There is nothing to escape from
And nothing to escape to. One is always alone.
T. S. ELIOT

The heart of man is the place the devils dwell in: I feel sometimes a hell
within myself.
SIR THOMAS BROWNE

When childhood dies, its corpses are called adults and they enter
society, one of the politer names of hell.
BRIAN ALDISS

Hell is a half-filled auditorium.
ROBERT FROST

Maybe this world is another planet's Hell.
ALDOUS HUXLEY

I read about an Eskimo hunter who asked the local missionary priest,
'If I did not know about God and sin, would I go to hell?' 'No,' said the
priest, 'not if you did not know.' 'Then why,' asked the Eskimo, 'did you
tell me?'
ANNIE DILLARD

If you are going through hell, keep going.
WINSTON CHURCHILL

Historians

It is a great pity that every human being does not, at an early stage of
his life, have to write a historical work. He would then realise that the

human race is in quite a jam about truth.
REBECCA WEST

It has been said that though God cannot alter the past, historians can;
it is perhaps because they can be useful to Him in this respect that He
tolerates their existence.
SAMUEL BUTLER

It might be a good idea if the various countries of the world would
occasionally swap history books, just to see what other people are
doing with the same set of facts.
BILL VAUGHAN

Ignorance is the first requisite of the historian – ignorance which
simplifies and clarifies, which selects, and omits.
LYTTON STRACHEY

There are more valid facts and details in works of art than there are in
history books.
CHARLIE CHAPLIN

History is a construct consequent upon the questions asked by the
historian.
E. H. CARR

I sometimes think of what future historians will say of us. A single
sentence will suffice for modern man: he fornicated and read the
papers.
ALBERT CAMUS

History

The future is dark, the present burdensome. Only the past, dead and
buried, bears contemplation.
G. R. ELTON

History is a pack of lies about events that never happened told by
people who weren't there.
GEORGE SANTAYANA

History is an endless repetition of the wrong way of living.
LAWRENCE DURRELL

History is the sound of hobnailed boots ascending the staircase and of
silk slippers coming down.
VOLTAIRE

History is little more than the register of the crimes, follies and misfortunes of mankind.
EDWARD GIBBON

History is but glorification of murderers and robbers.
KARL POPPER

Sin writes histories, goodness is silent.
GOETHE

History celebrates the battlefields whereon we meet our death, but scorns to speak of the ploughed fields whereby we live. It knows the names of the kings' bastards, but cannot tell us the origin of wheat.
JEAN HENRI FABRE

History is the science of what never happens twice.
PAUL VALÉRY

It would be a good thing if man concerned himself more with the history of his nature than with the history of his deeds.
FRIEDRICH HEBBEL

What then is, generally speaking, the truth of history? A fable agreed upon.
NAPOLEON BONAPARTE From the memoirs of his private secretary, Louis Antoine Fauvelet de Bourrienne, published in 1829, but sometimes also attributed either to Voltaire or to his friend the centenarian Bernard le Bovier de Fontenelle (1657–1757).

What experience and history teach is this – that people and governments have never learned anything from the study of history, or acted on principles deduced from it.
G. W. F. HEGEL

The number of victims of robbers, highwaymen, rapists, gangsters and other criminals at any period of history is negligible compared to the massive numbers of those cheerfully slain in the name of the true religion, just policy, or correct ideology.
ARTHUR KOESTLER

One history passes by in full view and, strictly speaking, is the history of crime, for if there were no crimes there would be no history. All the most important turning points and stages of this history are marked by crimes: murders, acts of violence, robberies, wars, rebellions, massacres, tortures, executions . . . This is one history, the history which everybody knows, the history which is taught in schools.

P. D. OUSPENSKY Pupil of Gurdjieff and avatar of the 'Fourth Way', a new consciousness in which Western rationalism and Eastern mysticism were reconciled. More accessible than it sounds: the down-to-earth Yorkshireman J. B. Priestley was an admirer.

Happy the people whose annals are boring to read.
CHARLES DE MONTESQUIEU

The study of history is a powerful antidote to contemporary arrogance. It is humbling to discover how many of our glib assumptions, which seem to us novel and plausible, have been tested before, not once but many times and in innumerable guises; and discovered to be, at great human cost, wholly false.
PAUL JOHNSON

Honesty

Honesty may be the best policy, but it's important to remember that apparently, by elimination, dishonesty is the second-best policy.
GEORGE CARLIN

A truth that's told with bad intent beats all the lies you can invent.
WILLIAM BLAKE

There's one way to find out if a man is honest – ask him. If he says, 'Yes,' you know he is a crook.
GROUCHO MARX

A man that should call everything by its right name would hardly pass the streets without being knocked down as a common enemy.
GEORGE SAVILE, 1ST MARQUESS OF HALIFAX One of the great pragmatists of British history, a brilliant orator and racy conversationalist, known as the 'Trimmer' because he refused to side with either the Whigs or the Tories. He smoothed the passage to the English throne of the Dutch monarchs William and Mary.

People who are brutally honest get more satisfaction out of the brutality than out of the honesty.
RICHARD J. NEEDHAM

Speak the truth, but leave immediately afterwards.
SLOVENIAN PROVERB

It is always the best policy to tell the truth, unless, of course, you are an exceptionally good liar.
JEROME K. JEROME

Hope

Hope is the gay skylarking pajamas we wear over yesterday's bruises.
BENJAMIN DE CASSERES Wrote books on many other writers and thinkers,
including Spinoza, his direct ancestor. He survives through some pithy one-liners
and his 1922 anthology-staple poem, 'Moth-Terror'.

The human body experiences a powerful gravitational pull in the
direction of hope.
NORMAN COUSINS

I steer my bark with hope in the head, leaving fear astern. My hopes
indeed sometimes fail, but not oftener than the forebodings of the
gloomy.
THOMAS JEFFERSON

Hope is patience with the lamp lit.
TERTULLIAN

He that lives upon hope will die fasting.
BENJAMIN FRANKLIN

Hope is not the conviction that something will turn out well, but the
certainty that something makes sense regardless of how it turns out.
VÁCLAV HAVEL

Everything one *records* contains a grain of hope, no matter how deeply
it may come from despair.
ELIAS CANETTI

Hope for the best but prepare for the worst.
ENGLISH PROVERB

Hope is the feeling we have that the feeling we have is not permanent.
MIGNON McLAUGHLIN

Things which you do not hope happen more frequently than things
which you do hope.
PLAUTUS

Hope is like a road in the country; there was never a road, but when
many people walk on it, the road comes into existence.
LIN YUTANG

The road that is built in hope is more pleasant to the traveler than the
road built in despair, even though they both lead to the same
destination.
MARIAN ZIMMER BRADLEY

Hope, in reality, is the worst of all evils, because it prolongs the torments of man.
FRIEDRICH NIETZSCHE

If one truly has lost hope, one would not be on hand to say so.
ERIC BENTLEY

In your hopelessness is the only hope, and in your desirelessness is your only fulfilment, and in your tremendous helplessness suddenly the whole existence starts helping you.
OSHO The controversial and influential Indian guru and mystic, formerly known as Bhagwan Shree Rajneesh. He changed his name in 1989 having embraced Zen. Despite persistent rumours of corruption (he owned ninety-three Rolls-Royce cars given to him by followers) many Indians now regard him as one of their most significant modern philosophers. His epitaph reads: 'Never Born, Never Died. Only Visited this Planet Earth between December 11 1931 and January 19 1990.'

Housework

Housework can kill you, if you do it right.
ERMA BOMBECK

How do you know if it's time to wash the dishes and clean your house? Look inside your pants. If you find a penis in there, it's not time.
JO BRAND

The phrase 'working mother' is redundant.
JANE SELLMAN

One of the advantages of being disorderly is that one is constantly making exciting discoveries.
A. A. MILNE

Never sweep. After four years the dirt gets no worse.
QUENTIN CRISP

I'm not going to vacuum 'til Sears makes one you can ride on.
ROSEANNE BARR

Human Beings

What is man? The slave of death, a passing wayfarer. How is man placed? Like a lantern in the wind.
ALCUIN Became the chief intellectual at the court of the Emperor Charlemagne, an extraordinary achievement for a boy from York. Pious, clever, notably tolerant of unbelievers and a brilliant teacher, for some reason he has never been made a saint.

Why the toil, yearning, honesty, aesthetics, exaltation, love, hate, deceit, brilliance, hubris, humility, shame and stupidity that collectively define our species?
EDWARD O. WILSON

What a strange machine man is! You fill him with bread, wine, fish and radishes, and out come sighs, laughter and dreams.
NIKOS KAZANTZAKIS

A human being should be able to change a diaper, plan an invasion, butcher a hog, conn a ship, design a building, write a sonnet, balance accounts, build a wall, set a bone, comfort the dying, take orders, give orders, cooperate, act alone, solve equations, analyze a new problem, pitch manure, program a computer, cook a tasty meal, fight efficiently, die gallantly. Specialization is for insects.
ROBERT A. HEINLEIN The king of 'hard' (i.e. plausible) sci-fi, in the words of his most famous character Lazarus Long who featured in a series of novels beginning with *Methuselah's Children* in 1941.

We are all of us sentenced to solitary confinement inside our own skins, for life.
TENNESSEE WILLIAMS

We are not human beings on a spiritual journey. We are spiritual beings on a human journey.
STEPHEN COVEY

All human beings should try to learn before they die what they are running from, and to, and why.
JAMES THURBER

There may be said to be two classes of people in the world: those who constantly divide the people of the world into two classes, and those who do not.
ROBERT BENCHLEY

A human being is not a human being while his tendencies include self-indulgence, covetousness, temper and attacking other people.
EL-GHAZALI

Man is the only creature that consumes without producing. He does not give milk, he does not lay eggs, he is too weak to pull the plough, he cannot run fast enough to catch rabbits. Yet he is lord of all the animals.
GEORGE ORWELL

Man is the only living creature whom Nature covers with materials derived from others. To the remainder she gives different kinds of coverings – shell, bark, spines, hides, fur, bristles, down, feathers, scales and fleeces. But only man is cast forth on the day of his birth naked on the bare earth.
PLINY THE ELDER

There is a perfect ant, a perfect bee, but man is perpetually unfinished. He is both an unfinished animal and an unfinished man. It is this incurable unfinishedness which sets man apart from other living things. For, in the attempt to finish himself, man becomes a creator. Moreover, the incurable unfinishedness keeps man perpetually immature, perpetually capable of learning and growing.
ERIC HOFFER

Human Body

The body is but to the soule as a clogge tied to the legge.
JAMES COLE *Of Death: A True Description and against It a True Preparation* (1629).

The body is a self-building machine, a self-stoking, self-regulating, self-repairing machine – the most marvellous and unique automatic mechanism in the universe.
SIR J. ARTHUR THOMSON

The body is but a set of pincers set over a bellows and a stew pan and the whole fixed upon stilts.
SAMUEL BUTLER

Poor brother donkey.
SAINT FRANCIS OF ASSISI Some legends relate that he used these words to thank his body as he lay dying in 1226, aged 43. Others claim there was an actual donkey present too, and it cried.

The human penis is a thing like a marmoset or some other unruly small pet that they carry around with them.
NORMAN RUSH

Chins are exclusively a human feature, not to be found amongst the beasts. If they had chins, most animals would look like each other. Man was given a chin to prevent the personality of his mouth and eyes from overwhelming the rest of his face, to prevent each individual from becoming a species unto himself.
MALCOLM DE CHAZAL

Elizabeth Taylor has more chins than the Chinese telephone directory.
JOAN RIVERS

Human Nature

Every man is as Nature made him, and sometimes a great deal worse.
MIGUEL DE CERVANTES

When we speak of Nature it is wrong to forget that we are ourselves a part of Nature. We ought to view ourselves with the same curiosity and openness with which we study a tree, the sky or a thought, because we too are linked to the entire universe.
HENRI MATISSE

The universe seems bankrupt as soon as we begin to discuss the characters of individuals.
HENRY DAVID THOREAU

Strong people have strong weaknesses.
PETER DRUCKER

What a chimera then is man! What a novelty! What a monster, what a chaos, what a subject of contradiction, what a prodigy! Judge of all things, feeble earthworm, depository of truth, a sink of uncertainty and error, the glory and the shame of the universe.
BLAISE PASCAL

Always remember that you are absolutely unique. Just like everyone else.
MARGARET MEAD

You don't really understand human nature unless you know why a child on a merry-go-round will wave at his parents every time around – and why the parents will always wave back.
BILL TAMMEUS

The real problem is in the hearts and minds of men. It is not a problem of physics but of ethics. It is easier to denature plutonium than to denature the evil from the spirit of man.
ALBERT EINSTEIN

Out of the crooked timber of humanity, no straight thing was ever made.
IMMANUEL KANT

Every man is as Heaven made him, and sometimes a great deal worse.
MIGUEL DE CERVANTES

It is the greatest mistake to think that man is always one and the same. A man is never the same for long. He is continually changing. He seldom remains the same even for half an hour.
G. I. GURDJIEFF

We cannot heal the wounds we do not feel.
S. R. SMALLEY

I have striven not to laugh at human actions, not to weep at them, nor to hate them, but to understand them.
BARUCH SPINOZA

For the first time I examined myself with a seriously practical purpose. And there I found what appalled me; a zoo of lusts, a bedlam of ambitions, a nursery of fears, a harem of fondled hatreds. My name was Legion.
C. S. LEWIS

Psychoanalytic doctrine reveals the pig in man, a pig saddled with a conscience; the disastrous result is that the pig is uncomfortable beneath that pious rider, and the rider fares no better in the situation, since his endeavour is not only to tame the pig, but also to render it invisible.
STANISLAS LEM In the classic sci-fi novel *His Master's Voice* (1968) in which Pentagon scientists attempt to interpret a radio transmission from outer space.

The only thing you will ever be able to say in the so-called 'social' sciences is 'some do, some don't'.
ERNEST RUTHERFORD

Humility

I believe that the first test of a truly great man is his humility. I don't mean by humility, doubt of his power. But really great men have a curious feeling that the greatness is not of them, but through them. And they see something divine in every other man and are endlessly, foolishly, incredibly merciful.
JOHN RUSKIN

Humility is the mother of giants. One sees great things from the valley; only small things from the peak.
G. K. CHESTERTON

Stay humble. Always answer the phone, no matter who else is in the car.
JACK LEMMON

The meek shall inherit the earth, but not the mineral rights.
J. PAUL GETTY

Almost any difficulty will move in the face of honesty. When I am honest I never feel stupid. And when I am honest I am automatically humble.
HUGH PRATHER Methodist personal development counsellor in Tuscon, Arizona, whose first book *Notes to Myself* (1970) sold five million copies. His work seeks out the spiritual in everyday life, producing a kind of Christian version of cognitive therapy.

Humility is attentive patience.
SIMONE WEIL

At home I am a nice guy – but I don't want the world to know. Humble people, I've found, don't get very far.
MUHAMMAD ALI

Early in life I had to choose between honest arrogance and hypocritical humility. I chose honest arrogance and never found an occasion to change.
FRANK LLOYD WRIGHT

Humility is just as much the opposite of self-abasement as it is of self-exaltation. To be humble is not to make comparisons. Secure in its reality, the self is neither better nor worse, bigger nor smaller than anything else in the universe. It is – it is nothing yet at the same time one with everything. It is in this sense that humility is absolute self-effacement.
MAHATMA GANDHI

Humility is the most difficult of all virtues to achieve, nothing dies harder than the desire to think well of oneself.
T. S. ELIOT

For the most part, I do the thing which my own nature prompts me to do. It is embarrassing to earn so much respect and love for it.
ALBERT EINSTEIN

If I only had a little humility, I would be perfect.
TED TURNER

Humour

Humour is not a mood, but a way of looking at the world. So, if it's right to say that humour was eradicated in Nazi Germany, that does not

mean that people were not in good spirits or anything of that sort, but something much deeper and more important.
LUDWIG WITTGENSTEIN

The secret source of humour itself is not joy, but sorrow. There is no humour in heaven.
MARK TWAIN

A passionate man is seldom witty.
STENDHAL

If you want to make people weep, you must weep yourself. If you want to make people laugh, your face must remain serious.
GIACOMO CASANOVA

In the whole of the New Testament there is not one joke. That fact alone would invalidate any book.
FRIEDRICH NIETZSCHE From *The Will to Power* (1888), the posthumous collection of Nietzsche's fragments reordered by his sister Elisabeth into an apparent magnum opus which chimed in with her own anti-Semitic leanings. There is no evidence Nietzsche intended such a book.

Jokes are better than war. Even the most aggressive jokes are better than the least aggressive wars. Even the longest jokes are better than the shortest wars.
GEORGE MIKES

Serious things cannot be understood without laughable things, nor opposites at all without opposites.
PLATO

Unmitigated seriousness is always out of place in human affairs. Let not the unwary reader think me flippant for saying so; it was Plato, in his solemn old age, who said it.
GEORGE SANTAYANA

I

Ideas

No man can describe how an idea comes to him.
ISAAC BASHEVIS SINGER

Ideas come from space.
THOMAS EDISON

If the idea is not at first absurd, then there is no hope for it.
ALBERT EINSTEIN

There are some ideas so wrong that only a very intelligent person could believe in them.
GEORGE ORWELL

Serious people have few ideas. People with ideas are never serious.
PAUL VALLELY Responsible for coining the mantra 'from charity to justice', writing the report for Tony Blair's 'Commission for Africa' and ghost-writing Bob Geldof's autobiography, *Is That It?* (1986).

Ideas are like rabbits. You get a couple and learn how to handle them, and pretty soon you have a dozen of them.
JOHN STEINBECK

The ideas I stand for are not mine. I borrowed them from Socrates. I swiped them from Chesterfield. I stole them from Jesus. And I put them in a book. If you don't like their rules, whose would you use?
DALE CARNEGIE

Marx, Darwin and Freud are the three most crashing bores of the Western World. Simplistic popularisation of their ideas has thrust our world into a mental straitjacket from which we can only escape by the most anarchic violence.
WILLIAM GOLDING

Men thought and fought and wept and laughed and even died in despair over the ideas that look so dull on these pages.
WILL DURANT

It is not once nor twice but times without number that the same ideas make their appearance in the world.
ARISTOTLE

Why is it I get my best ideas in the morning while I'm shaving?
ALBERT EINSTEIN

When I am, as it were, completely myself, entirely alone and of good cheer – say travelling in a carriage, or walking after a good meal or during the night when I cannot sleep; it is on such occasions that my ideas flow best and most abundantly. Whence and how they come I know not, nor can I force them . . .
WOLFGANG AMADEUS MOZART

The best ideas come to me when I polish my shoes early in the morning.
JOHANNES BRAHMS

The best way to have a good idea is to have lots of ideas.
LINUS PAULING Multi-disciplinary American physicist who worked on quantum mechanics, molecular biology, X-ray crystallography, atomic structure and the healing effects of vitamin C. He won two Nobel prizes: one for chemistry and one for peace, for his campaign against nuclear testing.

Two ideas are always needed: one to kill the other.
GEORGES BRAQUE

New ideas don't win really. What happens is that the old scientists die and new ones come along with new ideas.
MAX PLANCK

Queen Victoria was like a great paperweight that for half a century sat upon men's minds, and when she was removed their ideas began to blow about the place quite haphazardly.
H. G. WELLS

It is not easy to convey, unless one has experienced it, the dramatic feeling of sudden enlightenment that floods the mind when the right idea finally clinches into place.
FRANCIS CRICK

If you have an apple and I have an apple and we exchange these apples then you and I will still each have one apple. But if you have an idea and I have an idea and we exchange these ideas, then each of us will have two ideas.
GEORGE BERNARD SHAW

Man is ready to die for an idea, provided that the idea is not quite clear to him.
PAUL ELDRIDGE

Don't worry about people stealing your ideas. If your ideas are any good, you'll have to ram them down people's throats.
HOWARD AIKEN

An idea that is not dangerous is unworthy of being called an idea at all.
OSCAR WILDE

I can't understand why people are frightened of new ideas. I'm frightened of the old ones.
JOHN CAGE

Idleness

Idleness is not doing nothing. Idleness is being free to do anything.
FLOYD DELL Aesthete and early adopter of Greenwich village bohemia, his own work might not be read now but without his support that of Eugene O'Neill, Theodore Dreiser and Sherwood Anderson might be much less well known.

Far from idleness being the root of all evil, it is rather the only true good.
SØREN KIERKEGAARD

A faculty for idleness implies a catholic appetite and a strong sense of personal identity.
ROBERT LOUIS STEVENSON

It is better to have loafed and lost than never to have loafed at all.
JAMES THURBER

You can't leave footprints in the sands of time if you're sitting on your butt – and who wants to leave butt prints in the sands of time?
BOB MOAWAD

Ignorance

I know nothing except the fact of my ignorance.
SOCRATES Quoted in Diogenes Laertius' *Lives & Opinions of Eminent Philosophers* written some time after AD 200. It pithily sums up many of the sentiments about wisdom expressed in Plato's *Apology*, the account of Socrates' trial and execution in 399 BC.

Have the courage to be ignorant of a great number of things, in order

to avoid the calamity of being ignorant of everything.
SYDNEY SMITH

All ignorance toboggans into know and trudges up to ignorance again.
e. e. cummings

It may be that the ignorant man, alone, has any chance to mate his life with life.
WALLACE STEVENS

By ignorance the truth is known.
HEINRICH SUSO Fourteenth-century German mystic and pupil of Meister Eckhart, he wrote *The Little Book of Truth* while still a student. As well as refusing to bathe, so as to encourage lice, he slept on a door and wore an undershirt studded with brass nails.

The little I know, I owe to ignorance.
SACHA GUITRY

Everybody is ignorant, only on different subjects.
WILL ROGERS

The greatest obstacle to discovery is not ignorance – it is the illusion of knowledge.
DANIEL J. BOORSTIN

T'aint what a man don't know that hurts him, it's what he knows that just ain't so.
FRANK 'KIN' HUBBARD

I would rather have my ignorance than another man's knowledge, because I have got so much more of it.
MARK TWAIN

There is nothing new under the sun, but there are lots of old things we don't know.
AMBROSE BIERCE

If ignorance is bliss, there should be more happy people.
VICTOR COUSINS

We don't know a millionth of one per cent about anything.
THOMAS EDISON

I could paint for a hundred years, a thousand years without stopping and I would still feel as though I knew nothing.
PAUL CÉZANNE

My greatest strength as a consultant is to be ignorant and ask a few questions.
PETER DRUCKER

To be conscious that you are ignorant of the facts is a great step towards knowledge.
BENJAMIN DISRAELI

At the simplest level, only people who know they do not know everything will be curious enough to find things out.
VIRGINIA POSTREL

Illness

Without fear and illness, I could never have accomplished all I have.
EDVARD MUNCH

Refuse to be ill. Never tell people you are ill; never own it to yourself. Illness is one of those things which a man should resist on principle.
EDWARD BULWER-LYTTON

I've never met a healthy person who worried much about his health or a good person who worried much about his soul.
J. B. S. HALDANE

A hospital is no place to be sick.
SAMUEL GOLDWYN

When I have gout, I feel as if I was walking on my eyeballs.
SYDNEY SMITH

Pain seizes the great toe, then the forepart of the heel on which we rest; next it comes into the arch of the foot . . . the ankle joint swells last of all . . . no other pain is more severe than this, not iron screws, nor cords, not the wound of a dagger, nor burning fire . . .
ARETAEUS OF CAPPADOCIA Describing his gout.

Keep up the spirits of your patient with the music of the viol and the psaltery, or by forging letters telling of the death of his enemies, or (if he be a cleric) by informing him that he has been made a bishop.
HENRI DE MONDEVILLE

Quit worrying about your health. It'll go away.
ROBERT ORBEN

Imagination

Everything you can imagine is real.
PABLO PICASSO

The real is always way ahead of what we can imagine.
PAUL AUSTER

Imagination is intelligence with an erection.
VICTOR HUGO

Imagination is more important than knowledge, for knowledge is limited while imagination embraces the entire world.
ALBERT EINSTEIN

Imagination acts upon man as really as does gravitation, and may kill him as certainly as a dose of prussic acid.
SIR JAMES FRAZER

Fantasy, abandoned by reason, produces impossible monsters; united with it, she is the mother of the arts and the origin of marvels.
FRANCISCO GOYA

The man who can't visualise a horse galloping on a tomato is an idiot.
ANDRÉ BRETON

Impossibility

Impossible is a word to be found only in the dictionary of fools.
NAPOLEON BONAPARTE

It is difficult to say what is impossible, for the dream of yesterday is the hope of today and reality of tomorrow.
ROBERT GODDARD

When a distinguished but elderly scientist states that something is possible he is almost certainly right. When he states that something is impossible, he is very probably wrong.
ARTHUR C. CLARKE (Clarke's First Law)

The only way of discovering the limits of the possible is to venture a little way past them into the impossible.
ARTHUR C. CLARKE (Clarke's Second Law) Clarke actually came up with an idea that changed the world. He first mooted the idea of satellites travelling at the same speed as the Earth being used for telecommunications in 1945. Now there are over 300 of them.

Insignificance

Whatever you do will be insignificant, but it is very important that you do it.
MAHATMA GANDHI

The negligible is important.
JONATHAN MILLER

A tiny fly can choke a big man.
SOLOMON IBN GABIROL

It's almost impossible to overestimate the unimportance of most things.
JOHN LOGUE

No man thinks there is much ado about nothing when the ado is about himself.
ANTHONY TROLLOPE

Nothing in fine print is ever good news.
ANDY ROONEY

Only the ephemeral is of lasting value.
EUGENE IONESCO

Inspiration

Inspiration may be a form of superconsciousness, or perhaps of subconsciousness – I wouldn't know. But I am sure it is the antithesis of self-consciousness.
AARON COPLAND

Inspiration is wonderful when it happens, but the writer must develop an approach for the rest of the time . . . the wait is simply too long.
LEONARD BERNSTEIN

I sit down to the piano regularly at nine o'clock in the morning and *Mesdames les Muses* have learned to be on time for that rendezvous.
PYOTR TCHAIKOVSKY

The poet who is about to make a poem (and I know this from experience) has the vague feeling he is going on a nocturnal hunting trip in an incredibly distant forest. An inexplicable fear murmurs in his heart. In order to calm down, it is always a good idea to take a glass of fresh water and make meaningless black marks with your pen. I say black because, and this is a secret . . . I do not use coloured ink.
FEDERICO GARCÍA LORCA

My sole inspiration is a telephone call from a producer.
COLE PORTER

Integrity

Few men have virtue to withstand the highest bidder.
GEORGE WASHINGTON

There is no such thing as a minor lapse of integrity.
TOM PETERS

Integrity is the essence of everything successful.
R. BUCKMINSTER FULLER

Somebody once said that in looking for people to hire, you look for three qualities: integrity, intelligence and energy. But if you don't have the first, the other two could kill you.
WARREN BUFFETT

Integrity has no need of rules.
ALBERT CAMUS

Intelligence

Man is so intelligent that he feels impelled to invent theories to account for what happens in the world. Unfortunately, he is not quite intelligent enough, in most cases, to find correct explanations. So that, when he acts on his theories, he behaves very often like a lunatic.
ALDOUS HUXLEY

There is no limit to a woman's intelligence provided she is not required to be coherent.
MIGUEL DE CERVANTES

What a distressing contrast there is between the radiant intelligence of the child and the feeble mentality of the average adult.
SIGMUND FREUD

So far as I can remember, there is not one word in the Gospels in praise of intelligence.
BERTRAND RUSSELL

Intelligence is not all that important in the exercise of power, and is often, in point of fact, useless.
HENRY KISSINGER

For any serious purpose, intelligence is a very minor gift.
G. H. HARDY

Sharks are as tough as those football fans who take their shirts off during games in Chicago in January, only more intelligent.
DAVE BARRY

Smartness runs in my family. When I went to school I was so smart my teacher was in my class for five years.
GEORGE BURNS

Great novels are always a little more intelligent than their authors.
MILAN KUNDERA

It is no proof of a man's understanding to be able to confirm whatever he pleases; but to be able to discern that what is true is true, and that what is false is false, this is the mark and character of intelligence.
EMANUEL SWEDENBORG The passage from professional scientist, who had produced designs for flying machines and published an influential book on smelting iron and copper, to mystic who conversed with angels is one of the most intriguing and moving ever recorded. He has been a talismanic figure for many free thinkers, including William Blake, Goethe, Strindberg, Emerson and, more recently, Jorge Luis Borges.

The best human intelligence is still decidedly barbarous; it fights in heavy armour and keeps a fool at court.
GEORGE SANTAYANA

Interestingness

There are only two forces that unite men – fear and interest.
NAPOLEON BONAPARTE

It is more important that a proposition be interesting than that it be true . . . But of course a true proposition is more apt to be interesting than a false one.
A. N. WHITEHEAD Worked with Bertrand Russell to produce the epoch-making *Principia Mathematica* in 1910–13. The two diverged sharply thereafter: Whitehead's later 'process philosophy', a fascinating attempt to reconcile Platonic theories of 'timeless entitities' with Einsteinian physics, deserves to be better known.

I can think of nothing that an audience won't understand. The only problem is to interest them; once they are interested, they understand anything in the world.
ORSON WELLES

There is an incessant influx of novelty into the world, and yet we tolerate incredible dullness.
HENRY DAVID THOREAU

The thousand mysteries around us would not trouble but interest us, if only we had cheerful, healthy hearts.
FRIEDRICH NIETZSCHE

There never was yet an uninteresting life. Such a thing is an impossibility. Inside of the dullest exterior there is a drama, a comedy and a tragedy.
MARK TWAIN

The secret of a man who is universally interesting is that he is universally interested.
WILLIAM DEAN HOWELLS

What am I interested in? Everything.

THOMAS EDISON

Internet

Prior to the Internet, the last technology that had any real effect on the way people sat down and talked together was the table.
CLAY SHIRKY

You just have a different relationship to somebody when you're looking at them than you do when you're punching away at a keyboard and some symbols come back. I suspect that extending that form of abstract and remote relationship, instead of direct, personal contact, is going to have unpleasant effects on what people are like. It will diminish their humanity.
NOAM CHOMSKY

We've heard that a million monkeys at a million keyboards could produce the Complete Works of Shakespeare; now, thanks to the Internet, we know this is not true.
ROBERT WILENSKY

On the Internet, nobody knows you're a dog.
PETER STEINER His now famous cartoon featuring a conversation between two dogs sitting in front of a computer screen first appeared on 5 July 1993. It is claimed as the inspiration for Apple's prototype 1997 web browser, Cyberdog.

Intuition

I have had my solutions for a long time, but I do not yet know how I am to arrive at them.
KARL FRIEDRICH GAUSS

Logic, which alone can give certainty, is the instrument of demonstration; intuition is the instrument of invention.
HENRI POINCARÉ

Bach, Beethoven, Brahms, Stravinsky and a few other composers of the past have recognised the supremacy of intuition, based on the quality of the composer being a medium. He is a mouthpiece of the divine.
KARLHEINZ STOCKHAUSEN

Thinking up the Theory of Relativity was easy. Proving it was next to impossible.
ALBERT EINSTEIN

It is the heart which perceives God and not the reason.
BLAISE PASCAL

Sell your cleverness and buy bewilderment. Cleverness is mere opinion, bewilderment is intuition.
RUMI Everbody's favourite mystic. The order of the Whirling Dervishes was founded by his son on his death, but it is his love poetry – wise, profound and full of the belief that words and music bring us closer to God – that make him still 'the most popular poet in America'.

Inventions

The man who invented cat's eyes got the idea when he saw a cat facing him in the road. If the cat had been facing the other way, he'd have invented the pencil sharpener.
KEN DODD

The guy who invented the first wheel was an idiot. The guy who invented the other three, *he* was a genius.
SID CAESAR

Our inventions are wont to be pretty toys, which distract our attention from serious things. They are but improved means to an unimproved end, an end which it was already but too easy to arrive at.
HENRY DAVID THOREAU

It is well to observe the force and virtue and consequence of inventions, and these are nowhere to be seen more conspicuously than in those three which were unknown to the ancients, and of which the origins, though recent, are obscure and inglorious; namely, printing, gunpowder, and the magnet. For these three have changed the whole face and state of things throughout the world.
FRANCIS BACON

Because I readily absorb ideas from every source – frequently starting where the last person left off – I am sometimes accurately described as 'more of a sponge than an inventor'.
THOMAS EDISON

Nothing is more important than to see the sources of invention which are, in my opinion, more interesting than the inventions themselves.
GOTTFRIED LEIBNIZ

I just invent, then wait until man comes around to needing what I've invented.
R. BUCKMINSTER FULLER Best known for his geodesic dome or Buckyball, he was a true American visionary: a scientist, architect, environmentalist and writer who believed human survival depended on technological innovation. From 1915 to 1983 he documented every fifteen minutes of his life. It's hard not to like someone who can write a book called *I Seem to Be a Verb* (1970).

Sleep is the only source of invention.
MARCEL PROUST

Investments

Never invest your money in anything that eats or needs repainting.
BILLY ROSE

Never invest in any idea you can't illustrate with a crayon.
PETER LYNCH

Successful investing is anticipating the anticipations of others.
JOHN MAYNARD KEYNES

Wide diversification is only required when investors do not understand what they are doing.
WARREN BUFFETT

Everybody has a powerful conviction of what is going on (in the stock market), but the truth is not a soul knows what is going on. That's what makes markets so fascinating.
ROGER ALTMAN

Anybody who plays the stock market not as an insider is like a man buying cows in the moonlight.
DANIEL DREW

Never pay the slightest attention to what a company president ever says about his stock.
BERNARD BARUCH

You go to bed feeling very comfortable just thinking about two and a half billion males with hair growing while you sleep. No one at Gillette has trouble sleeping.
WARREN BUFFETT

If you gave me $100 billion and said take away the soft drink leadership of Coca-Cola in the world, I'd give it back to you and say it can't be done.
WARREN BUFFETT

Most people get interested in stocks when everyone else is. The time to get interested is when no one else is. You can't buy what is popular and do well.
WARREN BUFFETT

Throughout all my years of investing I've found that the big money was never made in the buying or the selling. The big money was made in the waiting.
JESSE LIVERMORE

Wall Street is the only place that people ride to in a Rolls-Royce to get advice from those who take the subway.
WARREN BUFFETT

If stock market experts were so expert, they would be buying stock, not selling advice.
NORMAN R. AUGUSTINE

J

Jokes

A serious and good philosophical work could be written consisting entirely of jokes.
LUDWIG WITTGENSTEIN

A joke goes a great way in the country. I have known one last pretty well for seven years.
SYDNEY SMITH

One nice thing about telling a clean joke is there's a good chance no one's heard it before.
DOUG LARSON

A pun is two strings of thought tied with an acoustic knot.
ARTHUR KOESTLER

I'm not offended by all the dumb blonde jokes because I know I'm not dumb . . . and I'm also not blonde.
DOLLY PARTON

I don't mind making jokes, but I don't want to look like one.
MARILYN MONROE

SANDY: Shouldn't I stop making movies and do something that counts, like, like helping blind people or becoming a missionary or something?
ALIEN: Let me tell you: You're not the missionary type. You'd never last. And, incidentally, you're not Superman. You're a comedian. You want to do mankind a real service? Tell funnier jokes!
WOODY ALLEN *Stardust Memories* (1980) Angst-ridden Bergman fan Sandy Bates (played by Allen) asks an alien for advice.

Journalism

Journalism is the art of explaining to others what one doesn't understand oneself.
LORD NORTHCLIFFE

Journalism largely consists in saying 'Lord Jones Dead' to people who never knew Lord Jones was alive.
G. K. CHESTERTON

Literature is the art of writing something that will be read twice; journalism what will be grasped at once.
CYRIL CONNOLLY

There is much to be said in favour of modern journalism. By giving us the opinions of the uneducated, it keeps us in touch with the ignorance of the community.
OSCAR WILDE

Put it before them briefly so they will read it, clearly so they will appreciate it, picturesquely so they will remember it and, above all, accurately so they will be guided by its light.
JOSEPH PULITZER Practically invented sensationalist tabloid journalism. His name lives on as the touchstone of literary excellence, unlike his great rival William Randolph Hearst, owing to the prizes Pulitzer endowed on his death in 1911.

Early in life I had noticed that no event is ever correctly reported in a newspaper.
GEORGE ORWELL

Facing the press is more difficult than bathing a leper.
MOTHER TERESA

To a newspaperman, a human being is an item with the skin wrapped around it.
FRED ALLEN

I believe in equality for everyone, except reporters and photographers.
MAHATMA GANDHI

It is inexcusable for scientists to torture animals; let them make their experiments on journalists and politicians.
HENRIK IBSEN

I hate journalists. There is nothing in them but tittering jeering emptiness. They have all made what Dante calls the Great Refusal. The shallowest people on the ridge of the earth.
W. B. YEATS

Is it against the law to kill a reporter?
BOBBY FISCHER

Being a newspaper columnist is like being married to a
nymphomaniac. It's great for the first two weeks.
LEWIS GRIZZARD

I usually get my stuff from people who promised somebody else that
they would keep it a secret.
WALTER WINCHELL

Lies in newspapers are like rat droppings in clear soup. Not only
disgusting but obvious.
CHINESE PROVERB

Were it left to me to decide whether we should have a government
without newspapers, or newspapers without a government, I should
not hesitate a moment to prefer the latter.
THOMAS JEFFERSON

The lowest depth to which people can sink before God is defined by
the word 'journalist'. If I were a father and had a daughter who was
seduced I should not despair over her; I would hope for her salvation.
But if I had a son who became a journalist and continued to be one for
five years, I would give him up.
SØREN KIERKEGAARD He had no children of his own. The nearest he came was
his engagement to Regine Olsen, which he broke off claiming he was too miserable
to be a good husband. Instead he turned in 7,000 pages of very unjournalistic,
angst-ridden journals.

I had rather be called a journalist than an artist.
H. G. WELLS

If Moses had been paid newspaper rates for the Ten Commandments,
he might have written the Two Thousand Commandments.
ISAAC BASHEVIS SINGER

Joy

Joy is the simplest form of gratitude.
KARL BARTH

People are constantly clamouring for the joy of life. As for me, I find the
joy of life in the hard and cruel battle of life – to learn something is a
joy to me.
AUGUST STRINDBERG

The most profound joy has more of gravity than of gaiety in it.
MICHEL DE MONTAIGNE

All who joy would win must share it. Happiness was born a Twin.
LORD BYRON

We would never learn to be brave and patient if there were only joy in the world.
HELEN KELLER

Seize from every moment its unique novelty and do not prepare your joys.
ANDRÉ GIDE

Judgement

Do not judge, and you will never be mistaken.
JEAN JACQUES ROUSSEAU

It is well, when judging a friend, to remember that he is judging you with the same godlike and superior impartiality.
ARNOLD BENNETT

Our judgements judge us, and nothing reveals us, exposes our weaknesses more ingeniously than the attitude of pronouncing upon our fellows.
PAUL VALÉRY

I shall tell you a great secret, my friend. Do not wait for the last judgement, it takes place every day.
ALBERT CAMUS

K

Kindness

Three things in human life are important. The first is to be kind. The second is to be kind. And the third is to be kind.
WILLIAM JAMES

Be kind, for everyone you meet is fighting a hard battle.
PLATO

Always be a little kinder than necessary.
J. M. BARRIE

The highest wisdom is loving kindness.
THE TALMUD

My true religion is kindness.
THE DALAI LAMA

That best portion of a good man's life;
His little, nameless, unremembered acts
Of kindness and of love.
WILLIAM WORDSWORTH

He that is kind is free, though he is a slave; he that is evil is a slave, though he be a king.
SAINT AUGUSTINE

To give pleasure to a single heart by a single kind act is better than a thousand head-bowings in prayer.
SADI

Kindness is in one's power: fondness is not.
SAMUEL JOHNSON

It is not by sitting still at a grand distance and calling the human race *larvae* that men are to be helped.
RALPH WALDO EMERSON

You can get much further with a kind word and a gun than you can with a kind word alone.
AL CAPONE

Beware of the people you've been kind to.
ALAN MARSHALL

If you can't be kind, at least be vague.
JUDITH MARTIN Better known as 'Miss Manners', the queen of etiquette and author of an advice column that has run for over thirty years in more than 200 newspapers worldwide. She earned the eternal ire of *Star Wars* fans for panning *The Empire Strikes Back* in 1980 (describing the guru Yoda as looking like 'an elderly, eastern rodent').

Knowledge

If a little knowledge is dangerous, where is the man who has so much as to be out of danger?
T. H. HUXLEY

To know what everybody else knows is to know nothing.
RÉMY DE GOURMONT

To know that you do not know is the best.
To pretend to know when you do not know is disease.
LAOZI (LAO-TZU)

Human knowledge will be erased from the world's archives before we possess the last word that a gnat has to say to us.
JEAN HENRI FABRE

The larger the island of knowledge, the longer the shoreline of wonder.
RALPH W. SOCKMAN

Knowledge is the small part of ignorance that we arrange and classify.
AMBROSE BIERCE

All we know so far is what doesn't work.
RICHARD FEYNMAN

Seek knowledge, even if it be in China.
MUHAMMAD Although the authenticity of this *hadith* is sometimes questioned, its significance is that the Prophet is encouraging Muslims to look outside Islam for wisdom and knowledge. China was then synonymous with advances in science, medicine and technology.

As we acquire knowledge, things do not become more comprehensible, but more mysterious.
ALBERT SCHWEITZER

All knowledge is enveloped in darkness.
SIR THOMAS BROWNE

Knowledge does not keep any better than fish.
ALFRED NORTH WHITEHEAD

That which has been accepted by everyone, everywhere, is almost
certain to be false.
PAUL VALÉRY

Real knowledge is to know the extent of one's ignorance.
CONFUCIUS

Abundance of knowledge does not teach men to be wise.
HERACLITUS

Knowledge comes, but wisdom lingers.
ALFRED, LORD TENNYSON

I am not young enough to know everything.
J. M. BARRIE

All we know is still infinitely less than all that remains unknown. Great
learning and great shallowness go together very well under one hat.
FRIEDRICH NIETZSCHE

Since we cannot know all that is to be known of everything, we ought
to know a little about everything.
BLAISE PASCAL

Some drink deeply from the river of knowledge. Others only gargle.
WOODY ALLEN

We are here and it is now. Further than that all human knowledge is
moonshine.
H. L. MENCKEN

Reports that say that something hasn't happened are always interesting to me because, as we know, there are known knowns; there are
things we know we know. We also know there are known unknowns;
that is to say we know there are some things we do not know. But there
are also unknown unknowns – the ones we don't know we don't know.
DONALD RUMSFELD From his now legendary Defense Department briefing on 12
February 2002. It won him that year's Gobbledegook award from the Plain English
Campaign, but 'unknown unknowns' have entered the language.

We can be knowledgeable with other men's knowledge but we cannot
be wise with other men's wisdom.
MICHEL DE MONTAIGNE

L

Language

Language is a virus from outer space.
WILLIAM S. BURROUGHS

Language is a city to the building of which every human being brought a stone.
RALPH WALDO EMERSON

Drawing on my fine command of language, I said nothing.
ROBERT BENCHLEY Key member of the Algonquin round table, his best work appeared in the *New Yorker* and *Vanity Fair*. He also acted in and narrated a short satirical 'public information' film, *How to Sleep*, which won an Oscar in 1935.

Language was invented to ask questions. Answers may be given by grunts and gestures, but questions must be spoken. Humanness came of age when man asked the first question.
ERIC HOFFER

I personally think we developed language because of our deep inner need to complain.
JANE WAGNER

I wonder what language truck drivers are using, now that everyone is using theirs?
SYDNEY PFIZER

There is in every child a painstaking teacher, so skilful that he obtains identical results in all children in all parts of the world. The only language men ever speak perfectly is the one they learn in babyhood, when no one can teach them anything.
MARIA MONTESSORI

Anthropologically speaking, the human race can be said to have evolved from primitive to civilised states, but there is no sign of language having gone through the same evolution. There are no 'bronze age' or 'stone age' languages.
DAVID CRYSTAL

The great thing about human language is that it prevents us from sticking to the matter at hand.
LEWIS THOMAS

A language is a dialect with an army and navy.
MAX WEINRICH

To have another language is to possess a second soul.
CHARLEMAGNE

Those who know nothing of foreign languages, know nothing of their own.
GOETHE

If the English language made any sense, lackadaisical would have something to do with a shortage of flowers.
DOUG LARSON

Status quo, you know, is Latin for 'the mess we're in'.
RONALD REAGAN

There is no 'cat language'. Painful as it is for us to admit, they don't need one.
BARBARA HOLLAND

Last Words

Hello.
RUPERT BROOKE

It has all been very interesting.
LADY MARY WORTLEY MONTAGU

I think I am beginning to understand something of it.
AUGUSTE RODIN

I wish I had spent more time in the office.
HENRY ROYCE

Wish I had time for just one more bowl of chili.
KIT CARSON

Don't let it end like this. Tell them I said something.
PANCHO VILLA

Die? I should say not, dear fellow. No Barrymore would allow such a conventional thing to happen to him.
JOHN BARRYMORE

What is done by what is called myself is, I feel, done by something greater than myself in me.
JAMES CLERK MAXWELL Developed the theory of electromagnetism and produced the first colour photograph. Einstein had his picture on his study wall, alongside images of Newton and Faraday.

Try to be forgotten. Go and live in the country. Stay in mourning for two years, then remarry, but choose somebody decent.
ALEXANDER PUSHKIN To his wife, Natalya.

You made one mistake. You married me.
BRENDAN BEHAN To his wife, Beatrice.

I just had eighteen straight whiskies, I think that's a record.
DYLAN THOMAS This is the most famous of several possibilities for his last words (sometimes it's nineteen whiskies) including: 'After thirty-nine years, this is all I've I done' and 'I love you but I'm alone' to his then lover Liz Reitell.

Be not solitary, be not idle.
ROBERT BURTON

I should never have switched from Scotch to Martinis.
HUMPHREY BOGART

The fog is rising.
EMILY DICKINSON

Decay is inherent in all compounded things. Strive on with diligence.
BUDDHA

So here it is at last, the distinguished thing!
HENRY JAMES

Laughter

Laughter, while it lasts, slackens and unbraces the mind, weakens the faculties and causes a kind of remissness and dissolution in all the powers of the soul; and thus it may be looked on as weakness in the composition of human nature. But if we consider the frequent reliefs we receive from it and how often it breaks the gloom which is apt to depress the mind and damp our spirits, with transient, unexpected gleams of joy, one would take care not to grow too wise for so great a pleasure of life.
JOSEPH ADDISON

Nobody ever died of laughter.
MAX BEERBOHM

There are some things so serious you have to laugh at them.
NIELS BOHR

At the height of laughter, the universe is flung into a kaleidoscope of new possibilities.
JEAN HOUSTON

Laughter is an orgasm triggered by the intercourse of reason with unreason.
JACK KROLL

The human race has one really effective weapon, and that is laughter.
MARK TWAIN

The gods too are fond of a joke.
ARISTOTLE

Never laugh feebly at what you know to be wrong
BISHOP MANDELL CREIGHTON A brilliant administrator who was instrumental in tidying up the rituals and doctrines of the Church of England. He was the first Bishop of London (1897–1900) to wear a mitre since the Reformation.

Laughter is man's most distinctive emotional expression. Man shares the capacity for love and hate, anger and fear, loyalty and grief, with other living creatures. But humour, which has an intellectual as well as an emotional element, belongs to man.
MARGARET MEAD

Man is the only animal that laughs and weeps, for he is the only animal that is struck with the difference between what things are, and what they might have been.
WILLIAM HAZLITT

If two or three Englishmen are together any length of time, and do not laugh, something has gone wrong.
WILLIAM CORY

Laughter is the shortest distance between two people.
VICTOR BORGE

He who laughs last has not yet heard the bad news.
BERTOLT BRECHT

Among those whom I like or admire, I can find no common denominator, but among those whom I love, I can: all of them make me laugh.
W. H. AUDEN

She has a laugh so hearty it knocks the whipped cream off an order of strawberry shortcake on a table fifty feet away.
DAMON RUNYON

She had a penetrating sort of laugh. Rather like a train going into a tunnel.
P. G. WODEHOUSE

You don't stop laughing because you grow old. You grow old because you stop laughing.
MICHAEL PRITCHARD Began life as a stand-up comedian; his mantra is now 'learning through laughter'.

Laws

Laws are like sausages. It's better not to see how they are made.
OTTO VON BISMARCK

The law, in its majestic equality, forbids the rich, as well as the poor, to sleep under bridges, to beg in the streets, and to steal bread.
ANATOLE FRANCE

The law was made for one thing alone, for the exploitation of those who don't understand it, or are prevented by naked misery from obeying it.
BERTOLT BRECHT

Law is a Bottomless-Pit, it is a Cormorant, a Harpy, that devours every thing.
JOHN ARBUTHNOT Friend to Swift, Pope, Newton and Pepys, he was a satirist, mathematician, doctor, antiquarian, the inventor of John Bull, author of a best-selling diet book and guardian of Peter the Wild Boy. No one has a bad word to say about Arbuthnot.

Someone has tabulated that we have thirty-five million laws on the books to enforce the Ten Commandments.
BERT MASTERSON

Chance too, which seems to rush along with slack reins, is bridled and governed by law.
BOETHIUS

If you ask me, 'Why should not the people make their own laws?' I need only ask you, 'Why should not the people write their own plays?' They cannot. It is much easier to write a good play than to make a good law. And there are not a hundred men in the world who can write

a play good enough to stand the daily wear and tear as long as a law must.
GEORGE BERNARD SHAW.

Lawyers

Lawyers, I suppose, were children once.
CHARLES LAMB

I was never ruined but twice, once when I lost a lawsuit and once when I won one.
VOLTAIRE

Lawyers are the only persons in whom ignorance of the law is not punished.
JEREMY BENTHAM

No brilliance is required in law, just common sense and relatively clean fingernails.
JOHN MORTIMER

We are more casual about qualifying the people we allow to act as advocates in the courtroom than we are about licensing electricians.
WARREN E. BERGER

Under the English legal system you are innocent until you are shown to be Irish.
TED WHITEHEAD

I defended about one hundred forty people for murder in this country and I think in all of the cases I received just one Christmas card from all of these defendants.
SAMUEL LEIBOWITZ

I get paid for seeing that my clients have every break the law allows. I have knowingly defended a number of guilty men. But the guilty never escape unscathed. My fees are sufficient punishment for anyone.
F. LEE BAILEY

An incompetent lawyer can delay a trial for months or years. A competent lawyer can delay one even longer.
EVELLE J. YOUNGER

I don't want a lawyer to tell me what I cannot do; I hire them to tell me how to do what I want to do.
JOHN PIERPONT MORGAN

I'm not an ambulance chaser. I'm usually there before the ambulance.
MELVIN BELLI

I used to be a lawyer but now I am a reformed character.
WOODROW WILSON

Leadership

I start with the premise that the function of leadership is to produce
more leaders not more followers.
RALPH NADER

All are born to observe order, but few are born to establish it.
JOSEPH JOUBERT One of the great aphorists and life-enhancers, friend of Diderot
and Chateaubriand, his mind was so fine and curious he never managed to publish
anything during his lifetime. His wife arranged for his collected *Pensées* to be
published in 1838.

No man will make a great leader who wants to do it all himself, or to
get all the credit for doing it.
ANDREW CARNEGIE

The way to get people to build a ship is not to teach them carpentry,
assign them tasks, and give them schedules to meet; but to inspire
them to long for the infinite immensity of the sea.
ANTOINE DE SAINT-EXUPÉRY

A boss creates fear, a leader confidence. A boss fixes blame, a leader
corrects mistakes. A boss knows all, a leader asks questions. A boss
makes work drudgery, a leader makes it interesting. A boss is
interested in himself or herself, a leader is interested in the group.
RUSSELL H. EWING

Great leaders are almost always great simplifiers, who can cut through
argument, debate and doubt, to offer a solution everybody can
understand.
COLIN POWELL

The real leader has no need to lead – he is content to point the way.
HENRY MILLER

I learned that a great leader is a man who has the ability to get other
people to do what they don't want to do and like it.
HARRY S. TRUMAN

Leadership is the art of getting someone else to do something you want done because he wants to do it.
DWIGHT D. EISENHOWER

I have a different vision of leadership. A leadership is someone who brings people together.
GEORGE W. BUSH On the campaign trail in Bartlett, Tennessee, 18 August 2000.

Learning

Learning is its own exceeding great reward.
WILLIAM HAZLITT

Try to learn something about everything and everything about something.
T. H. HUXLEY

Personally I'm always ready to learn, although I do not always like being taught.
WINSTON CHURCHILL

The important thing is not so much that every child should be taught, as that every child should be given the wish to learn.
JOHN LUBBOCK

Where did I learn to understand sculpture? In the woods by looking at the trees, along roads by observing the formation of clouds, in the studio by studying the model, everywhere except in the schools.
AUGUSTE RODIN

It's what you learn after you know it all that counts.
EARL WEAVER

Man can learn nothing except by going from the known to the unknown.
CLAUDE BERNARD

That is what learning is. You suddenly understand something you've understood all your life, but in a new way.
DORIS LESSING

There is nothing more notable in Socrates than that he found time, when he was an old man, to learn music and dancing, and thought it time well spent.
MICHEL DE MONTAIGNE

Legs

If you fall out of that window and break both your legs, don't come running to me.
GROUCHO MARX

If it has legs it will have a head.
TANZANIAN PROVERB

A horse has four legs, yet it often falls.
ZULU PROVERB

Falsehoods have short legs.
MACEDONIAN PROVERB

Men's legs have a terribly lonely life – standing in the dark in your trousers all day.
KEN DODD

When a dog runs, the dog is moving his legs; when a sea-urchin runs, the legs are moving the sea-urchin.
JAKOB JOHANN VON UEXKULL Based his work on the idea of *Umwelt* ('surrounding world') or how different animals perceive their world and the passage of time. To a tick, for example, a mammal is just three things: a milky smell, warm blood and hair.

Though the perfection of my anatomical leg is truly wonderful, I do not want every awkward, big-fatted or gamble-shanked person who always strided or shuffled along in a slouching manner with both his natural legs to think that one of these must necessarily transform him or his movements into specimens of symmetry, neatness and beauty as if by magic – as Cinderella's frogs were turned into sprightly coachmen.
DR DOUGLAS BLY American inventor of Dr Bly's Anatomical Leg in 1858.

Life

There is no generally accepted definition of life.
Encyclopaedia Britannica

Life is absurd.
ALBERT CAMUS

Life is anything that dies when you stomp on it.
DAVE BARRY

Life is a sexually transmitted terminal disease.
LEWIS GRIZZARD

How did I come into the world? Why was I not consulted? And if I am compelled to take part in it, where is the director? I want to see him.
SØREN KIERKEGAARD

The world is disgracefully managed, one hardly knows to whom to complain.
RONALD FIRBANK

The secret of life is honesty and fair dealing. If you can fake that, you've got it made.
GROUCHO MARX

We are born. We eat sweet potatoes. Then we die.
EASTER ISLAND PROVERB

Life is short and full of blisters.
AFRICAN-AMERICAN PROVERB

A blister on top of a tumour and a boil on top of that.
SHOLOM ALEICHEM Yiddish literature's most popular storyteller. His work was the inspiration for the musical *Fiddler on the Roof* (1964).

Life is a moderately good play with a badly written third act.
TRUMAN CAPOTE

The two entities who might enlighten us, the baby and the corpse, cannot do so.
E. M. FORSTER

The most salient feature of existence is the unthinkable odds against it. For every way that there is of being here, there are an infinity of ways of not being here. Statistics declare us ridiculous. Thermodynamics prohibits us. Life, by any reasonable measure, is impossible.
RICHARD POWERS

Who knows but life be that which men call death,
And death what men call life?

EURIPIDES

'Life', wrote a friend of mine, 'is a public performance on the violin, in which you must learn the instrument as you go along.'
E. M. FORSTER

In three words I can sum up everything I've learned about life. It goes on.
ROBERT FROST

Life is rather like a tin of sardines and we are all of us looking for the
key. We roll back the lid of the sardine tin of life, we reveal the sardines,
the riches of life therein, and we get them out, we enjoy them. But, you
know, there's always a little piece in the corner you can't get out. I
wonder – I wonder, is there a little piece in the corner of your life? I
know there is in mine.
ALAN BENNETT

Life is a beautiful and strange winged creature that appears at a
window, flies swiftly through the banquet hall, and is gone.
THE VENERABLE BEDE

Have you noticed that life, real honest-to-goodness life, with murders
and catastrophes and fabulous inheritances, happens almost
exclusively in the newspapers?
JEAN ANOUILH

Life loves to be taken by the lapel and told: 'I am with you kid. Let's go.'
MAYA ANGELOU

You fall out of your mother's womb, you crawl across open country
under fire, and drop into your grave.
QUENTIN CRISP

This is my creed: For man the vast marvel is to be alive. For man as for
flower and beast and bird the supreme triumph is to be most vividly,
most perfectly alive. Whatever the unborn and the dead may know
they cannot know the beauty, the marvel of being alive in the flesh.
The dead may look after the afterwards. But the magnificent here and
now of life in the flesh is ours alone, and ours only for a time. We ought
to dance with rapture that we should be alive and in the flesh and part
of the living incarnate cosmos.
D. H. LAWRENCE

What an awful thing life is. It's like soup with lots of hairs floating on
the surface. You have to eat it nevertheless.
GUSTAVE FLAUBERT

We are living in a world today where lemonade is made from artificial
flavors and furniture polish is made from real lemons.
ALFRED E. NEUMAN The jug-eared and gap-toothed mascot of *Mad* magazine
since 1955 whose catchphrase was 'What – me worry?' The image has certain

similarities to early twentieth-century caricatures of Irish immigrants, although some doctors have also suggested Williams syndrome, a rare genetic disorder that creates an elfin appearance and cheerful demeanour in sufferers.

There'll be two dates on your tombstone. And all your friends will read 'em. But all that's gonna matter is that little dash between 'em.
KEVIN WELCH

In the end, everything is a gag.
CHARLIE CHAPLIN

Light

We all know what light is but it is not easy to *tell* what light is.
SAMUEL JOHNSON

There are two kinds of light – the glow that illumines, and the glare that obscures.
JAMES THURBER

All the fifty years of conscious brooding have brought me no closer to the answer to the question: what are light quanta? Of course today every rascal thinks he knows the answer, but he is deluding himself.
ALBERT EINSTEIN

This world we live in is but thickened light.
RALPH WALDO EMERSON

Most of all I miss working with Sven Nyqvist, perhaps because we are both utterly captivated by the problems of light; the gentle, dangerous, dreamlike, living, dead, clear, misty, hot, violent, bare, sudden, dark, springlike, slanting, sensuous, subdued, limited, poisonous, calming, pale light.
INGMAR BERGMAN

Prejudice comes from being in the dark; sunlight disinfects it.
MUHAMMAD ALI

Light travels faster than sound – isn't that why some people appear bright until you hear them speak?
STEVEN WRIGHT

The difference between pornography and erotica is lighting.
GLORIA LEONARD Former porn actress and ardent feminist, who was publisher of the riotously successful *High Society* magazine from the mid-1980s where she introduced phone sex and celebrity nudes. A prominent anti-censorship campaigner, she lists chess as one of her hobbies.

Listening

Be a good listener. Unlike your mouth, your ears will never get you in trouble.
FRANK TYGER

When people talk, listen and listen completely. Most people never listen.
ERNEST HEMINGWAY

The first duty of love is to listen.
PAUL TILLICH

The only way to entertain some folks is to listen to them.
FRANK 'KIN' HUBBARD

Lenin could listen so intently that he exhausted the speaker.
ISAIAH BERLIN

If we ate what we listened to we'd all be dead.
EARL WILD

Of all modern phenomena, the most monstrous and ominous, the most manifestly rotting with disease, the most grimly prophetic of destruction, the most clearly and unmistakably inspired by evil spirits, the most instantly and awfully overshadowed by the wrath of heaven, the most near to madness and moral chaos, the most vivid with deviltry and despair, is the practice of having to listen to loud music while eating a meal in a restaurant.
G. K. CHESTERTON

Literature

Literature is news that stays new.
EZRA POUND

A literary movement consists of five or six people who live in the same town and hate each other cordially.
GEORGE MOORE

Literature is mostly about having sex and not much about having children. Life is the other way around.
DAVID LODGE

Mrs Glegg had doubtless the glossiest and crispest brown curls in her drawers, as well as curls in various degrees of fuzzy laxness.
GEORGE ELIOT

She touched his organ, and from that bright epoch even it, the old companion of his happiest hours, incapable as he had thought of elevation, began a new and defined existence.
CHARLES DICKENS

Mrs Goddard was mistress of a school . . . where young ladies for enormous pay might be screwed out of health and into vanity.
JANE AUSTEN

'Well,' said the duchess, 'apart from your balls, can't I be of any use to you?'
MARCEL PROUST

'Oh, I can't explain,' cried Roderick impatiently, returning to his work. 'I've only one way of expressing my deepest feelings – it's this.' And he swung his tool.
HENRY JAMES

Living

Everything has been figured out, except how to live.
JEAN-PAUL SARTRE

The art of living is more like that of wrestling than of dancing; the main thing is to stand firm and be ready for an unforeseen attack.
MARCUS AURELIUS

The goal of life is living in agreement with nature.
ZENO OF CITIUM The founder of Stoicism (from the *stoa*, or porch, he used to teach from). The core idea – freedom through harmony with nature and overcoming destructive habits – became the dominant philosophy of the Graeco-Roman elite for 600 years.

Begin at once to live, and count each separate day as a separate life.
SENECA

To live only for some future goal is shallow. It's the sides of the mountain that sustain life, not the top.
ROBERT M. PIRSIG

I love my past. I love my present. I'm not ashamed of what I've had, and I'm not sad because I have it no longer.
COLETTE

The world is ruled by letting things take their course.
LAOZI (LAO TZU)

May you live every day of your life.
JONATHAN SWIFT

Life is too short to be small.
BENJAMIN DISRAELI

It's not the length of life, but the depth of life.
RALPH WALDO EMERSON

Try to be one of the people on whom nothing is lost.
HENRY JAMES

Life is tough. Three out of three people die, so shut up and deal.
RING LARDNER

Life is not always a matter of holding good cards, but sometimes of
playing a poor hand well.
ROBERT LOUIS STEVENSON

Seize the moment. Remember all those women on the *Titanic* who
waved off the dessert cart.
ERMA BOMBECK

Study as if you were to live forever; live as if you were to die tomorrow.
SAINT EDMUND OF ABINGDON

This is what you should do: love the earth and sun and the animals,
despise riches, give alms to everyone that asks, stand up for the stupid
and crazy, devote your income and labor to others, hate tyrants, argue
not concerning God, have patience and indulgence toward the people,
take off your hat to nothing known or unknown or to any man or
number of men . . . re-examine all you have been told at school or
church or in any book, dismiss what insults your own soul, and your
very flesh shall be a great poem.
WALT WHITMAN

Life is short, art long, opportunity fleeting, experience treacherous,
judgement difficult.
HIPPOCRATES

A man must swallow a toad every morning if he wishes to be sure of
finding nothing still more disgusting before the day is over,
NICOLAS CHAMFORT

Three things in this life are self-destructive: Anger, Greed, Self-esteem.
MUHAMMAD

Speak the truth, do not yield to anger; give, if thou art asked for little; by these three steps thou wilt go near the gods.

THE DHAMMAPADA Buddhist scripture on ethics usually attributed to Buddha himself and dating from the early third century BC. It means 'Path of the Dhamma', the latter term meaning 'that which upholds', i.e. the ultimate reality.

Think nothing profitable to you which compels you to break a promise, to lose your self-respect, to hate any person, to suspect, to curse, to act the hypocrite, to desire anything that requires walls and curtains about it.

MARCUS AURELIUS

For a long time it has seemed to me that life was about to begin – Real Life. But there was always some obstacle in the way, something to be got through first, some unfinished business, time still to be served, a debt to be paid – then life would begin. At last it dawned on me that these obstacles were my life.

ALFRED D'SOUZA One of the most quoted of all inspirational passages, confidently attributed to a Father Alfred d'Souza, a writer/philosopher from Brisbane, Australia who died in 2004. Often it gets tangled up with another passage that begins 'Dance like no one is watching'. Well, that was definitely the work of an Australian singer songwriter, Jim Lesses, in 2000. As for the original quote, it's a one-off. No information of any kind exists about any philosophically minded Alfred d'Souzas, except for a much-loved radio operator in Mumbai, who died unexpectedly of a heart attack aged 45 in 2006.

My formula for living is quite simple. I get up in the morning and I go to bed at night. In between, I occupy myself as best I can.

CARY GRANT

It is often tragic to see how blatantly a man bungles his own life and the lives of others yet remains totally incapable of seeing how much the whole tragedy originates in himself, and how he continually feeds it and keeps it going.

CARL JUNG

Since we have explored the maze so long without result, it follows for poor human reasons, that we cannot have to explore much longer; close by must be the centre, with a champagne luncheon and a piece of ornamental water. How if there were no centre at all, but just one alley after another, and the whole world a labyrinth without end or issue?

ROBERT LOUIS STEVENSON

I feel an irresistible desire to wander, and go to Japan, where I will pass my youth, sitting under an almond tree, drinking amber tea out of a blue cup, and looking at a landscape without perspective.
OSCAR WILDE

I have come to an unalterable decision – to go and live forever in Polynesia. Then I can end my days in peace and freedom, without thoughts of tomorrow and this eternal struggle against idiots.
PAUL GAUGUIN

Life is like a B-movie. You don't want to leave in the middle of it but you don't want to see it again.
TED TURNER

If I had my life story offered to me to film, I'd turn it down.
KIRK DOUGLAS

If I had to do my life over, I would change every single thing I have done.
RAY DAVIES

Logic

What we call logic may just as well be described as 'the way adult Athenian males of the fifth century BC think'.
ALAN GARNER

Logic is neither a science nor an art, but a dodge.
BENJAMIN JOWETT

The use of logic in thought is as necessary and justified as the use of perspective in painting – but only as a medium of expression, not as a criterion of reality.
GOVINDA

To become truly immortal, a work of art must escape all human limits: logic and common sense will only interfere. But once these barriers are broken, it will enter the realms of childhood visions and dreams.
GIORGIO DE CHIRICO

A mind all logic is like a knife all blade.
RABINDRANATH TAGORE

Logic, like whiskey, loses its beneficial effect when taken in too large quantities.
LORD DUNSANY

There is no logical way to the discovery of elemental laws. There is only the way of intuition, which is helped by a feeling for the order lying behind the appearance.
ALBERT EINSTEIN

The French are a logical people, which is one reason why the English dislike them so intensely. The other is that they own France, a country we have always judged to be too good for them.
ROBERT MORLEY

The clinching proof of my reasoning is that I will cut anyone who argues further into dogmeat.
SIR GEOFFREY DE TOURNEVILLE Another one-quote-wonder, with no sources and no historical record of his existence other than 'Norman knight'. He might be Geoffrey de Turville, who was arrested and had his eyes put out by King Henry I in 1125 after joining the unsuccessful second Norman rebellion led by the Count of Meulan.

No, no, you're not thinking; you're just being logical.
NIELS BOHR

If the world were a logical place, men would ride side saddle.
RITA MAE BROWN

Loneliness

Music was invented to confirm human loneliness.
LAWRENCE DURRELL

If you are afraid of loneliness, don't marry.
ANTON CHEKHOV

The more you stay in this kind of job, the more you realize that a public figure, a major public figure, is a lonely man.
RICHARD NIXON

Loneliness is the inability to keep something or someone with us company. It is not a tree that stands alone in the middle of a plain, but the distance between the deep sap and the bark, between the leaves and the roots.
JOSÉ SARAMAGO

Loneliness is the way by which destiny endeavours to lead man to himself.
HERMANN HESSE

Love

What the world really needs is more love and less paperwork.
PEARL BAILEY

Love is metaphysical gravity.
R. BUCKMINSTER FULLER

Love will draw an elephant through a key-hole.
SAMUEL RICHARDSON

Some day, after mastering the winds, the waves, the tides and gravity, we shall harness for God the energies of love, and then, for a second time in the history of the world, man will have discovered fire.
TEILHARD DE CHARDIN Visionary Jesuit, palaeontologist and philosopher, who helped excavate Peking Man in 1926 and proposed the noosphere, a kind of early version of the Gaia hypothesis, although the Vatican refused him permission to publish it in his lifetime.

He gave her a look you could have poured on a waffle.
RING LARDNER

Love has but one word and it never repeats itself.
JEAN LACORDAIRE The most influential French Catholic writer and thinker of the nineteenth century, he was responsible for re-establishing the French Dominican order in 1850.

Love is a gross exaggeration of the difference between one person and everybody else.
GEORGE BERNARD SHAW

Art is love.
WILLIAM HOLMAN HUNT

Whatever else is unsure in this stinking dunghill of a world a mother's love is not.
JAMES JOYCE

Mother's love is peace. It need not be acquired, it need not be deserved.
ERICH FROMM

I loved my mother from the day she died.
MICHAEL HARTNETT

You do not have to deserve your mother's love. You have to deserve your father's. He's more particular.
ROBERT FROST

I wish people would love everybody else the way they love me. It would be a better world.
MUHAMMAD ALI

Love is the delightful interval between meeting a beautiful girl and discovering that she looks like a haddock.
JOHN BARRYMORE

Love affairs have always greatly interested me, but I do not greatly care for them in books or moving pictures. In a love affair, I wish to be the hero, with no audience present.
E. W. HOWE

At the beginning of a love affair, not even the neurotic is neurotic.
MIGNON McLAUGHLIN

Love takes off masks that we fear we cannot live without and know we cannot live within.
JAMES BALDWIN

All, everything that I understand, I understand only because I love. Everything is, everything exists, only because I love. Everything is united by it alone. Love is God, and to die means that I, a particle of love, shall return to the general and eternal source.
LEO TOLSTOY

Where love rules, there is no will to power; and where power predominates, there love is lacking. The one is the shadow of the other.
CARL JUNG

Love is a snowmobile racing across the tundra and then suddenly it flips over, pinning you underneath. At night, the ice weasels come.
MATT GROENING Creator of *The Simpsons*, quoted in the *LA Times* on St Valentine's Day, 1991.

Luck

Luck is an essential part of a career in physics.
LEON LEDERMAN

Nothing is as obnoxious as other people's luck.
F. SCOTT FITZGERALD

Shallow men believe in luck. Strong men believe in cause and effect.
RALPH WALDO EMERSON

What luck for rulers that men do not think.
ADOLF HITLER

I've done the calculation and your chances of winning the lottery are identical whether you play or not.
FRAN LEBOWITZ

What we call luck is the inner man externalized. We make things happen to us.
ROBERTSON DAVIES

I find that the harder I work, the more luck I seem to have.
THOMAS JEFFERSON

Luck affects everything. Let your hook always be cast. In the stream where you least expect it, there will be fish.
OVID

I'm so unlucky that if I was to fall into a barrel of nipples I'd come out sucking my thumb.
FREDDIE STARR

Lying

The foundation of all morality is to have done, once and for all, with lying.
THOMAS HARDY

Lying is done with words and also with silence.
ADRIENNE RICH

We tell lies when we are afraid . . . afraid of what we don't know, afraid of what others will think, afraid of what will be found out about us. But every time we tell a lie, the thing that we fear grows stronger.
TAD WILLIAMS

The most common lie is that which one lies to himself; lying to others is relatively an exception.
FRIEDRICH NIETZSCHE

M

Machinery

Man is only man at the surface. Remove his skin, dissect, and immediately you come to machinery.
PAUL VALÉRY

You cannot endow even the best machine with initiative; the jolliest steam-roller will not plant flowers.
WALTER LIPPMANN

The most technologically efficient machine that man ever invented is the book.
NORTHROP FRYE

It is so characteristic, that just when the mechanics of reproduction are so vastly improved, there are fewer and fewer people who know how the music should be played.
LUDWIG WITTGENSTEIN

The amount of genuine leisure available in a society is generally in inverse proportion to the amount of labour-saving machinery it employs.
E. F. SCHUMACHER

Madness

I sometimes wonder whether our planet is the asylum of the universe for disordered minds.
GOETHE

I doubt if a single individual could be found from the whole of mankind free from some form of insanity. The only difference is one of degree. A man who sees a gourd and takes it for his wife is called insane because this happens to very few people.
ERASMUS

Every man is wise when attacked by a mad dog; fewer when pursued by a mad woman; only the wisest survive when attacked by a mad notion.
ROBERTSON DAVIES

It is sometimes an appropriate response to reality to go insane.
PHILIP K. DICK

The foundation of all mental illness is the unwillingness to experience legitimate suffering.
CARL JUNG

Insanity: doing the same thing over and over again and expecting different results.
ALBERT EINSTEIN

The statistics on sanity are that one out of every four Americans is suffering from some form of mental illness. Think of your three best friends. If they're okay, then it's you.
RITA MAE BROWN

I don't suffer from insanity but enjoy every minute of it.
EDGAR ALLAN POE

There is a pleasure in being mad which none but madmen know.
JOHN DRYDEN

When dealing with the insane, it is best to pretend to be sane.
HERMAN HESSE

I am not strictly speaking mad, for my mind is absolutely normal in the intervals, and even more so than before. But during the attacks it is terrible – and then I lose consciousness of everything. But that spurs me on to work and to seriousness, as a miner who is always in danger makes haste in what he does.
VINCENT VAN GOGH

The history of saints is mainly the history of insane people.
BENITO MUSSOLINI

All of us are mad. If it weren't for the fact that every one of us is slightly abnormal, there wouldn't be any point in giving each person a separate name.
UGO BETTI With Pirandello, the greatest twentieth-century Italian playwright, sometimes known as the Italian Kafka. He was also a judge and managed to survive first being accused as a Jew by the fascists and then as fascist once the war ended.

Insanity in individuals is something rare – but in groups, parties, nations and epochs, it is the rule.
FRIEDRICH NIETZSCHE

Show me a sane man and I will cure him for you.
CARL JUNG

What garlic is to salad, insanity is to art.
AUGUSTUS SAINT-GAUDENS

Be mad.
SALVADOR DALÍ

Magic

Any sufficiently advanced technology is indistinguishable from magic.
ARTHUR C. CLARKE

Using words to describe magic is like using a screwdriver to cut roast beef.
TOM ROBBINS

The universe is full of magical things, patiently waiting for our wits to grow sharper.
EDEN PHILLPOTTS

When magic becomes scientific fact we refer to it as medicine or astronomy.
ANTON LAVEY

In the last analysis magic, religion and science are nothing but theories of thought.
SIR JAMES FRAZER

I am a member of a magic circle – The Secret Six – which is so secret I don't know the other five.
TOMMY COOPER

Magnetism

The secret of magnetism, now explain that to me! There is no greater secret, except love and hate.
GOETHE From his 1827 poem 'Gott, Gemüt und Welt' (God, Soul and World).

Magnetism is one of the Six Fundamental Forces of the Universe, with the other five being Gravity, Duct Tape, Whining, Remote Control, and The Force That Pulls Dogs Toward The Groins Of Strangers.
DAVE BARRY

I have not had a moment's peace or happiness in respect to electromagnetic theory since November 28, 1846. All this time I have been liable to fits of ether dipsomania, kept away at intervals only by rigorous abstention from thought on the subject.
LORD KELVIN British physicist and engineer, born William Thomson, who for one

half of his career was one of the great scientists of his day, with over seventy patents to his name. In the second half he too often got waylaid by theories (such as his belief, alluded to here, that electromagnetic waves travelled through a frictionless medium called the aether) which were eventually swept away by relativity and quantum physics.

Manners

Good manners: The noise you don't make when you're eating soup.
BENNETT CERF

Good manners can replace morals. It may be years before anyone knows if what you are doing is right. But if what you are doing is nice, it will be immediately evident.
P. J. O'ROURKE

Clothes and manners do not make the man; but, when he is made, they greatly improve his appearance.
HENRY WARD BEECHER

Manners are especially the need of the plain. The pretty can get away with anything.
EVELYN WAUGH

Marriage

The married state is the most complete image of heaven and hell we are capable of receiving in this life.
RICHARD STEELE

Marriage resembles a pair of shears, so joined that they cannot be separated; often moving in opposite directions, yet always punishing anyone who comes between them.
SYDNEY SMITH

I wouldn't be caught dead marrying a woman old enough to be my wife.
TONY CURTIS

Love is blind and marriage is the institution for the blind.
LEWIS GRIZZARD

The conception of two people living together for twenty-five years without having a cross word suggests a lack of spirit only to be admired in sheep.
A. P. HERBERT

I've been married so long I'm on my third bottle of Tabasco.
SUSAN VASS

No man should marry until he has studied anatomy and dissected at least one woman.
HONORÉ DE BALZAC

I never married because there was no need. I have three pets at home which answer the same purpose as a husband. I have a dog that growls every morning, a parrot that swears all afternoon, and a cat that comes home late at night.
MARIE CORELLI Born Mary McKay, she became an Edwardian literary sensation, producing twenty-four popular pot-boiler novels that combined the raciness of Jackie Collins with the cod-mysticism of *The Da Vinci Code*. Settling in Stratford-upon-Avon, she was famously eccentric – she travelled the Avon on a gondola.

The majority of husbands remind me of an orang-utan trying to play the violin.
HONORÉ DE BALZAC

By all means marry. If you get a good wife, you'll be happy; if you get a bad one, you'll become a philosopher.
SOCRATES

Marriage is like a bank account. You put it in, you take it out, you lose interest.
IRWIN CAREY

It doesn't much signify whom one marries, for one is sure to find out next morning that it was someone else.
SAMUEL ROGERS

I don't think I'll get married again. I'll just find a woman I don't like and give her a house.
LEWIS GRIZZARD

Mathematics

The good Christian should beware the mathematician and all those who make empty prophecies. The danger already exists that the mathematicians have made a covenant with the devil to darken the spirit and to confine man in the bonds of hell.
SAINT AUGUSTINE

The things of this world cannot be made known without a knowledge of mathematics.
ROGER BACON

Mathematics may be defined as the subject in which we never know what we are talking about.
BERTRAND RUSSELL

Life is good for only two things, discovering mathematics and teaching mathematics.
SIMÉON POISSON

Each generation has its few great mathematicians, and mathematics would not even notice the absence of the others. They are useful as teachers, and their research harms no one, but it is of no importance at all. A mathematician is great or he is nothing.
ALFRED ADLER

We used to think that if we knew one, we knew two, because one and one are two. We are finding that we must learn a great deal more about 'and'.
SIR ARTHUR EDDINGTON Famous for explaining Einstein's theories to the English-speaking world, he is the modern source for the idea that an infinite number of monkeys on an infinite number of typewriters could eventually write all the books in the British Museum.

One cannot escape the feeling that these mathematical formulas have an independent existence and an intelligence of their own, that they are wiser than we are, wiser even than their discoverers, that we get more out of them than was originally put into them.
HEINRICH HERTZ

Mathematics is the art of giving the same name to different things.
HENRI POINCARÉ

Beauty is the first test; there is no permanent place in the world for ugly mathematics.
G. H. HARDY

In the arithmetic of the world, one plus one equals everything, and two minus one equals nothing.
MIGNON McLAUGHLIN

In real life, I assure you, there is no such thing as algebra.
FRAN LEBOWITZ

An equation for me has no meaning unless it expresses a thought of God.
SRINIVASA RAMANUJAN

The pleasure we obtain from music comes from *counting*, but

counting unconsciously. Music is nothing but unconscious arithmetic.
GOTTFRIED LEIBNIZ

There can be mathematicians of the first order who cannot count.
NOVALIS

Anyone who cannot cope with mathematics is not fully human. At best
he is a tolerable subhuman, who has learned to wear shoes, bathe, and
not make messes in the house.
ROBERT A. HEINLEIN

Mathematics is like draughts in being suitable for the young, not too
difficult, amusing, and without peril to the state.
PLATO

'Obvious' is the most dangerous word in mathematics.
ERIC TEMPLE BELL

If people do not believe that mathematics is simple, it is only because
they do not realize how complicated *life* is.
JOHN VON NEUMANN Brilliant mathematician who helped develop the hydrogen
bomb, and made theoretical breakthroughs across a vast number of disciplines. He
was also a committed party animal, with a large appetite for life's pleasures. His wife
once said he could count anything but calories.

The hardest arithmetic to master is that which enables us to count our
blessings.
ERIC HOFFER

The mathematics are usually considered as being the very antipodes of
Poesy. Yet Mathesis and Poesy are of the closest kindred, for they are
both works of the imagination.
THOMAS HILL

As far as the laws of mathematics refer to reality, they are not certain;
and as far as they are certain, they do not refer to reality.
ALBERT EINSTEIN

The laws of nature are but the mathematical thoughts of God.
EUCLID

If there is a God, he's a great mathematician.
PAUL DIRAC

In most sciences one generation tears down what another has built
and what one has established another undoes. In mathematics alone
each generation adds a new story to the old structure.
HERMANN HANKEL

Why do we believe that in all matters the odd numbers are more powerful?
PLINY THE ELDER

Uneven numbers are the gods' delight.
VIRGIL

Pure mathematics is the world's best game. It is more absorbing than chess, more of a gamble than poker, and lasts longer than Monopoly. It's free. It can be played anywhere – Archimedes did it in a bathtub.
RICHARD J. TRUDEAU

A mathematician is a machine for turning coffee into theorems.
PAUL ERDOS

Meaning

It is not peace we seek but meaning.
LAWRENCE DURRELL

As far as we can discern, the sole purpose of human existence is to kindle a light of meaning in the darkness of mere being.
CARL JUNG

This is our purpose: to make as meaningful as possible this life that has been bestowed upon us; to live in such a way that we may be proud of ourselves; to act in such a way that some part of us lives on.
OSWALD SPENGLER Despite its pessimism, the self-taught historian and philosopher's *Decline of the West* (1919) was a hugely influential 'big-picture' book through the first half of the twentieth century, inspiring such different writers and thinkers as F. Scott Fitzgerald, the Beat Poets, Henry Kissinger and Malcolm X.

Even the dullest things have meaning.
STEPHEN BAYLEY Design guru once described as 'the second most intelligent man in Britain'. He is talking about coat hangers.

People want to find a 'meaning' in everything and everyone. That's the disease of our age – an age that is anything but practical but believes itself to be more practical than any other age.
PABLO PICASSO

Life and love are life and love, a bunch of violets is a bunch of violets, and to drag in the idea of a point is to ruin everything. Live and let live, love and let love, flower and fade, and follow the natural curve, which flows on, pointless.
D. H. LAWRENCE

When we have found all the meaning and lost all the mystery, we will be alone on an empty shore.
TOM STOPPARD

In our sad condition our only consolation is the expectancy of another life. Here below all is incomprehensible.
MARTIN LUTHER

'We are here on the wrong side of the tapestry,' answered Father Brown. 'The things that happen here do not seem to mean anything; they mean something somewhere else. Somewhere else retribution will come on the real offender. Here it often seems to fall on the wrong person.
G. K. CHESTERTON

The whole problem can be stated quite simply by asking, 'Is there a meaning to music?' My answer would be, 'Yes.' And 'Can you state in so many words what the meaning is?' My answer to that would be, 'No.'
AARON COPLAND

Fortunately, in her kindness and patience, Nature has never put the fatal question as to the meaning of their lives into the mouths of most people. And where no one asks, no one needs to answer.
CARL JUNG

It makes no sense to say the universe has no sense.
NIELS BOHR

It is not meaning that we need but sight.
LAWRENCE DURRELL

Memory

God gave us memories so that we might enjoy roses in December.
J. M. BARRIE

Poetry is all that is worth remembering in life.
WILLIAM HAZLITT

The true beloveds of this world are in their lover's eyes, lilacs opening, ship lights, school bells, a landscape, remembered conversations, friends, a child's Sunday, lost voices, one's favorite suit, autumn and all seasons, memory, yes, it being the earth and water of existence, memory.
TRUMAN CAPOTE

Everybody needs his memories. They keep the wolf of insignificance from the door.
SAUL BELLOW

Our memories are card indexes consulted, and then put back in disorder by authorities whom we do not control.
CYRIL CONNOLLY

Memories are like stones, time and distance erode them like acid.
UGO BETTI

To expect a man to retain everything he has read is like expecting him to carry about in his body everything that he has ever eaten.
ARTHUR SCHOPENHAUER

Those who receive with most pains and difficulty remember best; every one thing they learn being, as it were, burnt and branded on their minds.
PLUTARCH

Some men's memory is like a box, where a man should mingle his jewels with his old shoes.
GEORGE SAVILE, 1ST MARQUESS OF HALIFAX

Some people do not become thinkers simply because their memories are too good.
FRIEDRICH NIETZSCHE

The best way to remember your wife's birthday is to forget it once.
E. JOSEPH COSSMAN

Men

Women like silent men. They think they are listening.
MARCEL ACHARD

Men are boring to women, because there are only about twelve types of us, and they know all the keys. I only know this because I'm the type they talk to.
JACK NICHOLSON

Married men live longer than single men. But married men are a lot more willing to die.
JOHNNY CARSON

Men who make money rarely saunter; men who save money rarely swagger.
EDWARD BULWER-LYTTON Overblown novelist whose fame has persisted thanks mainly to his 1830 novel, *Paul Clifford*, which opens with the immortal line: 'It was a dark and stormy night.' He lived at the original Craven Cottage, now the home of Fulham FC.

Men don't care what's on TV. They only care what else is on TV.
JERRY SEINFELD

Men and Women

The main difference between men and women is that men are lunatics and women are idiots.
REBECCA WEST

A man's got to do what a man's got to do. A woman must do what he can't.
RHONDA HANSOME

Whatever women must do they must do twice as well as men to be thought half as good. Luckily, this is not difficult.
CHARLOTTE WHITTON

Behind every successful man is a surprised woman.
MARYON PEARSON

A successful man is one who makes more money than his wife can spend. A successful woman is one who can find such a man.
LANA TURNER

A woman need only know one man well in order to understand all men, whereas a man may know all women and not understand one of them.
HELEN ROWLAND

A man can sleep around, but if a woman makes nineteen or twenty mistakes she's a tramp.
JOAN RIVERS

If men knew all that women think, they would be twenty times more audacious.
ALPHONSE KARR Editor of *Le Figaro*, novelist and phrasemaker, he is responsible for coining the phrase *plus ça change, plus c'est la même chose* ('the more things change, the more they stay the same'). He loved flowers and has several, including a famous dahlia, named after him.

When novelist Margaret Atwood asked women what they feared most from men, they said: 'We're afraid they'll kill us.' When men were asked the same question about women, they said: 'We're afraid they'll laugh at us.'
NAOMI WOLF

When a woman is very, very bad she is awful, but when a man is correspondingly good, he is weird.
MINNA ANTRIM

The man's desire is for the woman, but the woman's desire is rarely other than for the desire of the man.
SAMUEL TAYLOR COLERIDGE

Men live by forgetting – women live on memories.
T. S. ELIOT

A woman's guess is much more accurate than a man's certainty.
RUDYARD KIPLING

Feminine passion is to masculine as an epic to an epigram.
KARL KRAUS

The woman possesses a theatrical exterior and a circumspect interior, while in the man it is the interior which is theatrical. The woman goes to the theatre; the man carries it inside himself and is the impresario of his own life.
JOSÉ ORTEGA Y GASSET His philosophy of vitalism ('I live, therefore I think') made him a major influence on the existentialists and meant he was an active political liberal. He's also the only philosopher we know to have a grape variety named after him (the Ortega, an aromatic German white wine grape created in 1948).

A man would create another man if one did not already exist, but a woman might live an eternity without even thinking of reproducing her own sex.
GOETHE

If women are often frustrated because men do not respond to their troubles by offering matching troubles, men are often frustrated because women do.
DEBORAH TANNEN

A woman knows how to keep quiet when she is in the right, whereas a man, when he is in the right, will keep on talking.
MALCOLM DE CHAZAL

The most important thing in a relationship between a man and a woman is that one of them should be good at taking orders.
LINDA FESTA

Mind

The empires of the future are the empires of the mind.
WINSTON CHURCHILL

The mind is a musical instrument with a certain range of tones, beyond which in both directions we have infinite silence.
JOHN TYNDALL

Is the mind more like a fancy system of domino chains or a bathtub full of spring-loaded mousetraps? I'm betting on the latter.
DOUGLAS HOFSTADTER

We know more about the interior of stars than we do about what's going on in our heads.
RICHARD GREGORY

Be very, very careful what you put into that head, because you will never, ever get it out.
CARDINAL WOLSEY

A mind that is stretched by a new experience can never go back to its old dimensions.
OLIVER WENDELL HOLMES

The mind is like a parachute. It doesn't work if it's not open.
FRANK ZAPPA

Your mind is a dangerous neighbourhood and you shouldn't go in there alone at night.
CHRISTIANE NORTHRUP

Our life is shaped by our mind; we become what we think. Suffering follows an evil thought as the wheels of a cart follow the oxen that draws it. Our life is shaped by our mind; we become what we think. Joy follows a pure thought like a shadow that never leaves.
BUDDHA

Our ordinary mind always tries to persuade us that we are nothing but acorns and that our greatest happiness will be to become bigger, fatter, shinier acorns; but that is of interest only to pigs. Our faith gives us knowledge of something better: that we can become oak trees.
E. F. SCHUMACHER

Like the earth a hundred years ago, our mind still lies in darkest Africa, unmapped Borneos and Amazonian basins. In relation to the fauna of these regions we are not yet zoologists, we are mere naturalists and collectors of specimens.
JULIAN HUXLEY

We carry with us the wonders we seek without us. There is all Africa and her prodigies in us.
SIR THOMAS BROWNE His 1646 book of 'vulgar errors' (*Pseudodoxia Epidemica*) was one of the first 'myth-busting' books to be published in English. Browne had a menagerie of live and stuffed animals including the heads of two whales, a pelican and an ostrich.

The mind of man is capable of anything – because everything is in it, all the past as well as all the future.
JOSEPH CONRAD

You never have to change anything you got up in the middle of the night to write.
SAUL BELLOW

When he was expected to use his mind, he felt like a right-handed person who has to do something with his left.
G. C. LICHTENBERG

The mind sleeps in the mineral kingdom, breathes in the vegetable kingdom, dreams in the animal kingdom, and awakes in man.
TEILHARD DE CHARDIN

Miracles

If it's free, it's advice; if you pay for it, it's counseling; if you can use either one, it's a miracle.
JACK ADAMS Legendary Canadian ice hockey player and later a hockey administrator who is the only player ever to have been credited with an own goal. This achievement dates from 1920 and is likely to stand unchallenged. There are no own goals in ice hockey – the goal is always given to the last attacking player to hit the puck.

There are only two ways to live your life. One is as though nothing is a miracle. The other is as though everything is a miracle.
ALBERT EINSTEIN

Where there is great love, there are always miracles.
WILLA CATHER

The happy do not believe in miracles.
GOETHE

Miracles are not contrary to nature, but only contrary to what we know about nature.
SAINT AUGUSTINE

To be always with a woman and not to have intercourse with her is more difficult than to raise the dead.
SAINT BERNARD OF CLAIRVAUX Known as the '*Doctor Mellifluus*', and driving force behind the rise of the Cistercian order in the twelfth century, founding over 160 monasteries and inspiring the Second Crusade in 1146. He had a 'special relationship' with the Virgin Mary, who had appeared to him and squirted milk from her breasts on to his lips . . .

Find something that isn't a miracle, you'll have cause to wonder then.
LAURENCE HOUSMAN

Misery

Pain and suffering are inevitable in our lives, but misery is an option.
CHIP BECK

Nobody really cares if you're miserable, so you might as well be happy.
CYNTHIA NELMS

Misery is almost always the result of thinking.
JOSEPH JOUBERT

Make a child a painting and he'll be happy for a day. Teach a child to paint and he'll be miserable for a lifetime.
CHRISTOPHER WILLARD

We are unhappy married, and unhappy unmarried. We are unhappy when alone, and unhappy in society: we are like hedgehogs clustering together for warmth, uncomfortable when too closely packed, and yet miserable when kept apart. It is all very funny . . . the life of every individual is really always a tragedy; but gone through in detail it has the character of comedy.
ARTHUR SCHOPENHAUER

There are two means of refuge from the miseries of life: music and cats.
ALBERT SCHWEITZER

Mistakes

Sometimes I lie awake at night, and I ask, 'Where have I gone wrong?' Then a voice says to me, 'This is going to take more than one night.'
CHARLES M. SHULZ A classic Charlie Brown quote from *Peanuts*, the legendary American cartoon strip that ran for nearly fifty years in more than 2,500 newspapers in seventy-five countries.

Mistakes are at the very base of human thought feeding the structure like root nodules. If we were not provided with the knack of being wrong, we could never get anything useful done.
LEWIS THOMAS His writings stylishly bridged the worlds of science and literature. The classic 1971 collection, *The Lives of a Cell*, draws its title from his insight that the world functions like a giant cell. He also loved word histories, and achieved a distinction, rare among etymologists, of being both amusing and inspiring.

I am willing to admit that I may not always be right, but I am never wrong.
SAMUEL GOLDWYN

There is only one innate error, and that is that we are here in order to be happy.
ARTHUR SCHOPENHAUER

A clever man commits no minor blunders.
GOETHE

You must learn from the mistakes of others. You can't possibly live long enough to make them all yourself.
SAM LEVENSON

Creativity is allowing yourself to make mistakes. Art is knowing which ones to keep.
SCOTT ADAMS Creator of the Dilbert comic strip.

There is no mistake so great as the mistake of not going on.
WILLIAM BLAKE

Do not fear mistakes, there are none.
MILES DAVIS

Money

Money is the root of all evil, and yet it is such a useful root that we cannot get on without it any more than we can without potatoes.
LOUISA MAY ALCOTT

Whoever said money can't buy happiness simply didn't know where to go shopping.
BO DEREK

Always live within your income, even if you have to borrow money to do so.
JOSH BILLINGS

To be clever enough to get a great deal of money, one must be stupid enough to want it.
GEORGE BERNARD SHAW

The only thing money gives is the freedom of not worrying about money.
JOHNNY CARSON

Then you will come to a hill, Bear-No-False-Witness. Turn right away from it, for it is thickly wooded with bribes and bristling with florins. At all costs, gather no blossoms here, or you will lose your soul.
WILLIAM LANGLAND From *Piers Plowman*, the great fourteenth-century satirical poem that deserves to stand alongside Chaucer's *Canterbury Tales*. We don't know much about Langland, but there is a rough consensus suggesting he was tall, from the west, well educated, a rebel and possibly a hermit.

I have enough money to last me the rest of my life unless I buy something.
JACKIE MASON

He who has money can eat sherbet in hell.
LEBANESE PROVERB

You don't seem to realize that a poor person who is unhappy is in a better position than a rich person who is unhappy, because the poor person has hope. He thinks money would help.
JEAN KERR

At the back of every great fortune lies a great crime.
HONORÉ DE BALZAC

It is said that for money you can have everything, but you cannot. You can buy food, but not appetite; medicine, but not health; knowledge but not wisdom; glitter, but not beauty; fun, but not joy; acquaintances, but not friends; servants, but not faithfulness; leisure, but not peace. You can have the husk of everything for money, but not the kernel.
ARNE GARBORG

I have a fair amount of money. However, I would estimate it to total less than $50 million. What is that after twenty-two years as head of state of such a big country?
PRESIDENT MOBUTU SESE SEKO

One may see the small value God has for riches by the people He gives them to.
ALEXANDER POPE

Of all the forms of money, slavery proved to be one of the least reliable because of their high mortality rate and their tendency to escape.
JACK WEATHERFORD

There are three principal ways to lose money: wine, women and engineers. While the first two are more pleasant, the third is by far the more certain.
BARON EDMOND DE ROTHSCHILD

I cannot afford to waste my time making money.
LOUIS AGASSIZ One of the founding fathers of modern science. He was the first to propose the idea of an ice age but was also an implacable opponent of the theory of evolution, preferring his own creationist and racist ideas.

Money never made a man happy yet, nor will it. The more a man has, the more he wants. Instead of filling a vacuum, it makes one.
BENJAMIN FRANKLIN

All I ask is a chance to prove that money can't make me happy.
SPIKE MILLIGAN

Morality

There's no more morality in world affairs, fundamentally, than there was at the time of Genghis Khan.
NOAM CHOMSKY

The moral high ground is wreathed in fog.
ARTHUR MILLER

Ours is a world of nuclear giants and ethical infants. We know more about war than we know about peace, more about killing than we know about living. We have grasped the mystery of the atom and rejected the Sermon on the Mount.
GENERAL OMAR BRADLEY One of the architects of the D-Day Landings, he became the first Chairman of NATO in 1950.

The ethical view of the universe involves us in so many cruel and absurd contradictions, that I have come to suspect that the aim of creation cannot be ethical at all.
JOSEPH CONRAD

Do not be too moral. You may cheat yourself out of much life. So aim above morality. Be not simply good; be good for something.
HENRY DAVID THOREAU

Mothers

She who forms the souls of the young is greater than any painter or sculptor.
SAINT JOHN CHRYSOSTOM

Every beetle is a gazelle in the eyes of its mother.
MOROCCAN PROVERB

My mother never saw the irony in calling me a son-of-a-bitch.
JACK NICHOLSON

If evolution really works, how come mothers only have two hands?
MILTON BERLE

What one owes to one's mother is never repaid.
BASQUE PROVERB

When your mother asks, 'Do you want a piece of advice?' it is a mere formality. It doesn't matter if you answer yes or no. You're going to get it anyway.
ERMA BOMBECK

If a writer has to rob his mother he will not hesitate; the 'Ode on a Grecian Urn' is worth any number of old ladies.
WILLIAM FAULKNER

The remarkable thing about my mother is that for thirty years she served us nothing but leftovers. The original meal has never been found.
CALVIN TRILLIN Best known as *The Nation*'s 'deadline poet'. He also wrote *Tepper's Not Going Out* (2001), possibly the only novel written about the subject of parking.

Mountains

My father considered a walk among the mountains as the equivalent of church-going.
ALDOUS HUXLEY

What we get from this adventure is just sheer joy. And joy is, after all, the end of life. We do not live to eat and make money. We eat and make money to be able to enjoy life. That is what life means and what life is for.
GEORGE MALLORY

I can't do with mountains at close quarters - they are always in the way, and they are so stupid, never moving and never doing anything but obtrude themselves.
D. H. LAWRENCE

Mountains are not fair or unfair, they are just dangerous.
REINHOLD MESSNER Considered by many as the greatest mountaineer of all time, and the first to climb all fourteen peaks over 8,000 metres. In his first Himalayan climb in 1970, Messner lost seven toes and three fingers to frostbite and was forced to abandon his brother Günther, whose remains weren't found for thirty-five years.

You climb for the hell of it.
SIR EDMUND HILLARY

They say that if the Swiss had designed these mountains they'd be rather flatter.
PAUL THEROUX On the Alps.

Movies

There are three secrets to the success of a film: casting, casting and casting.
WILLIAM WYLER

Film is one of the three universal languages, the other two: mathematics and music.
FRANK CAPRA

Pictures are for entertainment, messages should be delivered by Western Union.
SAMUEL GOLDWYN

The movies were custard compared to politics.
NANCY REAGAN

The length of a film should be directly related to the endurance of the human bladder.
ALFRED HITCHCOCK

Having your book turned into a movie is like seeing your oxen turned into bouillon cubes.
JOHN LE CARRÉ

When the script is finished, then we add the dialogue.
ALFRED HITCHCOCK

The only really good thing about acting in movies is that there's no heavy lifting.
CARY GRANT

I am a film-maker, not a director. I like the physical process of making movies. I might be a toy-maker if I wasn't a film-maker.
GEORGE LUCAS

This film cost $31 million. With that kind of money I could have invaded some country.
CLINT EASTWOOD

My favorite line about Hollywood is, 'Nobody wants to be first. But everyone wants to be the first to be second.'
LEN WEIN

In Hollywood a marriage is a success if it outlasts milk.
RITA RUDNER

Gandhi was everything the voting members of the Academy would like to have been: moral, tan and thin.
JOE MORGENSTERN In the *Los Angeles Herald-Examiner* after Richard Attenborough's film *Gandhi* swept the boards at the 1983 Academy Awards.

I'm not going to go to any more dinner-parties. They're so badly directed.
LOUIS MALLE His 1981 film *My Dinner with André* was a film, largely improvised, of a conversation between actor/directors André Gregory and Wallace Shawn in a New York restaurant.

You can take all the sincerity in Hollywood, place it in the navel of a fruit-fly and still have room for three caraway seeds and a producer's heart.
FRED ALLEN

Music

Of all noises, I think music is the least disagreeable.
SAMUEL JOHNSON

Music, which can be made anywhere, is invisible and does not smell.
W. H. AUDEN

Music is the only cheap unpunished rapture on earth.
SYDNEY SMITH

Music is no different from opium.
AYATOLLAH KHOMEINI

Don't play what's there, play what's not there.
MILES DAVIS

The notes I handle no better than many pianists. But the pauses between the notes – ah, that is where the art resides.
ARTUR SCHNABEL

Music has many resemblances to algebra.
NOVALIS Born Georg Philipp Friedrich Freiherr von Hardenberg, his great project, a Romantic encyclopaedia, or 'scientific Bible' comprising thousands of fragments that attempt to integrate knowledge about science, religion and the arts, was left unfinished at his death (aged 29) in 1801. He was also the manager of a salt mine.

Music is the arithmetic of sounds as optics is the geometry of light.
CLAUDE DEBUSSY

Music is the language spoken by angels.
HENRY WADSWORTH LONGFELLOW

It may be that when the angels go about their task praising God, they play only Bach. I am sure, however, that when they are together *en famille* they play Mozart.
KARL BARTH

Music is powerless to express anything.
IGOR STRAVINSKY

Music expresses that which cannot be said and on which it is impossible to be silent.
VICTOR HUGO

I like the fact that listen is an anagram of silent. Silence is not something that is there before the music begins and after it stops. It is the essence of the music itself, the vital ingredient that makes it possible for the music to exist at all.
ALFRED BRENDEL

My music is best understood by children and animals.
IGOR STRAVINSKY

Nothing separates the generations more than music. By the time a child is eight or nine, he has developed a passion for his own music that is even stronger than his passions for procrastination and weird clothes.
BILL COSBY

Every kind of music is good, except the boring kind.
GIOACCHINO ROSSINI

The British like any kind of music so long as it is loud.
SIR THOMAS BEECHAM

All the good music has already been written by people with wigs and stuff.
FRANK ZAPPA

There is two kinds of music, the good and bad. I play the good kind.
LOUIS ARMSTRONG

Since music is the only language with the contradictory attributes of being at once intelligible and untranslatable, the musical creator is a being comparable to the gods, and music itself the supreme mystery of the science of man.
CLAUDE LÉVI-STRAUSS

No culture so far discovered lacks music.
ANTHONY STORR

It seems obvious that painting, sculpture or drama imitated nature. But what does music imitate? The measurements suggest that music is imitating the characteristic way our world changes with time.
RICHARD FREDERICK VOSS In *Science and Uncertainty* (1985). He's referring to something specific here called '1/f' noise, whatever that is . . .

Music is the effort we make to explain to ourselves how our brains work. We listen to Bach transfixed because this is listening to a human mind.
LEWIS THOMAS

There is no feeling, except the extremes of fear and grief, that does not find relief in music.
GEORGE ELIOT

I know only two tunes: one of them is 'Yankee Doodle' and the other one isn't.
ULYSSES S. GRANT

Classical music is the kind we keep thinking will turn into a tune.
FRANK 'KIN' HUBBARD

All music is folk music. I ain't never heard no horse sing a song.
LOUIS ARMSTRONG

What do you get when you play country music backwards? You get your girl back, your dog back, your pick-up back, and you stop drinking.

LOUIS SAABERDA Great quote, a singleton, with absolutely no clues anywhere to Mr Saaberda's identity. The closest we've got are a couple of Luis Saavedras, but neither of them fit our preconceived notion of a grizzled old band leader or session musician or hip young music critic.

Country music is three chords and the truth.
HARLAN HOWARD

If it has more than three chords, it's jazz.
LOU REED

Jazz is not dead . . . it just smells funny.
FRANK ZAPPA

There are some experiences in life which should not be demanded twice from any man, and one of them is listening to the Brahms's *Requiem*.
GEORGE BERNARD SHAW

People usually complain that music is so ambiguous, that it leaves them in such doubt as to what to think, whereas words can be understood by everyone. But to me it seems exactly the opposite.
FELIX MENDELSSOHN

Remember: information is not knowledge; knowledge is not wisdom; wisdom is not truth; truth is not beauty; beauty is not love; love is not music; music is the best.
FRANK ZAPPA

Without music, life would be a mistake.
FRIEDRICH NIETZSCHE

My idea is that there is music in the air, music all around us; the world is full of it, and you simply take as much as you require.
EDWARD ELGAR

Music is the best means we have of digesting time.
W. H. AUDEN

I like Wagner's music better than any other music. It is so loud that one can talk the whole time without people hearing what one says. That is a great advantage.
OSCAR WILDE

A painter paints his pictures on canvas. But musicians paint their pictures on silence. We provide the music, and you provide the silence.
LEOPOLD STOKOWSKI English-born US conductor, reprimanding a talkative audience, May 1967.

If the King loves music, it is well with the land.
MENCIUS (MENG ZI) The best-known Confucian philosopher after Confucius. He worked as an official in the state of Qi, in what is now Shandong province. Such was his devotion to his mother that he took three years off work to mourn her death.

Music is essentially useless, as is life.
GEORGE SANTAYANA

Musical Instruments

It's easy to play any musical instrument: all you have to do is touch the right key at the right time and the instrument will play itself.
J. S. BACH

Any space is as much a part of the instrument as the instrument itself.
PAULINE OLIVEROS Accordionist and avant-garde composer, founder of the Deep Listening Institute, which performs her meditative work in spaces with reverberant acoustics such as caves and cathedrals.

There are two instruments worse than a clarinet – two clarinets.
AMBROSE BIERCE

The flute is not an instrument which has a good moral effect – it is too exciting.
ARISTOTLE

A flute with no holes is not a flute, and a doughnut with no hole is a Danish.
CHEVY CHASE

From the start, when it was the instrument of the wood-god Pan, the flute has been associated with pure (some might say impure) energy. Its sound releases something naturally untamed, as if a squirrel were let loose in a church.
SEAMUS HEANEY

The most difficult instrument to play in the orchestra is second fiddle. I can get plenty of first violinists, but to find someone who can play second fiddle with enthusiasm – that's the problem. Yet, if there is no one to play second fiddle, there is no harmony.
LEONARD BERNSTEIN

What is a harp but an over-sized cheese-slicer with cultural pretensions?
DENIS NORDEN

Harpists spend 90 per cent of their lives tuning their harps and 10 per cent playing out of tune.
IGOR STRAVINSKY

The sound of a harpsichord – two skeletons copulating on a tin roof in a thunderstorm.
SIR THOMAS BEECHAM

When she started to play, Steinway himself came down personally and rubbed his name off the piano.
BOB HOPE On fellow comedian Phyllis Diller.

Wagner did not like the saxophone; he said it sounds like the word *Reckankreuzungsklankewerkzeuge*.
RICHARD WAGNER An invented onomatopoeic insult directed at the saxophone, developed by Adolphe Sax in the 1840s, but not (as is often stated) at Paul Hindemith's *Sonata for Saxophone*, composed in 1943, sixty years after Wagner's death. This 'quote' first appeared in Nicholas Slonimsky's *Lexicon of Musical Invective* in 1952.

Never look at the trombones, it only encourages them.
RICHARD STRAUSS

The tuba is certainly the most intestinal of instruments, the very lower bowel of music.
PETER DE VRIES

The difference between a violin and a viola is that a viola burns longer.
VICTOR BORGE

Ah, music! What a beautiful art! But what a wretched profession!
GEORGES BIZET

Musicians

Did Beethoven look like a musician? No, of course she didn't.
TONY HANCOCK

A jazz musician is a juggler who uses harmonies instead of oranges.
BENNY GREEN

A typical day in the life of a heavy metal musician consists of a round of golf and an AA meeting.
BILLY JOEL

I've never known a musician who regretted being one. Whatever deceptions life may have in store for you, music itself is not going to let you down.
VIRGIL THOMSON

I would rather play Chiquita Banana and have my swimming pool than play Bach and starve.
XAVIER CUGAT The original Mambo King. 'Chiquita Banana' was one of the best known of all Latin tunes: it was the soundtrack to a popular animated advert for the leading banana brand, shot in the Disney studios in the 1940s.

My whole trick is to keep the tune well out in front. If I play Tchaikovsky, I play his melodies and skip his spiritual struggle.
LIBERACE

My biggest regret is that I didn't hit John Denver in the mouth while I had the chance.
DENNIS LEARY

I once played to an audience of one and he tapped me on the shoulder while I had my eyes closed, halfway through singing *Maggie's Farm*, to say he had to catch his bus.
DAVE STEWART

I have always adored Mahler, and Mahler was a major influence on the music of the Beatles. John and me used to sit and do the *Kindertoten-lieder* and *Wunderhorn* for hours, we'd take turns singing and playing the piano. We thought Mahler was gear.
PAUL McCARTNEY

The Beatles are dying in the wrong order.
VICTOR LEWIS-SMITH

The music business is a cruel and shallow money trench, a long plastic hallway where thieves and pimps run free and good men die like dogs. There's also a negative side.
HUNTER S. THOMPSON

Pop music is about stealing pocket money from children.
IAN ANDERSON

The whole business is built on ego, vanity, self-satisfaction, and it's total crap to pretend it's not.
GEORGE MICHAEL

Mystery

The mystical is not how the world is, but that it is.
LUDWIG WITTGENSTEIN

The concepts most familiar to us are often the most mysterious.
ÉTIENNE KLEIN

Penetrating so many secrets, we cease to believe in the Unknowable.
But there it sits, nevertheless, calmly licking its chops.
H. L. MENCKEN

Something unknown is doing we don't know what.
SIR ARTHUR EDDINGTON

It is the unknown that excites the ardor of scholars, who, in the known
alone, would shrivel up with boredom.
WALLACE STEVENS

Art evokes the mystery without which the world would not exist.
RENÉ MAGRITTE

People love mystery and that is why they love my paintings.
SALVADOR DALÍ

The job of the artist is always to deepen the mystery.
FRANCIS BACON

No one can explain how the notes of a Mozart symphony, or the folds
of a piece of Titian's drapery produce their essential effects. If you do
not feel it, no one can by reasoning make you feel it.
JOHN RUSKIN

If you want my opinion on the mystery of life and all that, I can give it
to you in a nutshell: the universe is like a safe to which there is a key.
But the key is locked up in the safe.
PETER DE VRIES

When I was young, I said to God, 'God, tell me the mystery of the
universe.' But God answered, 'That knowledge is for me alone.' So I
said, 'God, tell me the mystery of the peanut.' Then God said, 'Well,
George, that's more nearly your size.'
GEORGE WASHINGTON CARVER The son of slave parents, he became America's
leading agricultural chemist, devising 325 uses for peanut derivatives, including a
form of peanut cheese.

N

Nationalities

You know the world is going crazy when the best rapper is a white guy, the best golfer is a black guy, the tallest guy in the NBA is Chinese, the Swiss hold the America's Cup, France is accusing the US of arrogance, Germany doesn't want to go to war, and the three most powerful men in America are named 'Bush', 'Dick', and 'Colon'. Need I say more?
CHRIS ROCK

The English are not happy unless they are miserable, the Irish are not at peace unless they are at war, and the Scots are not at home unless they are abroad.
GEORGE ORWELL

England is a paradise for women, and hell for horses; Italy a paradise for horses, hell for women, as the diverb goes.
ROBERT BURTON From *The Anatomy of Melancholy* (1621). A 'diverb' is an antithetical proverb. Burton's gloomy masterpiece is full of them.

My one claim to originality amongst Irishmen is that I have never made a speech.
GEORGE MOORE

We do not regard Englishmen as foreigners. We look on them only as rather mad Norwegians.
HALVARD LANGE Norwegian Foreign Minister from 1946 to 1965, a member of the Nobel Committee, and strong advocate of NATO.

The Cuban movement is not a communist movement. Its members are Roman Catholics, mostly.
FIDEL CASTRO In April 1959, during his unsuccessful trip to the Unites States to woo President Eisenhower.

When you sing in Danish, it sounds like you have throat disease.
MORTEN CARLSSON Former head of Danish Eurovision song contest delegation and now executive producer of the Eurovision live broadcast.

The Swazis despise sheep.
EDWARD FOX Not the plummy-voiced actor but the American writer, now based in

London. Just one of many excellent one-liners from his diverting travel book *Obscure Kingdoms: Journeys to Distant Royal Courts* (1993).

Neither good winds nor good marriages come from Spain.
PORTUGUESE PROVERB

France is a country where the money falls apart in your hand and you can't tear the toilet paper.
BILLY WILDER

The French are sawed-off sissies who eat snails and slugs and cheese that smells like people's feet. Utter cowards who force their own children to drink wine, they gibber like baboons even when you try to speak to them in their own wimpy language.
P J. O'ROURKE

To all the world's nations let it be known that the Poles are not geese, but have a tongue of their own.
MIKOLAJ REY

Italians come to ruin most generally in three ways, women, gambling, and farming. My family chose the slowest one.
POPE JOHN XXIII

It is not impossible to govern Italians. It is merely useless.
BENITO MUSSOLINI

The Welsh are the Italians in the rain.
RENÉ CUTFORTH

There are still parts of Wales where the only concession to gaiety is a striped shroud.
GWYN THOMAS

Nature

Of all the wonders of nature, a tree in summer is perhaps the most remarkable; with the possible exception of a moose singing 'Embraceable You' in spats.
WOODY ALLEN

Nature teaches more than she preaches. There are no sermons in stones. It is easier to get a spark out of a stone than a moral.
JOHN BURROUGHS

Nature, my dear Sir, is only a hypothesis.
RAOUL DUFY

Laws of Nature are human inventions, like ghosts.
ROBERT M. PIRSIG

To a person uninstructed in natural history, his country or seaside stroll is a walk through a gallery filled with wonderful works of art, nine tenths of which have their faces turned to the wall.
T. H. HUXLEY

I once had a sparrow alight upon my shoulder for a moment, while I was hoeing in a village garden, and I felt that I was more distinguished by that circumstance that I should have been by any epaulette I could have worn.
HENRY DAVID THOREAU

Of all the things that oppress me, this sense of the evil working of nature herself – my disgust at her barbarity – clumsiness – darkness – bitter mockery of herself – is the most desolating.
JOHN RUSKIN

Unfortunately this earth is not a fairy-land, but a struggle for life, perfectly natural and therefore extremely harsh.
MARTIN BORMANN

I do not believe Nature has a heart; and I suspect that, like many another beauty, she has been credited with a heart because of her face.
FRANCIS THOMPSON

Nature uses as little as possible of anything.
JOHANNES KEPLER

Repetition is the only form of permanence that nature can achieve.
GEORGE SANTAYANA

There is nothing useless in nature; not even uselessness itself.
MICHEL DE MONTAIGNE

Neurosis

Everything great in the world comes from neurotics. They alone have founded our religions and composed our masterpieces.
MARCEL PROUST

I prefer neurotic people. I like to hear rumblings beneath the surface.
STEPHEN SONDHEIM

The good writing of any age has always been the product of *someone's* neurosis, and we'd have a mighty dull literature if all the writers that

came along were a bunch of happy chuckleheads.
WILLIAM STYRON From his interview with the *Paris Review* in 1958. He knew what
he was talking about: a severe bout of depression in 1985 produced his short
masterpiece *Darkness Visible: A Memoir of Madness* (1989). Styron described his
experience as 'despair beyond despair'.

Acting is the expression of a neurotic impulse. It's a bum's life. The
principal benefit acting has afforded me is the money to pay for my
psychoanalysis.
MARLON BRANDO

A mistake which is commonly made about neurotics is to suppose that
they are interesting. It is not interesting to be always unhappy,
engrossed with oneself, malignant and ungrateful, and never quite in
touch with reality.
CYRIL CONNOLLY

No good neurotic finds it difficult to be both opinionated and
indecisive.
MIGNON McLAUGHLIN

Neurotics build castles in the air, psychotics live in them. My mother
cleans them.
RITA RUDNER

Newspapers

News travels faster than the mail.
CONFUCIUS

It's amazing that the amount of news that happens in the world every
day always just exactly fits the newspaper.
JERRY SEINFELD

I always turn to the sports page first, which records people's
accomplishments. The front page has nothing but man's failures.
EARL WARREN

I am unable to understand how a man of honour could take a
newspaper in his hands without a shudder of disgust.
CHARLES BAUDELAIRE

I read the newspaper avidly. It is my one form of continuous fiction.
ANEURIN BEVAN

Newspapers always excite curiosity. No one ever lays one down
without a feeling of disappointment.
CHARLES LAMB

A weekday edition of the *New York Times* contains more information than the average person was likely to come across in a lifetime in seventeenth-century England.
RICH SAUL WURMAN

Night

A man is a small thing, and the night is very large and full of wonders.
LORD DUNSANY

Learn to reverence night and to put away the vulgar fear of it, for, with the banishment of night from the experience of man, there vanishes as well a religious emotion, a poetic mood, which gives depth to the adventure of humanity.
HENRY BESTON

Whoever thinks of going to bed before twelve o'clock is a scoundrel.
SAMUEL JOHNSON

Normality

The mind excels in its effortless ability to treat the world as if nothing it contains is entirely strange.
JOSEPH CAMPBELL

Nobody realises that some people expend tremendous energy merely to be normal.
ALBERT CAMUS

The only normal people are the ones you don't know very well.
JOE ANCIS

Society highly values its normal men. It educates children to lose themselves and to become absurd, and thus be normal. Normal men have killed perhaps 100,000,000 of their fellow normal men in the last fifty years.
R. D. LAING

Little minds are interested in the extraordinary; great minds in the commonplace.
ELBERT HUBBARD Leader of the American Arts and Craft movement, his short essay *A Message to Garcia* became one of the world's best-selling books, as its tale of a soldier who 'gets the job done' commended it to American employers as an inspirational text for staff. Written in an hour 'after supper' in 1899 it sold over forty million copies. Hubbard and his wife died on the *Lusitania* in 1915.

Nothingness

A hole is nothing at all, but you can break your neck in it.
AUSTIN O'MALLEY

There is one piece of advice, in a life of study, which I think no one will object to; and that is, every now and then to be completely idle – to do nothing at all.
SYDNEY SMITH

The best screen actor is one who can do nothing supremely well.
ALFRED HITCHCOCK

I have noticed that nothing I have never said ever did me any harm.
CALVIN COOLIDGE

Blessed is the man who, having nothing to say, abstains from giving evidence of the fact.
GEORGE ELIOT

One of the lessons of history is that nothing is often a good thing to do and always a clever thing to say.
WILL DURANT

Perfection is achieved, not when there is nothing more to add, but when there is nothing left to take away.
ANTOINE DE SAINT-EXUPÉRY

Nothing is particularly hard if you divide it into small jobs.
HENRY FORD

There is no such thing as nothing.
MARTIN HEIDEGGER

Nothing is more real than nothing.
SAMUEL BECKETT

We turn clay to make a vessel, but it is on the space where there is nothing that the usefulness of the vessel depends.
LAOZI (LAO-TZU)

Uh-oh, I've lost a button-hole.
STEVEN WRIGHT

Doughnut holes are made of the same thing as the hole in your toilet seat, but nobody ever publicizes that.
MEGAN COUGHLIN

God made everything out of nothing. But the nothingness shows through.
PAUL VALÉRY Many consider *La Jeune Parque* (1917) to be the greatest French poem of the twentieth century. It came nineteen years after the death of his mentor, Stéphane Mallarmé, during which time he didn't publish a single word. Luckily, he did continue to fill his notebooks with quotable aphorisms.

Nihilism has no substance. There is no such thing as nothingness, and zero does not exist. Everything is something. Nothing is nothing.
VICTOR HUGO

Numbers

Once is happenstance; twice is coincidence; three times is enemy action.
IAN FLEMING

The Pythagoreans say the world, and all that is in it, is determined by the number three.
ARISTOTLE

All is numbers.
PYTHAGORAS The first man to call himself a philosopher (i.e. 'lover of wisdom'), he is now more famous for his theorem about triangles than for his philosophy, which is, as this quote shows, based on mathematical ratios expressing the ultimate reality. Some have pointed out that his teachings show remarkable similarities to Buddha's, who was his close contemporary.

If an angel were to tell us something of his philosophy, I do believe that some of his propositions would sound like 2 + 2 = 13.
G. C. LICHTENBERG

There is no safety in numbers, or in anything else.
JAMES THURBER

Our brains have evolved to get us out of the rain, find where the berries are, and keep us from getting killed. Our brains did not evolve to help us grasp really large numbers or to look at things in a hundred thousand dimensions.
RONALD L. GRAHAM

I believe there are 15,747,724,136,275,002,577,605,653,961,181,555,468,964,717,914,527,116,709,366,231,425,076,185,631,031,296 protons in the universe and the same number of electrons.
SIR ARTHUR EDDINGTON – the number is more conveniently written as 2^{256} x 136.

I've dealt with numbers all my life, of course, and after a while you begin to feel that each number has a personality of its own. A twelve is very different from a thirteen, for example. Twelve is upright, conscientious, intelligent, whereas thirteen is a loner, a shady character who won't think twice about breaking the law to get what he wants. Eleven is tough, an outdoorsman who likes tramping through woods and scaling mountains; ten is rather simpleminded, a bland figure who always does what he's told; nine is deep and mystical, a Buddha of contemplation.

PAUL AUSTER

O

Obviousness

The obscure we see eventually. The completely obvious, it seems, takes longer.
ED MURROW

The concepts most familiar to us are often the most mysterious.
ÉTIENNE KLEIN He participated in the design of the CERN large particle collider and his writing has done much to make modern physics comprehensible as an extension of philosophy as well as hard science.

Familiar things happen and mankind does not bother about them. It requires a very unusual mind to undertake analysis of the obvious.
A. N. WHITEHEAD

The more original a discovery, the more obvious it seems afterwards.
ARTHUR KOESTLER

No question is so difficult to answer as that to which the answer is obvious.
GEORGE BERNARD SHAW

Everything you've learned in school as 'obvious' becomes less and less obvious as you begin to study the universe. For example, there are no solids in the universe . . . There are no absolute continuums. There are no surfaces. There are no straight lines.
R. BUCKMINSTER FULLER

The secret of all victory lies in the organisation of the non-obvious.
MARCUS AURELIUS

Opera

People are wrong when they say opera is not what it used to be. It is what it used to be. That is what is wrong with it.
NOËL COWARD

No good opera plot can be sensible, for people do not sing when they are feeling sensible.
W. H. AUDEN

I do not mind what language an opera is sung in so long as it is a language I do not understand.
SIR EDWARD APPLETON

Opera is when a guy gets stabbed in the back and, instead of bleeding, he sings.
ED GARDNER

Opera in English is, in the main, about as sensible as baseball in Italian.
H. L. MENCKEN

I went to watch Pavarotti once. He doesn't like it when you join in.
MICK MILLER

Opinions

A great many people mistake opinions for thoughts.
HERBERT VICTOR PROCHNOW

People seem not to see that their opinion of the world is also a confession of character.
RALPH WALDO EMERSON

A painting in a museum hears more ridiculous opinions than anything else in the world.
EDMOND DE GONCOURT

Every man . . . should periodically be compelled to listen to opinions which are infuriating to him. To hear nothing but what is pleasing to one is to make a pillow of the mind.
ST JOHN ERVINE

In religion and politics people's beliefs and convictions are in almost every case gotten at second-hand, and without examination, from authorities who have not themselves examined the questions at issue but have taken them at second-hand from other non-examiners, whose opinions about them were not worth a brass farthing.
MARK TWAIN

I share no man's opinions; I have my own.
IVAN TURGENEV

Opinion is ultimately determined by feeling, and not by the intellect.
HERBERT SPENCER English social philosopher who coined the phrase 'survival of the fittest' and invented the paperclip in 1845.

Everyone's entitled to my opinion.
MADONNA

Let your mind wander in simplicity, blend your spirit with the
vastness, follow along with things the way they are, and make no room
for personal views – then the world will be governed.
ZHUANGZI (CHUANG TZU)

Originality

It has bothered me all my life that I do not paint like everybody else.
HENRI MATISSE

Originality is unexplored territory. You get there by carrying a canoe.
You can't take a taxi.
ALAN ALDA

And many a night we would stroll back and forth between Gluckstrasse
and Schüsselstrasse engrossed in philosophical conversation. Little
did we know then that what seemed so original to us had occupied
great minds for centuries already.
ERWIN SCHRÖDINGER

Original thought is like original sin: both happened before you were
born to people you could not possibly have met.
FRAN LEBOWITZ

Everything has been thought of before, but the problem is to think of it
again.
GOETHE

What is originality? To *see* something that has no name as yet and hence
cannot be mentioned although it stares us all in the face. The way men
usually are, it takes a name to make something visible for them. Those
with originality have for the most part also assigned names.
FRIEDRICH NIETZSCHE

Make it a practice to keep on the lookout for novel and interesting
ideas that others have used successfully. Your idea has to be original
only in its adaptation to the problem you are working on.
THOMAS EDISON

Originality does not consist in saying what no one has ever said before,
but in saying exactly what you think yourself.
JAMES STEPHEN

P

Painters

A painter is a choreographer of space.
BARNETT NEWMAN

Cézanne! He was like the father of us all.
PABLO PICASSO

Cézanne, you see, is a sort of God of painting.
HENRI MATISSE

In a few generations you can breed a racehorse. The recipe for making a man like Delacroix is less well known.
PIERRE AUGUSTE RENOIR

When Chagall paints you do not know if he is asleep or awake. Somewhere or other inside his head there must be an angel.
PABLO PICASSO

Rembrandt painted 700 pictures. Of these, 3,000 are still in existence.
WILHELM VON BODE

Salvador Dalí seduced many ladies, particularly American ladies, but these seductions usually consisted of stripping them naked in his apartment, frying a couple of eggs, putting them on the woman's shoulders and, without a word, showing them the door.
LUIS BUÑUEL

Painting

Painting is just another way of keeping a diary.
PABLO PICASSO

The only time I feel alive is when I'm painting.
VINCENT VAN GOGH

For me, painting is a way to forget life. It is a cry in the night, a strangled laugh.
GEORGES ROUAULT

I want to die painting.
PAUL CÉZANNE

When I've painted a woman's bottom so that I want to touch it, then
the painting is finished.
PIERRE-AUGUSTE RENOIR

It's enough to disgust you with love forever after. Those buttocks he
gives those wenches ought not to be allowed.
GEORGES CLEMENCEAU Describing Renoir's nudes in conversation with his
secretary Paul Martet shortly before his death in 1929. Twice President of France,
Clemenceau was a great friend of Claude Monet.

If necessary, I would even paint with my bottom.
JEAN-HONORÉ FRAGONARD

The buttocks are the most aesthetically pleasing part of the body
because they are non-functional. Although they conceal an essential
orifice, these pointless globes are as near as the human form can ever
come to abstract art.
KENNETH TYNAN

How vain painting is – we admire the realistic depiction of objects
which in their original state we don't admire at all.
BLAISE PASCAL

It is a widely accepted notion among painters that it does not matter
what one paints as long as it is well painted. This is the essence of
academicism. There is no such thing as good painting about nothing.
MARK ROTHKO

Painting is silent poetry, and poetry is painting that speaks.
SIMONIDES In his time – the fifth century BC – could ask any price for his verse. He is
often credited with the invention of the 'memory theatre' system that enabled people
to remember long strings of poetry and prose before the invention of printing.

Painting is damned difficult . . . you always think you've got it, but you
haven't.
PAUL CÉZANNE

When I paint, the sea roars. The others splash about in the bath.
SALVADOR DALÍ

Painting is a nail to which I fasten my ideas.
GEORGES BRAQUE

Painting is stronger than me, it makes me do its bidding.
PABLO PICASSO

Shall I tell you what I think are the two qualities of a work of art? First, it must be indescribable, and, second, it must be inimitable.
PIERRE AUGUSTE RENOIR

The painting has a life of its own.
JACKSON POLLOCK

Every artist dips his brush in his own soul, and paints his own nature into his pictures.
HENRY WARD BEECHER

Every portrait that is painted with feeling is a portrait of the artist, not of the sitter.
OSCAR WILDE

A portrait is a painting with something wrong with the mouth.
JOHN SINGER SARGENT

A painting without something disturbing in it – what's that?
GEORGES BRAQUE

A good picture, any picture, has to be bristling with razor blades.
PABLO PICASSO

This is either a forgery or a damn clever original.
FRANK SULLIVAN

Paradox

A paradox is only the truth standing on its head to attract attention.
G. K. CHESTERTON

There are trivial truths and the great truths. The opposite of a trivial truth is plainly false. The opposite of a great truth is also true.
NIELS BOHR One of the great physicists, a Nobel Laureate who cracked the structure of the atom and 'father-confessor' on the Manhattan Project. He designed his own coat of arms that bore the motto: *contraria sunt complementa* (opposites are complementary).

All know that the drop merges into the ocean, but few know that the ocean merges into the drop.
KABIR

The word 'paradox' has always had a kind of magic for me, and I think my pictures have a paradoxical quality, a paradox of chaos and order in one.
BRIDGET RILEY

How wonderful that we have met with a paradox. Now we have some hope of making progress.
NIELS BOHR

Unless man can understand two contraries, that is, two contradictory things, together, then truly and without any doubt it is not easy to speak to him of such things. For, until he understands this, he has not yet started out on the path of the life that I am talking about.
HEINRICH SUSO

In painting you must give the idea of the true by means of the false.
EDGAR DEGAS

Although this may seem a paradox, all exact science is dominated by the idea of approximation.
BERTRAND RUSSELL

What is a paradox, if not a truth opposed to the prejudices of the vulgar, ignored by the bulk of mankind, and which current experience prevents their being aware of? What is a paradox for us today will be a demonstrable truth for posterity.
DENIS DIDEROT

Parents

Children need love, especially when they do not deserve it.
HAROLD S. HUBERT

Children need models rather than critics.
JOSEPH JOUBERT

There are times when parenthood seems nothing but feeding the mouth that bites you.
PETER DE VRIES

Selective ignorance, a cornerstone of child rearing. You don't put kids under surveillance. Parents should sit tall in the saddle and look upon their troops with a noble and benevolent and extremely nearsighted gaze.
GARRISON KEILLOR

Parents are not interested in justice, they're interested in quiet.
BILL COSBY

If you want your children to turn out well, spend twice as much time with them as you think you should and half the amount of money.
ESTHER SELSDON

If you want to see what children can do, you must stop giving them things.
NORMAN DOUGLAS

If your parents never had children, chances are you won't either.
DICK CAVETT

Patience

Adopt the pace of nature, her secret is patience.
RALPH WALDO EMERSON

You cannot have genius without patience.
MARGARET DELAND

Everything comes to him who hustles while he waits.
THOMAS EDISON

If you are patient in a moment of anger, you will escape a hundred days of sorrow.
CHINESE PROVERB

Patience and perseverance have a magical effect before which difficulties disappear and obstacles vanish.
JOHN QUINCY ADAMS

Impatient people always arrive too late.
JEAN DUTOURD

Beware the fury of a patient man.
JOHN DRYDEN

Peace

To injure an opponent is to injure yourself. To control aggression without inflicting injury is the Art of Peace.
MORIHEI UESHIBA

People sleep peaceably in their beds at night only because rough men stand ready to do violence on their behalf.
GEORGE ORWELL

Peace on earth would be the end of civilization as we know it.
JOSEPH HELLER

Five enemies of peace inhabit with us – avarice, ambition, envy, anger, and pride; if these were to be banished, we should infallibly enjoy perpetual peace.
PETRARCH

How come the dove gets to be the peace symbol? How about the
pillow? It has more feathers than the dove, and it doesn't have that
dangerous beak.
JACK HANDEY

If a sufficient number of people who wanted to stop war really did gather
together, they would first of all begin by making war upon those who
disagreed with them. And it is still more certain that they would make
war on people who also want to stop wars but in another way.
G. I. GURDJIEFF

Peace is costly but it is worth the expense.
KIKUYU PROVERB

Peanuts

I hate television. I hate it as much as peanuts. But I can't stop eating
peanuts.
ORSON WELLES

No man in the world has more courage than the man who can stop
after eating one peanut.
CHANNING POLLOCK The highest-paid magician of his time, and the
acknowledged master of conjuring doves from thin air. Always immaculately
dressed, his devastating good looks won him a cult following as an actor in
European art house movies. In 1969 he retired to his organic farm in California.

Peanut butter is the paté of childhood.
FLORENCE FABRICANT

If you don't mind smelling like peanut butter for two or three days,
peanut butter is darn good shaving cream.
BARRY GOLDWATER

Pencils

Even what can appear to be the most common, small and simple of
objects, can reveal itself to be on its own terms as complex and as
grand as a space shuttle or a great suspension bridge.
HENRY PETROSKI

A formal manipulator in mathematics often experiences the
discomforting feeling that his pencil surpasses him in intelligence.
HOWARD WHITLEY EVES

Farming looks mighty easy when your plow is a pencil and you're a thousand miles from the corn field.
DWIGHT D. EISENHOWER

Lying in bed would be an altogether perfect and supreme experience if only one had a coloured pencil long enough to draw on the ceiling.
G. K. CHESTERTON

I am a little pencil in the hand of a writing God who is sending a love letter to the world.
MOTHER TERESA

Personality

Whenever two people meet there are six present. There is the man as he sees himself, each as the other person sees him, and each man as he really is.
WILLIAM JAMES

It is also true that one can write nothing readable unless one constantly struggles to efface one's own personality. Good prose is like a windowpane.
GEORGE ORWELL

There used to be a me behind the mask, but I had it surgically removed.
PETER SELLERS

You cannot develop a personality with physics alone, the rest of life must be worked in.
RICHARD FEYNMAN

We should take care not to make the intellect our god; it has, of course, powerful muscles, but no personality.
ALBERT EINSTEIN

For I was: I was alive: I could feel: I could guard my personality, the imprint of that mysterious unity from which my being was derived.
SAINT AUGUSTINE

The achievements which society rewards are won at the cost of diminution of personality.
BENJAMIN JOWETT

A river is a personality, with its rages and loves, its strength, its god of chance, its illnesses, its greed for adventure.
JEAN GIONO Best known for his internationally best-selling fable, *The Man who Planted Trees* (1953), the rights in which he offered for free to anyone who cared to

publish it. 'The goal was to make planting trees likeable,' he once commented.

He liked to observe emotions; they were like red lanterns strung along the dark unknown of another's personality, marking vulnerable points.
AYN RAND

The Texan turned out to be good-natured, generous, and likeable. In three days no one could stand him.
JOSEPH HELLER

Persuasion

Few are open to conviction, but the majority of men are open to persuasion.
GOETHE

Example is not the main thing in influencing others. It is the only thing.
ALBERT SCHWEITZER A doctor who was also an acclaimed concert pianist, Lutheran priest and author of groundbreaking biographies of Jesus and J. S. Bach. In 1905 he set up a missionary hospital in the depths of Gabon which won him the 1952 Nobel Peace Prize.

The object of oratory is not truth but persuasion.
THOMAS BABINGTON MACAULAY

Nothing is so unbelievable that oratory cannot make it acceptable.
CICERO

The ability to have our own way, and yet convince others that they are having their own way, is a rare thing among men. Among women, it is as common as eyebrows.
THOMAS BAILEY ALDRICH

The best way to persuade people is with your ears – by listening to them.
DEAN RUSK

The real persuaders are our appetites, our fears and, above all, our vanity. The skilful propagandist stirs and coaches these internal persuaders.
ERIC HOFFER

Philosophy

All are lunatics, but he who can analyse his delusion is called a philosopher.
AMBROSE BIERCE

One cannot conceive anything so strange and so implausible that it has not already been said by one philosopher or another.
RENÉ DESCARTES

Philosophy is not a theory but an activity.
LUDWIG WITTGENSTEIN

There's a difference between a philosophy and a bumper sticker.
CHARLES M. SCHULZ

It is a great advantage for a system of philosophy to be substantially true.
GEORGE SANTAYANA

I'm not a philosopher. Guilty bystander, that's my role.
PETER O'TOOLE

You could read Kant by yourself, if you wanted to, but you must share a joke with someone else.
ROBERT LOUIS STEVENSON

Philosophy: unintelligible answers to insoluble problems.
HENRY BROOKS ADAMS An intellectual whose grandfather and great-grandfather were both US presidents. His best work is part autobiography, part social history. He proposed a theory of history based on the second law of thermodynamics and believed the dynamo was as symbolic of the modern age as the Virgin Mary had been of the medieval.

Nothing so absurd can be said that some philosopher has not said it.
CICERO

Why is philosophy so complicated? It ought to be entirely simple. Philosophy unties the knots in our thinking that we have, in a senseless way, put there. Although the result of philosophy is simple, its method cannot be if it is to succeed. The complexity of philosophy is not the complexity of its subject matter, but of our knotted understanding.
LUDWIG WITTGENSTEIN

Philosophy is a wonderful subject, but it is necessarily unfinished and unfinishable. You really can't solve anything. At the end of my life I want to know more than I did at the beginning. And I couldn't get that from philosophy.
SIR ISAIAH BERLIN

Wonder is what the philosopher endures most; for there is no other beginning of philosophy than this.
PLATO

Philosophy begins in wonder. And, at the end, when philosophic thought has done its best, the wonder remains.
A. N. WHITEHEAD

What is the first business of one who practises philosophy? To get rid of self-conceit. For it is impossible for anyone to begin to learn that which he already knows.
EPICTETUS

Almost all of the hypotheses that have dominated modern philosophy were first thought of by the Greeks.
BERTRAND RUSSELL

Philosophy triumphs easily over past evils and future evils, but present evils triumph over it.
LA ROCHEFOUCAULD

The point of philosophy is to start with something so simple as not to seem worth stating, and to end with something so paradoxical that no one will believe it.
BERTRAND RUSSELL

For what is philosophy but the study of death?
SOCRATES

There may be some branches of human study – mechanics perhaps – where the personal spirit of the investigator does not affect the result; but philosophy is not one of them.
JOHN JAY CHAPMAN

One becomes a Stoic, but one is born Epicurean.
DENIS DIDEROT

Organic Life, we are told, has developed gradually from the protozoon to the philosopher and this development, we are assured, is indubitably an advance. Unfortunately it is the philosopher, not the protozoon, who gives us this assurance.
BERTRAND RUSSELL

Be a philosopher, but amidst all your philosophy, still be a man.
DAVID HUME

So in the end when one is doing philosophy one gets to the point where one would like just to emit an inarticulate sound.
LUDWIG WITTGENSTEIN

Photography

The camera is an instrument that teaches people how to see without a camera.
DOROTHEA LANGE

There are no fat war photographers.
PETER HOWE Former *New York Times Magazine* and *Life* magazine picture editor and author of the definitive record of modern war photography, *Shooting Under Fire.*

It takes a lot of imagination to be a good photographer. You need less imagination to be a painter because you can invent things. But in photography everything is so ordinary; it takes a lot of looking before you learn to see the extraordinary.
DAVID BAILEY

One should photograph objects, not only for what they are, but for what else they are.
MINOR WHITE

A photograph is neither taken nor seized by force. It offers itself up. It is the photo that takes you. One must not take photos.
HENRI CARTIER-BRESSON

Photography freed painting from a lot of tiresome chores, starting with family portraits.
PIERRE AUGUSTE RENOIR

Consulting the rules of composition before taking a photograph is like consulting the laws of gravity before going for a walk.
EDWARD WESTON

The best zoom lens is your legs.
ERNST HAAS

Physics

In science there is only physics; all the rest is stamp collecting.
LORD KELVIN

Physics. A subject that induces fear and loathing in students and most of their teachers. Synonyms include incomprehensible, waste of money and mind-numbing.
LEON LEDERMAN Nobel Physics laureate in 1988 for his work on neutrinos, particles that have no charge, and if they do have mass, it is very small. Did you know that more than fifty trillion of them pass through your body every second?

There is nothing new to be discovered in physics now. All that remains is more and more precise measurement.
LORD KELVIN

Anyone who is not shocked by the quantum theory does not understand it.
NIELS BOHR

In physics the truth is rarely perfectly clear, and that is certainly universally the case in human affairs. Hence, what is not surrounded by uncertainty cannot be the truth.
RICHARD FEYNMAN

Most of the papers which are submitted to the *Physical Review* are rejected, not because it is impossible to understand them, but because it is possible. Those which are impossible to understand are usually published.
FREEMAN DYSON Dyson manages to be both a Christian and a scientist, with a gift for visionary predictions. 'It's better to be wrong than vague' is one of his mantras. He has had many papers published in *Physical Review*.

A physicist is just an atom's way of looking at itself.
NIELS BOHR

Take quantum theory, the laws of the subatomic world. Over the past century it has passed every single test with flying colours, with some predictions vindicated to ten places of decimals. Not surprisingly, physicists claim quantum theory as one of their greatest triumphs. But behind their boasts lies a guilty secret: they haven't the slightest idea why the laws work, or where they come from.
ROBERT MATTHEWS

There is no democracy in physics. We can't say that some second-rate guy has as much right to opinion as Fermi.
LUIS WALTER ALVAREZ

Before I die, I hope someone will explain quantum physics to me. After I die, I hope God will explain turbulence to me.
WERNER HEISENBERG

It is often stated that of all the theories proposed in this century, the silliest is quantum theory. In fact, some say that the only thing that quantum theory has going for it is that it is unquestionably correct.
MICHIO KAKU

I like relativity and quantum theories
because I don't understand them
and they make me feel as if space shifted about like a swan that can't
    settle,
refusing to sit still and be measured;
and as if the atom were an impulsive thing
always changing its mind.
D. H. LAWRENCE 'Relativity'

Quantum mechanics is very impressive. But an inner voice tells me
that it is not yet the real thing. The theory yields a lot, but it hardly
brings us any closer to the secret of the Old One. In any case I am
convinced that He doesn't play dice.
ALBERT EINSTEIN

What I am going to tell you about is what we teach our physics
students in the third or fourth year of graduate school . . . It is my task
to convince you *not* to turn away because you don't understand it. You
see my physics students don't understand it. That is because *I* don't
understand it. Nobody does.
RICHARD FEYNMAN Flamboyant, bongo-playing, joke-telling physicist whose
clear and imaginative way of communicating the most complex subjects gained him
a huge following. He was the expert witness who took NASA to task over the
Challenger disaster.

Physics is not religion. If it were, we'd have a much easier time raising
money.
LEON LEDERMAN

Places

There was no there, there.
GERTRUDE STEIN On her home town, Oak Park, Illinois.

I grew up in Europe, where the history comes from.
EDDIE IZZARD

All places are distant from Heaven alike.
ROBERT BURTON

To be everywhere is to be nowhere.
MICHEL DE MONTAIGNE

There is something that can be found in one place. It is a great treasure
which may be called the fulfilment of existence. The place where this
treasure can be found is the place where one stands.
MARTIN BUBER

Play

Play is the highest form of research.
ALBERT EINSTEIN

The supreme accomplishment is to blur the line between work and play.
ARNOLD TOYNBEE

The master in the art of living makes little distinction between his work and his play, his labour and his leisure, his mind and his body, his education and his recreation, his love and his religion. He hardly knows which is which; he simply pursues his vision of excellence in whatever he does, leaving others to decide whether he is working or playing. To him he is always doing both.
BUDDHA

The understanding of atomic physics is child's play, compared with the understanding of child's play.
DAVID KRESH

We do not cease to play because we grow old. We grow old because we cease to play.
GEORGE BERNARD SHAW

Pleasure

Pleasure is very seldom found where it is sought.
SAMUEL JOHNSON

The greatest pleasure I know is to do a good action by stealth, and to have it found out by accident.
CHARLES LAMB

If there is a pure and elevated pleasure in this world, it is a roast pheasant with bread sauce.
SYDNEY SMITH

Show me another pleasure like dinner which comes every day and lasts an hour.
TALLEYRAND

There is but one pleasure in life equal to that of being called on to make an after-dinner speech, and that is not being called on to make one.
CHARLES DUDLEY WARNER

It is a pleasure to stand upon the shore, and to see ships tost upon the sea: a pleasure to stand in the window of a castle, and to see a battle and the adventures thereof below: but no pleasure is comparable to standing upon the vantage ground of truth . . . and to see the errors, and wanderings, and mists, and tempests, in the vale below.
FRANCIS BACON

The greatest and noblest pleasure which men can have in this world is to discover new truths; and the next is to shake off old prejudices.
FREDERICK THE GREAT

The great pleasure in life is doing what people say you cannot do.
WALTER BAGEHOT

There is no pleasure in having nothing to do; the fun is having lots to do and not doing it.
ANDREW JACKSON

No entertainment is so cheap as reading, nor any pleasure so lasting.
LADY MARY WORTLEY MONTAGU The intrepid and controversial aristocrat and bluestocking who travelled and wrote vividly about her visits to the Ottoman empire. She also brought back the Arab techniques of inoculating against smallpox, a disease which had left her badly disfigured.

Nothing gives an author so much pleasure as to find his works respectfully quoted by other learned authors.
BENJAMIN FRANKLIN

I can think of nothing less pleasurable than a life devoted to pleasure.
JOHN D. ROCKEFELLER

In diving to the bottom of pleasure we bring up more gravel than pearls.
HONORÉ DE BALZAC

I advise you to go on living solely to enrage those who are paying your annuities. It is the only pleasure I have left.
VOLTAIRE

I have a most peaceable disposition. My desires are for a modest hut, a thatched roof, but a good bed, good food, very fresh milk and butter, flowers in front of my window and a few pretty trees by my door. And should the good Lord wish to make me really happy, he will allow me the pleasure of seeing about six or seven of my enemies hanged upon those trees.
HEINRICH HEINE

Buying is a profound pleasure.
SIMONE DE BEAUVOIR

There is no such thing as pure pleasure; some anxiety always goes with it.
OVID

Remorse, the fatal egg by pleasure laid.
WILLIAM COWPER Eighteenth-century English nature poet whose life was scarred by depressive episodes. He once tried to drown himself in the Thames near Billingsgate, but failed because the tide was out at the time.

All fits of pleasure are balanced by an equal degree of pain or languor; it is like spending this year part of the next year's revenues.
JONATHAN SWIFT

The true pleasure of life is to live with your inferiors.
WILLIAM MAKEPEACE THACKERAY

I despise the pleasure of pleasing people that I despise.
LADY MARY WORTLEY MONTAGU

When a man says he had pleasure with a woman he does not mean conversation.
SAMUEL JOHNSON

Pleasure is not happiness. It has no more importance than a shadow following a man.
MUHAMMAD ALI

I get up every morning determined to both change the world and have one hell of a good time. Sometimes this makes planning my day difficult.
E. B. WHITE One of the small band of brilliantly funny writers that made the *New Yorker* America's most influential magazine. Joining the staff in 1927 he remained a contributor until his death in 1985. His children's novels *Stuart Little* (1945) and *Charlotte's Web* (1952) remain best-sellers, and his revision of *The Elements of Style* is still on every writer's desk.

Plots

When in doubt, have a man come through the door with a gun in his hand.
RAYMOND CHANDLER

An actor entering through a door, you've got nothing. But if he enters through the window, you've got a situation.
BILLY WILDER

If there is a gun hanging on the wall in the first act, it must fire in the last.
ANTON CHEKHOV

Poetry

Publishing a volume of verse is like dropping a rose petal down the Grand Canyon and waiting for the echo.
DON MARQUIS

A poet is someone who stands outside in the rain hoping to be struck by lightning.
JAMES DICKEY

The poet is the priest of the invisible.
WALLACE STEVENS

Genuine poetry can communicate before it is understood.
T. S. ELIOT

A haiku is an open door that looks shut.
REGINALD H. BLYTH

Poets utter great and wise things which they do not themselves understand.
PLATO

When it comes to atoms, language can only be used as in poetry.
NIELS BOHR

Keats and Shelley were the last poets who were up to date with their chemical knowledge.
J. B. S. HALDANE

Poets are masters of us ordinary men in knowledge of the mind, because they drink at streams which we have not yet made accessible to science.
SIGMUND FREUD

Whoever wins to a great scientific truth will find a poet before him in the quest.
FREDERIC WOOD-JONES

In science one tries to tell people, in such a way as to be understood by everyone, something that no one ever knew before. But in poetry, it's the exact opposite.
PAUL DIRAC Nobel laureate in 1933, famous for predicting the existence of

antimatter and for producing *Principles of Quantum Mechanics* (1930), a model of scientific clarity still used today. His hard-line outlook is evidenced in this admonishment of his colleague J. Robert Oppenheimer's enthusiasm for poetry.

There is no money in poetry, but then there is no poetry in money, either.
ROBERT GRAVES

Money is a kind of poetry.
WALLACE STEVENS

No man was ever yet a great poet, without being at the same time a profound philosopher. For poetry is the blossom and the fragrancy of all human knowledge, human thoughts, human passions, emotions, language.
SAMUEL TAYLOR COLERIDGE

I can't understand these chaps who go round American universities explaining how they write poems: it's like going round explaining how you sleep with your wife.
PHILIP LARKIN

A poet looks at the world the way a man looks at a woman.
WALLACE STEVENS

Poetry is the synthesis of hyacinths and biscuits.
CARL SANDBURG

The chief use [of the overt content of poetry] . . . is to satisfy one habit of the reader, to keep his mind diverted and quiet, while the poem does its work upon him: much as the imaginary burglar is always provided with a nice bit of meat for the house-dog.
T. S. ELIOT

My favourite poem is the one that starts 'Thirty days hath September' because it actually tells you something.
GROUCHO MARX

The most important thing for poets to do is to write as little as possible.
T. S. ELIOT

I envy the poet. He is encouraged towards drunkenness and wallows with nubile wenches while the painter must endure wretchedness and pain for his art.
REMBRANDT

All poets are mad.
ROBERT BURTON

Politicians

It is terrible to contemplate how few politicians are hanged.
G. K. CHESTERTON

A fool and his money are soon elected.
WILL ROGERS

We offer the party as a big tent. How we do that [recognise the big tent philosophy] within the platform, the preamble to the platform or whatnot, that remains to be seen. But that message will have to be articulated with great clarity.
DAN QUAYLE This remark won him a special mention at the 1991 Plain English Foot in Mouth Awards.

90 per cent of the politicians give the other 10 per cent a bad reputation.
HENRY KISSINGER

There are two problems in my life. The political ones are insoluble and the economic ones are incomprehensible.
SIR ALEC DOUGLAS-HOME

Successful politicians are insecure and intimidated men. They advance politically only as they placate, appease, bribe, seduce, bamboozle or otherwise manage to manipulate the demanding and threatening elements in their constituencies.
WALTER LIPPMANN

A politician is a statesman who approaches every question with an open mouth.
ADLAI STEVENSON

Since a politician never believes what he himself says, he is surprised when others believe it.
GENERAL DE GAULLE

The dreadful truth is that when people come to see their MP they have run out of better ideas.
BORIS JOHNSON

Next week there can't be any crisis. My schedule is already full.
HENRY KISSINGER

Politics

Politics is the entertainment branch of industry.
FRANK ZAPPA

Sex and politics are a lot alike. You don't have to be good at them to enjoy them.
SENATOR BARRY GOLDWATER

The American political system is like fast food – mushy, insipid, made out of disgusting parts of things and everybody wants some.
P. J. O'ROURKE

Politics is the art of preventing people from becoming involved in affairs which concern them.
PAUL VALÉRY

One of the penalties for refusing to participate in politics is that you end up being governed by your inferiors.
PLATO

Politics is the gentle art of getting votes from the poor and campaign funds from the rich by promising to protect each from the other.
OSCAR AMERINGER

It makes no difference who you vote for – the two parties are really one party representing four percent of the people.
GORE VIDAL

A liberal is a man who leaves the room when the fight starts.
HEYWOOD C. BROUN Campaigner and champion of the underdog, member of Algonquin Round Table and friend to the Marx brothers. His 'It Seems to Me' column was so popular that 3,000 mourners attended his funeral in New York in 1939.

Liberals feel unworthy of their possessions. Conservatives feel they deserve everything they have stolen.
MORT SAHL

I have wondered at times what the Ten Commandments would have looked like if Moses had run them through the US Congress.
RONALD REAGAN

Finishing second in the Olympics gets you silver. Finishing second in politics gets you oblivion.
RICHARD M. NIXON

Not every problem that someone has with his girlfriend is necessarily due to the capitalist mode of production.
HERBERT MARCUSE

Too bad that all the people who know how to run this country are busy driving taxis and cutting hair.
GEORGE BURNS

Popes

I admire the Pope. I have a lot of respect for anyone who can tour without an album.
RITA RUDNER

I would have made a good pope.
RICHARD M. NIXON

It often happens that I wake at night and begin to think about a serious problem and decide I must tell the Pope about it. Then I wake up completely and remember that I *am* the Pope.
POPE JOHN XXIII

Why should we take advice on sex from the Pope? If he knows anything about it, he shouldn't.
GEORGE BERNARD SHAW

My feelings of smallness and nothingness always kept me good company.
POPE JOHN XXIII Known as Il Papa Buono ('the good pope') he convened the Second Vatican Council in 1962 which did much to liberalise the Catholic Church. Beatified in 2000, his body was put on display (he died in 1963) and seemed remarkably well preserved, although the Church officially denied this the status of miracle.

Possessions

A man is rich in proportion to the number of things he can let alone.
HENRY DAVID THOREAU

Amongst my most prized possessions are the words that I have never spoken.
ORSON REGA CARD

Asceticism is not that you should own nothing, but that nothing should own you.
ALI IBN ABU TALIB Known more simply as Ali, he was Muhammad's right-hand man, and married his daughter. He was the last of the four caliphs who succeeded

the Prophet, but the first infallible Imam for the Shia sect, who defied the authority of the others in the great Sunni/Shia split that continues to divide Islam.

You possess only whatever will not be lost in a shipwreck.
EL-GHAZALI

In this life, all that I have is my word and my balls and I do not break them for nobody.
AL CAPONE

Potatoes

The man who has nothing to boast of but his ancestors is like a potato – the only good belonging to him is under ground.
SIR THOMAS OVERBURY Slowly poisoned while incarcerated in the Tower of London. The devious adulteress Frances Howard had decided to remove him, to clear her way to marrying Robert Carr, a match Overbury had advised his friend against in a poem, *The Wife*. Once the plot was uncovered in 1614, the poem became a best-seller.

What I say is that, if a fellow really likes potatoes, he must be a pretty decent sort of fellow.
A. A. MILNE

None for me. I appreciate the potato only as a protection against famine; except for that, I know of nothing more eminently tasteless.
JEAN-ANTHELME BRILLAT-SAVARIN

Found a little patched-up inn in the village of Bulson. Proprietor had nothing but potatoes; but what a feast he laid before me. Served them in five different courses – potato soup, potato fricassee, potatoes creamed, potato salad and finished with potato pie. It may be because I had not eaten for 36 hours, but that meal seems about the best I ever had.
GENERAL DOUGLAS MACARTHUR During his progress across north-east France in 1944.

Practice

Practice is nine-tenths.
RALPH WALDO EMERSON

Practice means to perform, over and over again in the face of all obstacles, some act of vision, of faith, of desire. Practice is a means of inviting the perfection desired.
MARTHA GRAHAM

I have a theory that there is something abnormal about children who like to practise instruments They are either geniuses or, more often, completely untalented. I certainly did not like to practise, and the teacher who hit me, and the view of the park, did not help to improve my attitude.
GEORG SOLTI

He who knoweth the precepts by heart, but faileth to practise them, is like unto one who lighteth a lamp and then shutteth his eyes.
SIDDHA NAGARJUNA The the most important Buddhist thinker after Buddha himself, active in the second century AD. He developed the concept of 'emptiness': because everything is always changing, nothing is ever fixed or present, therefore reality is 'empty'. Quantum physics tends to back him up.

Prayer

If the only prayer you said in your whole life was 'thank you', that would suffice.
MEISTER ECKHART

There are few men who dare publish to the world the prayers they make to Almighty God.
MICHEL DE MONTAIGNE

Whatever a man prays for, he prays for a miracle. Every prayer reduces itself to this; Great God, grant that two and two be not four.
IVAN TURGENEV

Often when I pray, I wonder if I am not posting letters to a non-existent address.
C. S. LEWIS

In prayer it is better to have a heart without words than words without a heart.
MAHATMA GANDHI

The fewer words the better prayer.
MARTIN LUTHER

The idea that He would take his attention away from the universe in order to give me a three-speed bicycle is just so unlikely I can't go along with it.
QUENTIN CRISP

When I was a kid I used to pray every night for a new bicycle. Then I realised that the Lord doesn't work that way so I stole one and asked

Him to forgive me.
EMO PHILLIPS

Predictions

It's tough to make predictions – especially about the future.
YOGI BERRA

There are two classes of forecasters: those who don't know, and those who don't know they don't know.
J. K. GALBRAITH

Old men and comets have long been reverenced for the same reason; their long beards and pretences to foretell events.
JONATHAN SWIFT

The time will come when people will travel in stages moved by steam engines, from one city to another, almost as fast as birds fly, fifteen or twenty miles an hour.
OLIVER EVANS

I see no reason to suppose that these machines will ever force themselves into general use.
DUKE OF WELLINGTON On steam locomotives in 1827.

The Americans have need of the telephone, but we do not. We have plenty of messenger boys.
SIR WILLIAM PREECE Chief Engineer, the British Post Office, 1876.

The 'telephone' has too many shortcomings to be seriously considered as a means of communication.
WESTERN UNION INTERNAL MEMO, 1876

Such startling announcements as these should be deprecated as being unworthy of science and mischievous to its true progress.
SIR WILLIAM SIEMENS On Edison's announcement of a successful light bulb in 1880.

Radio has no future.
LORD KELVIN

I can state flatly that heavier than air flying machines are impossible.
LORD KELVIN

I confess that in 1901 I said to my brother Orville that man would not fly for fifty years. Two years later we ourselves made flights. This demonstration of my impotence as a prophet gave me such a shock

that ever since I have distrusted myself and avoided all predictions.
WILBUR WRIGHT Speech to the Aero Club de France, 1908.

No flying machine will ever fly from New York to Paris, because no known motor can run at the requisite speed for four days without stopping.
ORVILLE WRIGHT

The motor car will help solve the congestion of traffic.
ARTHUR JAMES BALFOUR

Aeroplanes are interesting toys, but of no military value.
MARSHAL FERDINAND FOCH

Make no mistake, this weapon will change absolutely nothing.
GENERAL DOUGLAS HAIG On the machine gun, 1914.

There is not the slightest indication that nuclear energy will ever be obtainable. It would mean that the atom would have to be shattered at will.
ALBERT EINSTEIN

The energy produced by the breaking down of the atom is a very poor kind of thing. Anyone who expects a source of power from the transformation of these atoms is talking moonshine.
ERNEST RUTHERFORD

Space travel is utter bilge.
SIR RICHARD VAN DER RIET WOOLLEY British Astronomer Royal (1956–71) in 1956, a year before the launch of Sputnik 1.

Space travel is bunk.
SIR HAROLD SPENCER-JONES British Astronomer Royal (1933–55) in 1957, two weeks before the launch of Sputnik 1.

Computers in the future may weigh no more than 1.5 tons.
POPULAR MECHANICS, 1949

Landing and moving around on the moon offer so many serious problems for human beings that it may take science another 200 years to lick them.
LORD KELVIN

It will be years before a woman either leads the party or becomes Prime Minister. I certainly do not expect to see it happening in my time.
MARGARET THATCHER Quoted in an interview with the *Liverpool Post* in 1974.

Presidents

The President of today is just the postage stamp of tomorrow.
GRACIE ALLEN

I sit here all day trying to persuade people to do the things they ought to have the sense to do without my persuading them. That's all the powers of the President amount to.
HARRY S. TRUMAN

Being a president is like being a jackass in a hailstorm. There's nothing to do but stand there and take it.
LYNDON B. JOHNSON

The time is at hand when the wearing of a prayer shawl and skullcap will not bar a man from the White House, unless, of course, the man is Jewish.
WALLACE MARKFIELD Through the character of Jewish stand-up comedian Jules Farber in his 1974 comic novel, *You Could Live if They Let You.*

McKinley shows all the backbone of a chocolate eclair.
THEODORE ROOSEVELT

No president has ever enjoyed himself as much as I.
THEODORE ROOSEVELT

Sure, it's a big job – but I don't know anyone who can do it better than I can.
JOHN F. KENNEDY

When the President does it, that means it is not illegal.
RICHARD M. NIXON

I guess it just proves that anyone in America can be President.
GERALD FORD

I am a man of limited talents from a small town. I don't seem to grasp that I am President.
WARREN G. HARDING

The battle for the mind of Ronald Reagan was like the trench warfare of World War I. Never have so many fought so hard for such barren terrain.
PEGGY NOONAN Commentator and Reagan speechwriter, she was also responsible for George Bush Sr's famous 1988 quote: 'Read my lips, no new taxes.'

The thought of being President frightens me and I do not think I want the job.
RONALD REAGAN Fortieth President (1977–1981), in 1973, while he was Governor of California.

But there are advantages to being elected President. The day after I was elected, I had my high school grades classified Top Secret.
RONALD REAGAN

Ronald Reagan doesn't dye his hair – he's just prematurely orange.
GERALD FORD

I have opinions of my own – strong opinions – but I don't always agree with them.
GEORGE BUSH SR

Principle

In principle, I am against principles.
TRISTAN TZARA

When you say that you agree to a thing in principle, you mean that you have not the slightest intention of carrying it out in practice.
OTTO VON BISMARCK

In matters of style, swim with the current; in matters of principle, stand like a rock.
THOMAS JEFFERSON

It is easier to fight for one's principles than to live up to them.
ALFRED ADLER

Those are my principles and, if you don't like them . . . well, I've got others.
GROUCHO MARX

Prison

No one who has not sat in prison knows what the State is like.
LEO TOLSTOY

The worst evil of being in prison is that one can never bar one's door.
STENDAHL

What is a ship but a prison?
ROBERT BURTON

A man without a boat is a prisoner.
FAROESE PROVERB

Don't do drugs because if you do drugs you'll go to prison, and drugs are really expensive in prison.
JOHN HARDWICK

The only difference between me and my fellow actors is that I've spent more time in jail.
ROBERT MITCHUM

Problems

The problem when solved will be simple.
CHARLES FRANKLIN KETTERING

The solutions all are simple – after you have arrived at them. But they're simple only when you know already what they are.
ROBERT M. PIRSIG

I have yet to see any problem, however complicated, which when you looked at it in the right way, did not become still more complicated.
POUL ANDERSON

For every problem there is a solution that is neat and simple – and wrong.
H. L. MENCKEN

The problem is not that there are problems. The problem is expecting otherwise and thinking that having problems is a problem.
THEODORE RUBIN

You've got to take the bull by the teeth.
SAMUEL GOLDWYN

It is in the whole process of meeting and solving problems that life has meaning. Problems are the cutting edge that distinguishes between success and failure. Problems call forth our courage and our wisdom; indeed, they create our courage and our wisdom. It is only because of problems that we grow mentally and spiritually. It is through the pain of confronting and resolving problems that we learn.
M. SCOTT PECK

Mishaps are like knives, that either serve us or cut us, as we grasp them by the blade or the handle.
JAMES RUSSELL LOWELL

Don't get involved in partial problems, but always take flight to where there is a free view over the whole single great problem, even if this view is still not a clear one.
LUDWIG WITTGENSTEIN

When you worry, you go over the same ground endlessly and come out

the same place you started. Thinking makes progress from one place to another; worry remains static. The problem of life is to change worry into thinking and anxiety into creative action.
HAROLD B. WALKER

Problems that remain persistently insoluble should always be suspected as questions asked in the wrong way.
ALAN WATTS One of the most urbane and approachable of modern mystics, drawing on Hinduism, Chinese philosophy, pantheism, and modern science to remind us that the way we think of ourselves as 'an ego in a bag of skin' is a dangerous illusion, supported by neither science nor intuition.

Early on in the space race, NASA spent much time and effort seeking a metal robust enough to withstand the heat of re-entry and protect the astronauts. The endeavor failed. At some point, a clever person changed the problem. The real problem was to protect the astronauts, and perhaps this could be done without a material that could withstand re-entry. The solution, the ablative heat shield, had characteristics just opposite to those originally sought. Rather than withstanding the heat, it slowly burnt away and carried the heat away from the vehicle.
D. N. PERKINS

There are children playing in the street who could solve some of my top problems in physics, because they have modes of sensory perception that I lost long ago.
ROBERT OPPENHEIMER

If you break your neck, if you have nothing to eat, if your house is on fire – then you got a problem. Everything else is inconvenience.
ROBERT FULGHUM Unitarian who hit upon a winning formula in his 1986 book, *All I Really Need to Know I Learned in Kindergarten*, in which he uses simple prose and a child's-eye perspective to explore spiritual issues. His books have sold over sixteen million copies.

Life is not a problem to be solved, but a mystery to be lived.
THOMAS MERTON

Procrastination

Know the true value of time; snatch, seize and enjoy every moment of it. No idleness, no laziness, no procrastination; never put off till tomorrow what you can do today.
LORD CHESTERFIELD

Only put off until tomorrow what you are willing to die having left undone.
PABLO ICASSO

Never do today what you can put off till tomorrow. Delay may give clearer light as to what is best to be done.
AARON BURR Controversial US politician and third vice-president who famously killed his rival Alexander Hamilton in a duel in 1804. Soon afterwards he was accused of attempting to steal the Louisiana Purchase and crown himself Emperor of Mexico. He was acquitted, but spent the rest of his life on the run, even living in London for a while with Jeremy Bentham.

Progress

Progress is not created by contented people.
FRANK TYGER

Progress, far from consisting in change, depends on retentiveness; when experience is not retained, as among savages, infancy is perpetual. Those who cannot remember the past are condemned to repeat it. This is the condition of children and barbarians, in whom instinct has learned nothing from experience.
GEORGE SANTAYANA His writings are universally anthologised, and this passage from *The Life of Reason* (1905) is almost always misquoted as 'Those who cannot remember history are condemned to repeat it.' Originally, it was not a quote about learning lessons from history, but about how knowledge is acquired.

A man learns to skate by staggering about making a fool of himself; indeed, he progresses in all things by making a fool of himself.
GEORGE BERNARD SHAW

Stupidity does not give way to science, technology, modernity, progress; on the contrary, it progresses right along with progress.
MILAN KUNDERA

Language is the biggest barrier to human progress because language is an encyclopaedia of ignorance. Old perceptions are frozen into language and force us to look at the world in an old-fashioned way.
EDWARD DE BONO

Emergencies have always been necessary to progress. It was darkness which produced the lamp. It was fog that produced the compass. It was hunger that drove us to exploration. And it took a depression to show us the value of a job.
VICTOR HUGO

Technological progress has merely provided us with more efficient means for going backwards.
ALDOUS HUXLEY

Any comfortable American who is cynical of progress – or the competent decency of modern civilization – hasn't pondered how life was for our ancestors. Any day that cossacks haven't burned your home should start out a happy one, overflowing with optimism.
M. N. PLANO A mystery solved. The pseudonym of multi-award-winning hard sci-fi writer David Brin. Best known for dramatising the impact of future technologies on human society, he has also conducted savage but thoughtful attacks on both *Star Wars* and *The Lord of the Rings* for their elitism and nostalgia-tinged conservatism.

Belief in progress is a doctrine of idlers and Belgians. It is the individual relying upon his neighbours to do his work.
CHARLES BAUDELAIRE

Is it progress if a cannibal uses knife and fork?
STANIS?AUS LEC Lifelong opponent of all forms of totalitarianism. He escaped from a concentration camp in 1943 and joined the resistance, only to end up battling the Polish communist authorities to allow his work to be published. One of the great twentieth-century aphorists, his massive popularity earned him a state funeral in Warsaw in 1966.

Proverbs

Proverbs are short sentences drawn from long experience.
MIGUEL DE CERVANTES

Proverbs, like the sacred books of each nation, are the sanctuary of the intuitions.
RALPH WALDO EMERSON

A proverb is the horse which can carry one swiftly to the discovery of ideas.
YORUBA PROVERB

Almost every wise saying has an opposite one, no less wise, to balance it.
GEORGE SANTAYANA

Nothing ever becomes real till it is experienced. Even a proverb is no proverb to you till your life has illustrated it.
JOHN KEATS

Proverbs are the palm-oil with which words are eaten.
CHINUA ACHEBE

My own view is that Scotch proverbs are often a little vague to outsiders, since one can't see the sense for the Scotch. For example: 'Better thole a grumph than a sumph.' That doubtless expresses a high grade of wisdom, painfully arrived at by those who have tholed sumphs, perhaps through no fault of their own, only to discover when it is too late that they were the grumph type all along. Again: 'If a man's gaun doon the brae ilka ane gies him a jundie.' I have a strange feeling that I've been through that very thing myself, but I'll never be sure.
WILL CUPPY *New Yorker* regular of the 1930s and 1940s whose easy style belied the depth of his research. His favourite method was to copy out notes on to 3- x 5-inch index cards, sometimes filling hundreds for one short article.

Psychology

Men will always be mad, and those who think they can cure them are the maddest of all.
VOLTAIRE

Behavioral psychology is the science of pulling habits out of rats.
DOUGLAS BUSCH

Personalities, which means personal criticism and analysis, presuppose a whole world laboratory of human psyches waiting to be vivisected. If you cut a thing up, of course it will smell. Hence, nothing raises such an infernal stink, at last, as human psychology.
D. H. LAWRENCE *St Mawr* (1925) in reference to the 'fiendish psychologist' Mrs Witt.

The aim of psychoanalysis is to relieve people of their neurotic unhappiness so that they can be normally unhappy.
SIGMUND FREUD

I do not have a psychiatrist and I do not want one, for the simple reason that if he listened to me long enough, he might become disturbed.
JAMES THURBER

Purpose

I don't know why we are here, but I'm pretty sure that it is not in order to enjoy ourselves.
LUDWIG WITTGENSTEIN

We are here on Earth to do good to others. What the others are here for, I don't know.
W. H. AUDEN

It is well to remember that the entire universe, with one trifling exception, is composed of others.
JOHN ANDREW HOLMES

Everything happens for a reason; if you can't find a reason for something, there's a reason for that.
CHRIS LEVI

Man's ideal state is realised when he has fulfilled the purpose for which he is born. And what is it that reason demands of him? Something very easy – that he live in accordance with his own nature.
SENECA

The purpose of life is not to be happy. It is to be useful, to be honorable, to be compassionate, to have it make some difference that you have lived and lived well.
RALPH WALDO EMERSON

If you ask me why I came to this Earth, I'll tell you: I came to live out loud.
ÉMILE ZOLA

Every man is occasionally visited by the suspicion that the planet on which he is riding is not really going anywhere; that the Force which controls its measured eccentricities hasn't got anything special in mind. If he broods on this sombre theme long enough he gets the doleful idea that the laughing children on a merry-go-round or the thin, fine hands of a lady's watch are revolving more purposely than he is.
JAMES THURBER

There is one thing that we all must do. If we do everything else but that one thing, we will be lost. And if we do nothing else but that one thing, we will have lived a glorious life.
RUMI

In the dim background of our mind, we know what we ought to be doing but somehow we cannot start.
WILLIAM JAMES

Q

Quality

Quality means doing it right when no one is looking.
HENRY FORD

Quality is never an accident; it is always the result of intelligent effort... The bitterness of poor quality lingers long after the sweetness of low price is forgotten.
JOHN RUSKIN Allegedly: no one has yet found a source for these statements.

In communities where men build ships for their own sons to fish or fight from, quality is never a problem.
J. DEVILLE

You can't fake quality any more than you can fake a good meal.
WILLIAM S. BURROUGHS

I have offended God and mankind because my work didn't reach the quality it should have.
LEONARDO DA VINCI

To affect the quality of the day, that is the highest of arts.
HENRY DAVID THOREAU

Questions

Where am I? Who am I? How did I come to be here? What is this thing called the world?
SØREN KIERKEGAARD

It is better to know some of the questions than all of the answers.
JAMES THURBER

'Why' and 'How' are words so important that they cannot be too often used.
NAPOLEON BONAPARTE

It is not the answer that enlightens, but the question.
EUGENE IONESCO

A question is like a knife that slices through the stage backdrop and gives us a look at what lies hidden behind it.
MILAN KUNDERA

Millions saw the apple fall, but Newton was the one who asked why.
BERNARD BARUCH

The 'silly' question is the first intimation of some totally new development.
A. N. WHITEHEAD

To realise that the question does not matter is the first step towards answering it correctly.
G. K. CHESTERTON

We feel that even if all possible scientific questions be answered, the problems of life have still not been touched at all.
LUDWIG WITTGENSTEIN

There are innumerable questions to which the inquisitive mind can in this state receive no answer: Why do you and I exist? Why was this world created? Since it was to be created, why was it not created sooner?
SAMUEL JOHNSON

In the search for truth, there are certain questions that are not important. Of what material is the universe constructed? Is the universe eternal? Are there limits or not to the universe? What is the ideal form of organisation for human society? If a man were to postpone his search for Enlightenment until such questions were solved, he would die before he found the path.
BUDDHA

Questions are fiction, and answers are anything from more fiction to science-fiction.
SAUL STEINBERG

The great question that has never been answered, and which I have not yet been able to answer despite my thirty years of research into the feminine soul, is: What does a woman want?
SIGMUND FREUD

Scientific opinion abhors questions unlikely to be answered soon, whence the general belief that the origin of the Universe is now nearly understood.
JOHN MADDOX Editor of *Nature* for twenty-two years. This is known as 'Maddox's Third Law'.

You can tell whether a man is clever by his answers. You can tell whether a man is wise by his questions.
NAGUIB MAHFOUZ

Every sentence that I utter must be understood not as an affirmation, but as a question.
NIELS BOHR

The outcome of any serious research can only be to make two questions grow where only one grew before.
THORSTEIN VEBLEN

All that non-fiction can do is answer questions. It's fiction's business to ask them.
RICHARD HUGHES

I keep six honest serving-men,/ (They taught me all I knew);/ Their names are What and Why and When,/ And How and Where and Who.
RUDYARD KIPLING

I haven't had a chance to ask the questioners the question they've been questioning.
GEORGE W. BUSH In front of a Senate committee as President-elect in January 2001, being pressed on his ill-fated attempt to appoint Linda Chavez as Labor Secretary in his first cabinet.

Toddlers ask many questions, and so do school children – until about grade three. By that time, many of them have learned an unfortunate fact, that in school, it can be more important for self-protection to hide one's ignorance about a subject than to learn more about it, regardless of one's curiosity.
JAN HUNT Parenting counsellor, founder of The Natural Child Project and advocate of 'unschooling'.

The riddle does not exist. If a question can be put at all, then it can also be answered.
LUDWIG WITTGENSTEIN

Be patient with all that is unresolved in your heart. And try to love the questions themselves. Do not seek for the answers that cannot be given. For you wouldn't be able to live with them. And the point is to live everything, live the questions now, and perhaps without knowing it, you will live along some day into the answers.
RAINER MARIA RILKE

Quotations

It is a good thing for an uneducated man to read books of quotations.
WINSTON CHURCHILL

To be apt in quotation is a splendid and dangerous gift. Splendid, because it ornaments a man's speech with other men's jewels; dangerous, for the same reason.
ROBERTSON DAVIES

Anyone can tell the truth, but only very few of us can make epigrams.
W. SOMERSET MAUGHAM

Genuinely good remarks surprise their author as well as his audience.
JOSEPH JOUBERT

I always love to quote Albert Einstein because nobody dares contradict him.
STUDS TERKEL

When a thing has been said, and said well, have no scruple. Take it and copy it.
ANATOLE FRANCE

I quote others only in order the better to express myself.
MICHEL DE MONTAIGNE

If it were not for quotations, conversation between gentlemen would consist of an endless succession of 'what-ho's!'.
P. G. WODEHOUSE

The great writers of aphorisms read as if they had all known each other well.
ELIAS CANETTI

Quotations will tell the full measure of meaning – if you have enough of them.
JAMES MURRAY

Stronger than an army is a quotation whose time has come.
W. I. E. GATES Surely the work of a hoaxer. Only listed against this quote and one other about a man who drowned crossing a stream six inches deep. The earliest citation seems to be mid-1990s. Also *wie geht's* (pronounced 'gates') means 'how's it going?' in German. If you were going to make up a quote, wouldn't it read a little like this?

Nothing is so useless as a general maxim.
THOMAS BABINGTON MACAULAY

Misquotations are the only quotations that are never misquoted.
HESKETH PEARSON

Misquotation is, in fact, the pride and privilege of the learned. A widely read man never quotes accurately, for the rather obvious reason that he has read too widely.
HESKETH PEARSON

R

Rain

It wasn't raining when Noah built the ark.
HOWARD RUFF Larger-than-life Mormon who advised his readers that the US was heading for a hyper-inflationary depression in the early 80s, and that they should store a year's worth of food just in case. A decade earlier he practically invented the modern survivalist movement with his 1974 book *Famine and Survival in America*.

A wet man does not fear rain.
RUSSIAN PROVERB

The best thing one can do when it's raining is to let it rain.
HENRY WADSWORTH LONGFELLOW

If a kid asks where rain comes from, I think a cute thing to tell him is, 'God is crying.' And if he asks why God is crying, another cute thing to tell him is, 'Probably because of something you did.'
JACK HANDEY

Oregonians don't tan, they rust.
OREGON SAYING

Reading

People say that life is the thing, but I prefer reading.
LOGAN PEARSALL SMITH American bookman, scholar and aphorist who settled in England (Cyril Connolly was his secretary). Best remembered for a sequence called *Trivia* he began in 1902: short, polished essays, vignettes and musings. They have a great deal more charm and intelligence than most modern 'trivia' books, but are definitely for dipping into.

If you believe everything you read, better not read.
JAPANESE PROVERB

Always read stuff that will make you look good if you die in the middle of it.
P. J. O'ROURKE

No entertainment is so cheap as reading, not any pleasure so lasting.
LADY MARY MONTAGU WORTLEY

Most people read poetry listening for echoes because the echoes are familiar to them. They wade through it the way a boy wades through water, feeling with his toes for the bottom: The echoes are the bottom.
WALLACE STEVENS

I would not exchange my early and invincible love of reading for all the treasures in India.
EDWARD GIBBON

Some people read because they are too lazy to think.
G. C. LICHTENBERG

He has left off reading altogether, to the great improvement of his originality.
CHARLES LAMB

He [Hobbes] had read much, but his contemplation was much more than his reading. He was wont to say that if he had read as much as other men, he should have known no more than other men.
JOHN AUBREY

Reality

Of this there is no academic proof in the world;
For it is hidden, and hidden, and hidden.
RUMI

We are all captives of the picture in our head – our belief that the world we have experienced is the world that really exists.
WALTER LIPPMANN

Nothing exists but thoughts! The universe is composed of impressions, ideas, pleasures and pains!
SIR HUMPHREY DAVY On surfacing from a nitrous oxide trip in 1799.

It may be a good thing to copy reality; but to invent reality is much, much better.
GIUSEPPE VERDI

They are imbeciles who call my work abstract. That which they call abstract is the most realistic, because what is real is not the exterior but the idea, the essence of things.
CONSTANTIN BRANCUSI

The nature of this one Reality is such that it cannot be directly apprehended except by those who have chosen to fulfil certain

conditions, making themselves loving, pure in heart, and poor in spirit. Why should this be so? We do not know. It is just one of those facts that we have to accept, whether we like them or not and however implausible and unlikely they seem.
ALDOUS HUXLEY

One thing I have learned in a long life: that all our science measured against reality is primitive and childlike.
ALBERT EINSTEIN

There is no such thing as reality. There is only perception.
GUSTAVE FLAUBERT

Reality is nothing but a collective hunch.
LILY TOMLIN

Reality is that which, when you stop believing in it, doesn't go away.
PHILIP K. DICK

'Reality' is some kind of ontological silly-putty.
ROBERT ANTON WILSON One of the big figures of the 1970s American underground, futurologist and friend of Timothy Leary and Buckminster Fuller, whose interests ranged from the occult to quantum physics and from Sufism to neuro-linguistic programming. He died in 2007, his last blog urging friends to 'keep the lasagna flying'.

One day it will have to be officially admitted that what we have christened reality is an even greater illusion than the world of dreams.
SALVADOR DALÍ

Reason

The vast majority of human beings are not interested in reason or satisfied with what it teaches.
ALDOUS HUXLEY

Nihil est sine ratione. Nothing is without reason. There is a reason for everything. Nothing happens without a reason.
GOTTFRIED LEIBNIZ

Those who will not reason, are bigots, those who cannot, are fools, and those who dare not, are slaves.
LORD BYRON

Reason is the shepherd trying to corral life's vast flock of wild irrationalities.
PAUL ELDRIDGE

If you follow reason far enough it always leads to conclusions that are contrary to reason.
SAMUEL BUTLER

The last function of reason is to recognise that there is an infinity of things which surpass it.
BLAISE PASCAL

Truly, that reason upon which we plume ourselves, though it may answer for little things, yet for great decisions is hardly surer than a toss-up.
C. S. PEIRCE His work was neglected in his lifetime (most of it has still not been published). A friend of William James and thought by Bertrand Russell to be 'the greatest American thinker ever', his decision to live with a woman before they married destroyed his academic career and condemned him to a life of dire poverty.

Relativity

Imagine yourself alone in the midst of nothingness, and then try to tell me how large you are.
SIR ARTHUR EDDINGTON

There is no absolute up or down, as Aristotle taught; no absolute position in space; but the position of a body is relative to that of other bodies. Everywhere there is incessant relative change in position throughout the universe, and the observer is always at the centre of things.
GIORDANO BRUNO The first to propose that the universe was infinite, all made from the same elements and that matter was composed of intelligent atoms. He was burnt at the stake as a heretic in 1600. The Church admitted its error 400 years later and expressed 'profound sorrow' at his death.

Put your hand on a hot stove for a minute, and it seems like an hour. Sit with a pretty girl for an hour, and it seems like a minute. That's relativity.
ALBERT EINSTEIN

I don't understand my husband's theory of relativity, but I know my husband, and I know he can be trusted.
ELSA EINSTEIN

Religion

Religion is different from everything else; because in religion seeking is finding.
WILLA CATHER

There is only one religion, though there are a hundred versions of it.
GEORGE BERNARD SHAW

There are many religions, but there is only one morality.
JOHN RUSKIN

I care not much for a man's religion whose dog and cat are not the better for it.
ABRAHAM LINCOLN

The only good thing to come out of religion was the music.
GEORGE CARLIN

I give money for church organs in the hope the organ music will distract the congregation's attention from the rest of the service.
ANDREW CARNEGIE

I have never read any theologian who claims God is particularly interested in religion, anyway.
ANNIE DILLARD

The religion of one age is the literary entertainment of the next.
RALPH WALDO EMERSON

Joy in the universe, and keen curiosity about it all – that has been my religion.
JOHN BURROUGHS With Thoreau, the inventor of the American nature essay and one of the most popular writers of any kind active in the late nineteenth century. All the great men of the day – Teddy Roosevelt, Edison, Ford – visited his cabin in the Catskills. Burroughs was also responsible for securing the literary reputation of his great friend and mentor, Walt Whitman.

We must respect the other fellow's religion, but only in the sense and to the extent that we respect his theory that his wife is beautiful and his children smart.
H. L. MENCKEN

The whole religious complexion of the modern world is due to the absence from Jerusalem of a lunatic asylum.
HAVELOCK ELLIS

Being a Jew is like walking in the wind or swimming: you are touched at all points and conscious everywhere.
LIONEL TRILLING

An Islamic regime must be serious in every field. There are no jokes in Islam. There is no humour in Islam. There is no fun in Islam.
AYATOLLAH KHOMEINI

The theory that you should always treat the religious convictions of other people with respect finds no support in the Gospels.
ARNOLD LUNN Originally found fame as a mountaineer and skier, inventing the slalom race in 1922. His father Henry was a Methodist minister and founder of the Lunn Poly travel company. Arnold rejected religion until 1933, when a debate with Ronald Knox transformed him into one of modern Catholicism's most tough-minded and persuasive zealots.

Just in terms of allocation of time resources, religion is not very efficient. There's a lot more I could be doing on a Sunday morning.
BILL GATES

Like a bee gathering honey from different flowers, the wise man accepts the essence of different scriptures and sees only the good in all religions.
THE SRIMAD BHAGAVATAN Also known as the *Bhagavata Purana*, its 18,000 verses describe the life and incarnations of Krishna. Often referred to as the 'Hindu Bible', it may date from as early as 3,000 BC. According to Hindu commentators, it is to the *Bhagavad Gita* what the New Testament is to the Sermon on the Mount.

If revealed religions have revealed anything it is that they are usually wrong.
FRANCIS CRICK

We must be on our guard against giving interpretations that are hazardous or opposed to science, and so exposing the Word of God to the ridicule of unbelievers.
SAINT AUGUSTINE

I have always thought it curious that, while most scientists claim to eschew religion, it actually dominates their thoughts more than it does the clergy.
FRED HOYLE

True religion is the life we lead, not the creed we profess.
LOUIS NIZER

Science tells us how the heavens go. Religion tells us how to go to heaven.
GALILEO GALILEI

All religions are founded on the fear of the many and the cleverness of the few.
STENDHAL

One is all for religion until one visits a really religious country. Then, one is all for drains, machinery and a minimum wage.
ALDOUS HUXLEY

The clergy of England have no more influence over the people at large than the cheesemongers of England.
SYDNEY SMITH

As for the British churchman, he goes to church as he goes to the bathroom, with the minimum of fuss and with no explanation if he can help it.
RONALD BLYTHE

Every day people are straying away from church and going back to God.
LENNY BRUCE

Defoe says that there were a hundred thousand country fellows in his time ready to fight to the death against popery, without knowing whether popery was a man or a horse.
WILLIAM HAZLITT

Man desires a world where good and evil can be clearly distinguished, for he has an irrepressible desire to judge before he understands. Religions and ideologies are founded on this desire.
MILAN KUNDERA

The common error of ordinary religious practice is to mistake the symbol for the reality, to look at the finger pointing the way and then to suck it for comfort rather than follow it.
ALAN WATTS

All national institutions of churches, whether Jewish, Christian, or Turkish, appear to me no other than human inventions, set up to terrify and enslave mankind, and monopolize power and profit.
THOMAS PAINE

As to the squabbles of the Jews and the Christians, I can only say that these sects remind me of a cluster of bats or ants escaping a nest, a bunch of frogs holding council in a swamp, or a clutch of worms assembling in the muck: all of them disagreeing over who is the worst sinner.
CELSUS From *The True Word*, an anti-Christian polemic probably written in Alexandria in the second century AD.

I have heard with admiring submission the experience of the lady who declared that the sense of being well-dressed gives a feeling of inward tranquillity, which religion is powerless to bestow.
RALPH WALDO EMERSON

. . . and with the bowels of the last priest let us strangle the last king.
DENIS DIDEROT

Research

Research! Research! A mere excuse for idleness; it has never achieved
and will never achieve any results of the slightest value.
BENJAMIN JOWETT

Basic research is what I am doing when I don't know what I am doing.
WERNER VON BRAUN

The trouble with research is it tells you what people are thinking about
yesterday. It's like driving a car using a rear-view mirror.
BERNARD LOOMIS One of the great toy visionaries, developer of Barbie and Hot
Wheels, the man who made film merchandising into a huge industry, even coining a
word – 'toyetic' – to describe properties ripe for exploitation. Famously he told
Spielberg that *Close Encounters* wasn't one of these, so Spielberg put him on to his
friend George Lucas, then struggling to make an apparently unpromising sci-fi film
called *Star Wars*. You know the rest.

Revenge

To choose one's victims, to prepare one's plan minutely, to slake an
implacable vengeance, and then to go to bed . . . there is nothing
sweeter in the world.
JOSEF STALIN To Lev Kamenev while they were exiled in Siberia in 1915. Kamenev
was Trotstky's brother-in-law and a member of the first Politburo in 1917. He and
most of his family perished in Stalin's purges of the 1930s.

Something of vengeance I had tasted for the first time; as aromatic
wine it seemed, on swallowing, warm and racy: its after-flavour,
metallic and corroding, gave me a sensation as if I had been poisoned.
CHARLOTTE BRONTË

A man that studieth revenge keeps his own wounds green, which
otherwise would heal and do well.
FRANCIS BACON

When you go out to seek revenge, dig two graves.
CHINESE PROVERB

To refrain from imitation is the best revenge.
MARCUS AURELIUS

There is no revenge so complete as forgiveness.
JOSH BILLINGS

Risk

There is the risk you cannot afford to take; there is the risk you cannot afford not to take.
PETER DRUCKER

What you risk reveals what you value.
JEANETTE WINTERSON

He that leaves nothing to chance will do few things ill, but he will do very few things.
GEORGE SAVILE, 1ST MARQUESS OF HALIFAX

Why not go out on a limb? That's where the fruit is.
WILL ROGERS

Death is not the biggest fear we have; our biggest fear is taking the risk to be alive – the risk to be alive and express what we really are.
DON MIGUEL RUIZ

Rules

Four Rules For Life. Show up. Pay attention. Tell the truth. Don't be attached to the results.
ANGELES ARRIEN

There are two rules for success: 1) Never tell everything you know.
ROGER H. LINCOLN

If you obey all the rules, you miss all the fun.
KATHARINE HEPBURN

There ain't no rules around here! We're trying to accomplish something.
THOMAS ALVA EDISON

The golden rule is that there are no golden rules.
GEORGE BERNARD SHAW

White's Rule: The magnitude of any non-trivial task can only be known after the information has ceased to be of any practical value.
BRENT WHITE Another mystery. Obviously not the Nashville singer or the editor of the Apatow brothers' comedies. One other attribution suggests a computer programmer at work in the mid-1980s but there are no obvious candidates. Otherwise, Mr White might be a New York corporate lawyer, a Chicago market research exec, a professor of psychology in Kentucky or an evangelical blogger.

There are those whose sole claim to profundity is the discovery of exceptions to the rules.
PAUL ELDRIDGE

S

Science

Science is a procedure for testing and rejecting hypotheses, not a compendium of certain knowledge.
STEPHEN JAY GOULD

The important thing in science is not so much to obtain new facts as to discover new ways of thinking about them.
SIR WILLIAM HENRY BRAGG

Science is built up with facts, as a house is with stones. But a collection of facts is no more a science than a heap of stones is a house.
HENRI POINCARÉ

Religions die when they are proved to be true. Science is the record of dead religions.
OSCAR WILDE

Every scientific truth goes through three stages. First, people say it conflicts with the Bible. Next they say it had been discovered before. Lastly they say they always believed in it.
LOUIS AGASSIZ

Science is a cemetery of dead ideas.
MIGUEL DE UNAMUNO Although an ardent Spanish nationalist, he fell foul of the Franco regime, was removed from his university post in Salamanca and died under house arrest in 1936. All his work refused the 'big picture': he thought historical truth was best observed in the lives of ordinary, anonymous people.

I find it analytic, pretentious, superficial, largely because it does not address itself to dreams, chance, laughter, feelings or paradox – all the things I love the most.
LUIS BUÑUEL

Chaos theory is a new theory invented by scientists panicked by the thought that the public were beginning to understand the old ones.
MIKE BARFIELD

Science should leave off making pronouncements: the river of knowledge has too often turned back on itself.
SIR JAMES JEANS

If science tends to thicken the crust of ice on which, as it were, we are skating, it is all right. If it tries to find, or professes to have found, the solid ground at the bottom of the water, it is all wrong.

SAMUEL BUTLER

Science is one thing, wisdom is another. Science is an edged tool, with which men play like children, and cut their own fingers.

SIR ARTHUR EDDINGTON

In science, one can learn the most by studying what seems to be the least.

MARVIN MINSKY

Two impressions remaining, after a life of scientific research:
1. The inexhaustible oddity of nature.
2. The capacity of the human system for recovery.

J. B. S. HALDANE

Scientists have long been baffled by the existence of spontaneous order in the universe. The laws of thermodynamics seem to dictate the opposite, that nature should inexorably degenerate toward a state of greater disorder, greater entropy. Yet all around us we see magnificent structures – galaxies, cells, ecosystems, human beings – that have somehow managed to assemble themselves. This enigma bedevils all of science today.

STEVEN STROGATZ

Although this may seem a paradox, all exact science is dominated by the idea of approximation.

BERTRAND RUSSELL

Science is like sex: sometimes something useful comes out, but that's not the reason we are doing it.

RICHARD FEYNMAN

This is what non-scientists don't know, and this is what scientists are too bashful to talk about publicly, at least until they grow old enough to become shameless. Science at its highest level is ultimately the organization of, the systematic pursuit of, and the enjoyment of wonder, awe, and mystery.

ABRAHAM MASLOW

Just as knowing how a magic trick is done spoils all its wonder, so let us be grateful that wherever science and reason turn they plunge finally into Stygian darkness.

MARTIN GARDNER

Science is really in the business of disproving current models or changing them to conform to new information. In essence, we are constantly proving our latest ideas wrong.
DAVID SUZUKI

Traditional scientific method has always been, at the very best, 20–20 hindsight. It's good for seeing where you've been. It's good for testing the truth of what you think you know, but it can't tell you where you ought to go.
ROBERT M. PIRSIG

Science has 'explained' nothing; the more we know, the more fantastic the world becomes and the profounder the surrounding darkness.
ALDOUS HUXLEY

The science of life is a superb and dazzlingly lighted hall which may be reached only by passing through a long and ghastly kitchen.
CLAUDE BERNARD One of the great innovators of the late nineteenth century and a passionate advocate of applying scientific methods to medicine. His 1865 classic, *An Introduction to the Study of Experimental Medicine*, won him the epithet 'the father of physiology' and he became the first French scientist of any kind to be given a state funeral in 1878.

Genetics has always turned out to be much more complicated than it seemed reasonable to imagine. Biology is not like physics. The more we know, the less it seems that there is one final explanation waiting to be discovered.
STEVE JONES

Sculpture

Sculpture is the art of the hole and the lump.
PIERRE AUGUSTE RODIN

It is not what you do to the stone, but what the stone does to you.
HENRY DAVID THOREAU

I say that the art of sculpture is eight times as great as any other art based on drawing, because a statue has eight views and they must all be equally good.
BENVENUTO CELLINI

Do not trouble yourself too much about the light on your statue: the light of the public square will test its value.
MICHELANGELO BUONAROTTI

Sculpture is the stuff you trip over when you are backing up trying to look at a painting.
JULES OLITSKI

It took me 40 years to find out that painting is not sculpture.
PAUL CÉZANNE

The essence of a sculpture must enter on tip-toe, as light as animal footprints on snow.
HANS ARP One of the co-founders of the Dada movement in 1916, describing it as an attack on fine art and 'a magic opening of the bowels' which had 'administered an enema to the Venus of Milo'. When speaking German he called himself Hans; when speaking French, he was Jean.

Moonlight is sculpture.
NATHANIEL HAWTHORNE

A statue has no tongue and needs none.
RALPH WALDO EMERSON

A great sculpture can roll down a hill without breaking.
MICHELANGELO BUONAROTTI

Sea

They that go down to the sea in ships, that do business in great waters, these see the works of the Lord and his wonders in the deep.
PSALMS 107:23–24.

The sea pronounces something, over and over, in a hoarse whisper; I cannot quite make it out.
ANNIE DILLARD

The snotgreen sea. The scrotumtightening sea.
JAMES JOYCE

There is nothing so desperately monotonous as the sea, and I no longer wonder at the cruelty of pirates.
JAMES RUSSELL LOWELL Prolific satirist and anti-slavery activist, he was for five years the American Ambassador to Britain under President Arthur and acted as a pall-bearer at Charles Darwin's funeral in 1882.

The most advanced nations are always those who navigate the most. The power which the sea requires in the sailor makes a man of him very fast, and the change of shores and population clears his head of much nonsense of his wigwam.
RALPH WALDO EMERSON

The sea rises, the light fails, lovers cling to each other, and children cling to us. The moment we cease to hold each other, the moment we break faith with one another, the sea engulfs us and the light goes out.
JAMES BALDWIN

Seeing

There are three classes of people. Those who see; those who see when they are shown; those who do not see.
LEONARDO DA VINCI

Thinking is more interesting than knowing, but less interesting than looking.
GOETHE

Don't think: Look!
LUDWIG WITTGENSTEIN

The whole of life lies in the verb *to see*.
TEILHARD DE CHARDIN

You can observe a lot by watching.
YOGI BERRA Much loved US baseball player who was famous for his verbal gaffs, now called 'Yogiisms.' Later in life he claimed: 'I never said half the things I really said.'

There are some people who see a great deal and some who see very little in the same things.
T. H. HUXLEY

Most people cannot see anything, but I can see what is in front of my nose with extreme clearness; the greatest writers can see through a brick wall. My vision is not so penetrating.
W. SOMERSET MAUGHAM

It takes little talent to see clearly what lies under one's nose, a good deal of it to know in which direction to point that organ.
W. H. AUDEN

Normally, we do not so much look at things as overlook them.
ALAN WATTS

You and I do not see things as they are. We see things as we are.
HERB COHEN

Everything one looks at is false.
TRISTAN TZARA

It is only with the heart that one can see rightly; what is essential is invisible to the naked eye.
ANTOINE DE SAINT-EXUPÉRY

The true mystery of the world is the visible, not the invisible.
OSCAR WILDE

I shut my eyes in order to see.
PAUL GAUGUIN

When I see anything, I see everything.
STANLEY SPENCER

From my long walks through the forest I discovered the sky, the sky that formerly I believed I had seen every day, until one day I did see it.
AUGUSTE RODIN

Thanks to the Interstate Highway System, it is now possible to travel from coast to coast without seeing anything.
CHARLES KURALT He knew what he was talking about – Kuralt presented the 'On the Road' feature on CBS news for twenty-five years, seeking out stories from the backwaters of America, and wearing out six motor homes in the process.

The greatest thing a human soul ever does in this world is to see something and tell what it saw in a plain way. Hundreds of people can talk for one who can think, but thousands can think for one who can see. To see clearly is poetry, prophecy and religion, all in one.
JOHN RUSKIN

A fool sees not the same tree the wise man sees.
WILLIAM BLAKE

It is a terrible thing to see and have no vision.
HELEN KELLER

X-rays. Their moral is this – that a right way of looking at things will see through almost anything.
SAMUEL BUTLER

Self

The importance and unimportance of the self cannot be exaggerated.
REGINALD H. BLYTH

If you live only for yourself you are always in immediate danger of being bored to death with the repetition of your own views and interests.
W. BERAN WOLFE

The whole object of comedy is to be yourself, and the closer you get to that, the funnier you will be.
JERRY SEINFELD

Honour and dishonour both move us, because we are troubled by having a self.
DAODEJING (TAO TE CHING)

I have had more trouble with myself than with any other man.
DWIGHT L. MOODY Perhaps the most famous American evangelist preacher of the nineteenth century, he honed his act in England performing more than a hundred times in spring 1872, accompanied by his friend, gospel singer Ira D. Sankey (known as the 'Sweet Singer of Methodism'). By the end of the trip they were attracting crowds of up to 30,000, a pattern they sustained for many years after they returned home.

Trying to define yourself is like trying to bite your own teeth.
ALAN WATTS

I always wanted to be somebody, but next time I'll be more specific.
LILY TOMLIN

There is as much difference between us and ourselves as between us and others.
MICHEL DE MONTAIGNE

We are all serving a life-sentence in the dungeon of self.
CYRIL CONNOLLY

The most excellent Jihad is that for the conquest of self.
MUHAMMAD

The perfect man has no self.
ZHUANGZI (CHUANG TZU)

To transform the world, we must begin with ourselves; and what is important in beginning with ourselves is the intention. The intention must be to understand ourselves, and not to leave it to others to transform themselves. This is our responsibility, yours and mine; because, however small may be the world we live in, if we can bring about a radically different point of view in our daily existence, then perhaps we shall affect the world at large.
J. KRISHNAMURTI

Self-Knowledge

Who in the world am I? Ah, that's the great puzzle.
LEWIS CARROLL

Any life, no matter how long and complex it may be, is made up of a single moment; the moment in which a man finds out, once and for all, who he is.
JORGE LUIS BORGES

Know thyself.
ANONYMOUS *Gnothi seauton* in Greek. This fundamental tenet has been ascribed to Socrates and at least five other Greek philosophers. It was one of three things inscribed on the temple of Apollo at Delphi, making it older than all of them.

'Know thyself?' If I knew myself, I'd run away.
GOETHE

Know thyself! A maxim as pernicious as it is ugly. Whoever observes himself arrests his own development. A caterpillar who wanted to know itself well would never become a butterfly.
ANDRÉ GIDE

There are three things that are extremely hard: steel, a diamond, and to know one's self.
BENJAMIN FRANKLIN

The humble knowledge of thyself is a surer way to God than the deepest search after science.
THOMAS À KEMPIS

I am the only person in the world I should like to know thoroughly.
OSCAR WILDE

Finding out who you are is the first step. Accepting who you are can be the hard part. Enhancing who you are is the fun part.
B'ANNE YOUNKER All we know about Ms Younker is that she lives in Preston, Arizona and makes rather interesting quilts and very good peanut brittle. This quote appeared on the Painter's Keys website of Canadian artist Robert Genn in 2005.

A man has many skins in himself, covering the depths of his heart. Man knows so many things; he does not know himself. Why, thirty or forty skins or hides, just like an ox's or a bear's, so thick and hard, cover the soul. Go into your own ground and learn to know yourself there.
MEISTER ECKHART

Our opinion of others is not so variable as our opinion of ourselves.
LUC DE CLAPIERS, MARQUIS DE VAUVENARGUES

I should not talk so much about myself if there were anybody else whom I knew so well.
HENRY DAVID THOREAU

The unexamined life is not worth living.
SOCRATES In Plato's *Apology*.

The examined life can make you want to kill yourself.
SAUL BELLOW

He who knows others is learned. He who knows himself is wise.
LAOZI (LAO-TZU)

I know who I am. No one else knows who I am. If I was a giraffe, and someone said I was a snake, I'd think, no, actually I'm a giraffe.
RICHARD GERE This outburst won the actor the 2002 Foot in Mouth award organised in the UK by the Plain English Campaign. It was in response to a question about his sexual orientation.

The last thing we discover about ourselves is our effect.
WILLIAM BOYD

Self-pity is easily the most destructive of the nonpharmaceutical narcotics; it is addictive, gives momentary pleasure and separates the victim from reality.
JOHN WILLIAM GARDNER

I never saw a wild thing sorry for itself. A small bird will drop frozen dead from a bough without ever having felt sorry for itself.
D. H. LAWRENCE

Trust thyself: every heart vibrates to that iron string.
RALPH WALDO EMERSON

To be thrown upon one's own resources is to be cast into the very lap of fortune, for our faculties then undergo a development and display an energy of which they were previously unsusceptible.
BENJAMIN FRANKLIN

It is not love of self but hatred of self which is at the root of the troubles that afflict our world.
ERIC HOFFER

He who lives in harmony with himself, lives in harmony with the Universe.
MARCUS AURELIUS

Sentimentality

Sentimentality is a superstructure covering brutality.
CARL JUNG

I find that the more a fellow weeps, the less he feels.
LORD CHESTERFIELD

Sentimentality, the ostentatious parading of excesssive and spurious emotion, is the mark of dishonesty, the inability to feel: the wet eyes of the sentimentalist betray his aversion to experience, his fear of life, his arid heart; and it is always, therefore, the signal of secret and violent inhumanity, the mask of cruelty.
JAMES BALDWIN

A sentimentalist is simply one who desires to have the luxury of an emotion without paying for it.
OSCAR WILDE

The difference between sentiment and being sentimental is the following: Sentiment is when a driver swerves out of the way to avoid hitting a rabbit on the road. Being sentimental is when the same driver, when swerving away from the rabbit, hits a pedestrian.
FRANK HERBERT Most famous for his 1965 novel, *Dune*, which as well as being full of ideas – it is often cited as the first 'ecological' novel – also brought a psychological complexity to the genre. It went on to become the best-selling sci-fi novel of all time.

Sex

Personally I know nothing about sex because I have always been married.
ZSA ZSA GABOR

The art of procreation and the members employed therein are so repulsive, that if it were not for the beauty of the faces and the adornments of the actors and the pent-up impulse, nature would lose the human species.
LEONARDO DA VINCI

There is no greater mystery in the world, as it seems to me, than the existence of the sexes.
CHARLES DARWIN

The finest people marry the two sexes in their own person.
RALPH WALDO EMERSON

Sex is something the children never discuss in the presence of their elders.
ARTHUR S. ROCHE

Sex hasn't been the same since women started enjoying it.
LEWIS GRIZZARD The original 'grumpy old man' and one of the South's most

popular and irreverent columnists and comedians. His personal life was messy: four wives, a congenital heart defect, a battle with alcoholism. He was once voted 'The Author from Hell' by a publishers' conference because of his bad behaviour on tour.

While farmers generally allow one rooster for ten hens, ten men are scarcely sufficient to service one woman.
BOCCACCIO

Erotica is using a feather, pornography is using the whole chicken.
ISABEL ALLENDE

I don't see much of Alfred anymore since he got so interested in sex.
CLARA McMILLAN Better known as Mrs Alfred Kinsey, or Mac, as he called her. This line is apocryphal – after all she was a qualified chemist and actively helped her husband (directly and indirectly) with his epoch-making reports on human sexuality.

If sex is such a natural phenomenon, how come there are so many books on how to do it.
BETTE MIDLER

You know 'that look' women get when they want sex? Me neither.
STEVE MARTIN

There are a number of mechanical devices which increase sexual arousal, particularly in women. Chief among these is the Mercedes-Benz 500SL.
LYNN LAVNER

Madame Bovary is the sexiest book imaginable. The woman's virtually a nyphomaniac but you won't find a vulgar word in the entire thing.
NOËL COWARD

Sex is one of the nine reasons for reincarnation. The other eight are unimportant.
HENRY MILLER

Sex is the poor man's polo.
CLIFFORD ODETS

An intellectual is a person who has discovered something more interesting than sex.
ALDOUS HUXLEY

I've made so many movies playing a hooker that they don't pay me in the regular way anymore. They leave it on the dresser.
SHIRLEY MACLAINE

The big difference between sex for money and sex for free is sex for money usually costs a lot less.
BRENDAN BEHAN

There are a number of mechanical devices which increase sexual arousal. The nice thing about masturbation is that you don't have to dress up for it.
TRUMAN CAPOTE

I regret to say that we of the FBI are powerless to act in cases of oral-genital intimacy, unless it has in some way obstructed interstate commerce.
J. EDGAR HOOVER

It's hard for me to get used to these changing times. I can remember when the air was clean and sex was dirty.
GEORGE BURNS

Sex between a man and a woman can be a beautiful thing, provided you're between the right man and the right woman.
WOODY ALLEN

There is nothing wrong with going to bed with someone of your own sex. People should be very free with sex, but they should draw the line at goats.
ELTON JOHN

There comes a moment in the day, when you have written your pages in the morning, attended to your correspondence in the afternoon, and have nothing further to do. Then comes the hour when you are bored; that's the time for sex.
H. G. WELLS Letter to Charlie Chaplin quoted in the 1973 Wells biography by Norman and Jeanne Mackenzie.

The difference between sex and love is that sex relieves tension and love causes it.
WOODY ALLEN

That's a bit like asking a man crawling across the Sahara whether he would prefer Perrier or Malvern Water.
ALAN BENNETT

Sheep

What is a sheep? This simple question is more than enough to have kept scientists occupied for hundreds of years, and will continue to do

so for many years to come.
PHILIP BALL

To say a sheep has five legs doesn't make it so.
ABRAHAM LINCOLN

And what is the Scientific Community doing about these problems,
young people? *They're cloning sheep.* Great! Just what we need! Sheep
that look *more alike* than they already do! Thanks a lot, Scientific
Community!
DAVE BARRY

It's better to be a lion for a day than a sheep all your life.
ELIZABETH KENNY Self-taught Australian 'bush nurse' who developed a
treatment for polio (despite the opposition of the medical establishment) which
evolved into what we now call physiotherapy. Her story was filmed as *Sister Kenny* in
1946, for which Rosalind Russell won a Best Actress Oscar nomination.

I am more afraid of an army of a hundred sheep led by a lion than an
army of a hundred lions led by a sheep.
TALLEYRAND

I once complained to my father that I didn't seem to be able to do
things the same way other people did. Dad's advice? 'Margo, don't be a
sheep. People hate sheep. They eat sheep.'
MARGO KAUFMAN

I am the pink sheep of the family.
ALEXANDER McQUEEN

It is useless for the sheep to pass resolutions in favour of
vegetarianism, while the wolf remains of a different opinion.
WILLIAM RALPH INGE

New Zealand is a country of thirty thousand million sheep, three
million of whom think they are human.
BARRY HUMPHRIES

To create man was a quaint and original idea, but to add the sheep was
tautology.
MARK TWAIN

Think of the fierce energy concentrated in an acorn! You bury it in the
ground, and it explodes into an oak! Bury a sheep, and nothing
happens but decay.
GEORGE BERNARD SHAW

Shoes

The reason the Romans built their great paved highways was because they had such inconvenient footwear.
CHARLES DE MONTESQUIEU

The high-heeled shoe is a marvellously contradictory item; it brings a woman to a man's height but makes sure she cannot keep up with him.
GERMAINE GREER

I did not have three thousand pairs of shoes, I had 1,060.
IMELDA MARCOS

I have very narrow feet, so I have to wear Ferragamo.
MRS GRACE MUGABE

Silence

Nothing is more useful than silence.
MENANDER Author of more than a hundred comedies, the majority of which have been lost to posterity.

When I have to cut tapes, in the spaces where people sometimes pause for a moment – or sigh, or take a breath, or there is absolute silence – I don't throw that away, I collect it!
HEINRICH BÖLL

Silence is one of the hardest arguments to refute.
JOSH BILLINGS

Silence is argument carried out by other means.
'CHE' GUEVARA

I found I had less and less to say, until, finally, I became silent, and began to listen. I discovered in the silence, the voice of God.
SØREN KIERKEGAARD

The Arctic expresses the sum of all wisdom: silence.
WALTER BAUER

Never assume that habitual silence means ability in reserve.
GEOFFREY MADAN

Whereof one cannot speak, thereof one must be silent.
LUDWIG WITTGENSTEIN

The answer to the existence of a fool is silence.
RUMI

He can keep silence well. That man's silence is wonderful to listen to.
THOMAS HARDY

I have often regretted my speech, never my silence.
XENOCRATES

Blessed are they who have nothing to say and who cannot be
persuaded to say it.
JAMES RUSSELL LOWELL

The silence went straight from rapt to fraught without pausing at
pregnant.
BERNARD LEVIN

Every man who delights in a multitude of words, even though he says
admirable things, is empty within. If you love truth be a lover of
silence. Silence like the sunlight will illuminate you in God and will
deliver you from the phantoms of ignorance.
ISAAC OF NINEVEH An ascetic born in modern-day Qatar, he lasted only five
months as Bishop of Nineveh, requesting a sabbatical which turned out to be
permanent as he settled in the desert to become a hermit, living on raw vegetables
and three loaves of bread a week.

The most beautiful thing of all is the complete stillness of an audience
so intent that it hardly breathes.
CHARLES LAUGHTON

Soon silence will have passed into legend. Man has turned his back on
silence. Day after day he invents machines and devices that increase
noise and distract humanity from the essence of life, contemplation,
meditation . . . tooting, howling, screeching, booming, crashing,
whistling, grinding, and trilling to bolster his ego. His anxiety subsides.
His inhuman void spreads monstrously like a grey vegetation.
JEAN ARP

In the End, we will remember not the words of our enemies, but the
silence of our friends.
MARTIN LUTHER KING

Simplicity

Above all, keep it simple.
AUGUSTE ESCOFFIER

Simplicity is the ultimate sophistication.
LEONARDO DA VINCI

Truth is ever to be found in the simplicity, not in the multiplicity and confusion of things.
ISAAC NEWTON

Simplicity does not precede complexity, but follows it.
ALAN J. PERLIS

The trouble with simple living is that, though it can be joyful, rich, and creative, it isn't simple.
DORIS JANZEN LONGACRE Mennonite Christian author who fulfilled the 'healing and hope' mission of her faith by producing *The More-with-Less Cookbook* in 1976, which showed a generation how to cook and eat less wastefully.

It is far more difficult to be simple than to be complicated.
JOHN RUSKIN

All the great things are simple.
WINSTON CHURCHILL

When the solution is simple, God is answering.
ALBERT EINSTEIN

Very simple ideas lie within the reach only of complex minds.
RÉMY DE GOURMONT

Everything is both simpler than we can imagine and more entangled than we can conceive.
GOETHE

Simplicity of life is not a misery but the foundation of refinement.
WILLIAM MORRIS

Seek simplicity, and distrust it.
ALFRED NORTH WHITEHEAD

Everything that is exact is short.
JOSEPH JOUBERT

Sin

How wise are thy commandments, Lord. Each of them applies to somebody I know.
SAM LEVENSON

There is sin in every single one of us and if we would fight evil then let us fight that wrong within our own being.
JAMES MAWDSLEY Campaigner for human rights in Myanmar (Burma) who was imprisoned there for fourteen months in 1999 and is now a Roman Catholic blogger and prospective parliamentary candidate for the Conservative Party.

The Seven Deadly Sins are: Wealth without work, Pleasure without conscience, Knowledge without character, Business without morality, Science without humanity, Worship without sacrifice, Politics without principle.
MAHATMA GANDHI

Gluttony is not a secret vice.
ORSON WELLES

Sin lies only in hurting others unnecessarily. All other 'sins' are invented nonsense.
ROBERT A. HEINLEIN

Everything that used to be a sin is now a disease.
BILL MAHER

Size

There is always something larger or smaller.
ANAXAGORAS A Presocratic who helped develop atomic theory and made the first scientific study of the sun, planets and other celestial bodies.

To make us feel small in the right way is a function of art; men can only make us feel small in the wrong way.
E. M. FORSTER

There is no big man who has not felt small. Some men never feel small; but these are the few men who are.
G. K. CHESTERTON

If you think you are too small to be effective, you have never been in bed with a mosquito.
BETTY REESE A popular one-off quote from an obscure source. She is often listed as an American officer and pilot, but the only one we could find was the Pilot Club chaplain in Mount Pleasant, Texas. Not impossible, and nor is the painter from Pennsylvania but we like the idea it was the drop-dead gorgeous PR director for design giants Raymond Loewy in the 1950s who commissioned a tiny but influential A-frame beachfront house in the Hamptons in 1956.

Enjoy the little things, for one day you may look back and realize they were the big things.
ROBERT BRAULT

Worry gives a small thing a big shadow.
SWEDISH PROVERB

University politics are vicious precisely because the stakes are so small.
HENRY KISSINGER

Sleep

Sleep is the only source of invention.
MARCEL PROUST

Sleep is the cousin of death.
CONGOLESE PROVERB

A sleeping child gives me the impression of a traveller in a very far country.
RALPH WALDO EMERSON

Sleep is no mean art: for its sake one must stay awake all day.
FRIEDRICH NIETZSCHE

Decency must be an even more exhausting state to maintain than its opposite. Those who succeed seem to need a stupefying amount of sleep.
QUENTIN CRISP

I have left orders to be awakened at any time in case of national emergency, even if I'm in a cabinet meeting.
RONALD REAGAN

Smell

Smell is the sense of memory and desire.
JEAN-JACQUES ROUSSEAU

I cannot smell mothballs because it's so difficult to get their little legs apart.
STEVE MARTIN

There are seventy-five perfumes, which it is very necessary that a criminal expert should be able to distinguish from each other.
SIR ARTHUR CONAN DOYLE From *The Hound of the Baskervilles* (1902), in which Sherlock Holmes identifies a woman from the scent of her notepaper.

Praise is like ambergris; a little whiff of it, by snatches, is very agreeable; but when a man holds a whole lump of it to his nose, it is a stink and strikes you down.
ALEXANDER POPE

Money has no smell.
EMPEROR VESPASIAN *Pecunia non olet*. Said when quashing an objection to a tax on urine.

Smoking

A custom loathsome to the eye, hateful to the nose, harmful to the brain, dangerous to the lungs, and the black stinking fume thereof nearest resembling the horrible Stygian smoke of the pit that is bottomless!
KING JAMES I OF ENGLAND

If you will study the history of almost any criminal, you will find he is an inveterate cigarette smoker.
HENRY FORD

To me, cigarettes are food.
FRANK ZAPPA

If smoking is not allowed in heaven, I shall not go.
MARK TWAIN

It was a really nice picture, but I happened to be smoking a cigarette. Now I'm being blamed not only for anorexia but for lung cancer.
KATE MOSS Famous for launching waif-chic in the 1990s. The quote dates from an interview with *People* magazine in 1996, but the precise photograph is hard to pin down (there are so many). A decade late she remains a defiant chain-smoker: 'I won't be quitting the fags because it's who I am,' she told *Now* magazine in July 2008.

I have every sympathy with the American who was so horrified by what he had read of the effects of smoking that he gave up reading.
HENRY STRAUSS, LORD CONESFORD

Snowflakes

How full of the creative genius is the air in which these are generated! I should hardly admire more if real stars fell and lodged on my coat.
HENRY DAVID THOREAU

An avalanche begins with a snowflake.
JOSEPH COMPTON

No snowflake in an avalanche ever feels responsible.
STANIS?AW LEC Often attributed to Voltaire or American comedian George Burns, this is first recorded in Lec's 1964 *More Unkempt Thoughts*.

The most delightful advantage of being bald – one can hear snowflakes.
R. G. DANIELS Attributed to an otherwise forgotten, presumably bald, English magistrate in the *Observer*'s 'Sayings of the Week' on 11 July 1976.

Solitude

Our language has wisely sensed the two sides of being alone. It has created the word loneliness to express the pain of being alone. And it has created the word solitude to express the glory of being alone.
PAUL TILLICH

Conversation enriches the understanding, but solitude is the school of genius; and the uniformity of a work denotes the hand of a single artist.
EDWARD GIBBON

No man ever will unfold the capacities of his own intellect who does not at least chequer his life with solitude.
THOMAS DE QUINCEY

One can acquire everything in solitude except character.
STENDHAL

Solitude is dangerous to reason, without being favourable to virtue.
SAMUEL JOHNSON

The man who goes alone can start today; but he who travels with another must wait till that other is ready.
HENRY DAVID THOREAU

Sorrow

It is foolish to tear one's hair in grief, as though sorrow would be made less with baldness.
CICERO

Grief is the agony of an instant; the indulgence of grief the blunder of a lifetime.
BENJAMIN DISRAELI

Sadness is almost never anything but a form of fatigue.
ANDRÉ GIDE

There are few sorrows, however poignant, in which a good income is of no avail.
LOGAN PEARSALL SMITH

I can't think of any sorrow in the world that a hot bath wouldn't help, just a little bit.
SUSAN GLASPELL Shamefully neglected winner of the Pulitzer for her play *Alison's House* in 1930. She survives on the web mostly through this quote from her 1911 novel, *The Visioning*, although it is usually credited to 'Susan Glasee', probably a misprint.

Sorrow happens, hardship happens, the hell with it, who never knew the price of happiness, will not be happy.
YEVGENY YEVTUSHENKO

You cannot prevent the birds of sorrow from flying over your head, but you can prevent them from building nests in your hair.
CHINESE PROVERB

Most people live dejectedly in worldly joys or sorrows. They sit on the sidelines and do not join in the dance.
SØREN KIERKEGAARD

Soul

The soul is the mirror of an indestructible universe.
GOTTFRIED LEIBNIZ

When we can drain the Ocean into mill-ponds, and bottle up the Force of Gravity, to be sold by retail, in gas jars; then may we hope to comprehend the infinitudes of man's soul.
THOMAS CARLYLE

The soul is the wife of the body. They do not have the same kind of pleasure or, at least, they seldom enjoy it at the same time.
PAUL VALÉRY

The pagan soul is like a bird fluttering about in the gloom, beating against the windows when all the time the doors are open to the air and sun.
EVELYN WAUGH

Frisbeetarianism is the belief that when you die, your soul goes up on the roof and gets stuck.
GEORGE CARLIN

Sound

The flat sound of my wooden clogs on the cobblestones, deep, hollow and powerful, is the note I seek in my painting.
PAUL GAUGUIN

Isn't it interesting how the sounds are the same for an awful nightmare and great sex?
RUE McCLANAHAN

The temple bell stops but I still hear the sound coming out of the flowers.
BASHO

Because half a dozen grasshoppers under a fern make the field ring with their importunate chink, while thousands of cattle, reposed beneath the shadow of the British oak, chew the cud and are silent, pray do not imagine that those who make the noise are the only inhabitants of the field.
EDMUND BURKE

Space

Six specks of dust inside Waterloo Station represent – or rather over-represent – the extent to which space is crowded with stars.
SIR JAMES JEANS

What is it that haunts space where matter is found?
ARTHUR EDDINGTON

Interestingly, according to modern astronomers, space is finite. This is a very comforting thought – particularly for people who cannot remember where they left things.
WOODY ALLEN

Space isn't remote at all. It's only an hour's drive away if your car could go straight upwards.
SIR FRED HOYLE Iconoclastic Yorkshire-born scientist, best remembered for naming the Big Bang theory (though he refused to accept it, preferring his own 'steady state' model). He also first proposed that all the chemical elements were produced from the helium and hydrogen in stars, which is now widely accepted, and that life evolved in space, which isn't.

Speech

It is impossible to speak in such a way that you cannot be misunderstood.
KARL POPPER

The voice of the dolphin in the air is like that of the human in that they can pronounce vowels and combinations of vowels, but have difficulties with the consonants.
ARISTOTLE

People have to talk about something just to keep their voice boxes in working order so they'll have good voice boxes in case there's ever anything really meaningful to say.
KURT VONNEGUT JR

If everybody thought before they spoke, the silence would be deafening.
GEORGE BARZAN

A thing is not necessarily true because badly uttered, nor false because spoken magnificently.
SAINT AUGUSTINE

An artist cannot talk about his art any more than a plant can discuss horticulture.
JEAN COCTEAU

Many a time I have wanted to stop talking and find out what I really believed.
WALTER LIPPMANN

The trouble with talking too fast is you may say something you haven't thought of yet.
ANN LANDERS

Never speak more clearly than you can think.
JEREMY BERNSTEIN

Speeches

Be sincere; be brief; be seated.
FRANKLIN D. ROOSEVELT

I will be brief. Not nearly so brief as Salvador Dalí, who gave the world's shortest speech. He said, 'I will be so brief I have already finished' and sat down.
EDWARD O. WILSON

The secret of a good sermon is to have a good beginning and a good ending, then having the two as close together as possible.
GEORGE BURNS

If I am to speak ten minutes, I need a week for preparation; if fifteen minutes, three days; if half an hour, two days; if an hour, I am ready now.
WOODROW WILSON

Speed

There is more to life than increasing its speed.
MAHATMA GANDHI

Have you ever noticed? Anybody going slower than you is an idiot, and anyone going faster than you is a moron.
GEORGE CARLIN

Speed, which becomes a virtue when it is found in a horse, by itself has no advantages.
EL-GHAZALI

Don't look for speed in a cheap horse: be content if it neighs.
HAUSA PROVERB

Haste is good only for catching flies.
RUSSIAN PROVERB

People forget how fast you did a job, but they remember how well you did it.
GENERAL GEORGE S. PATTON

Be not afraid of going slowly but only afraid of standing still.
CHINESE PROVERB

Anything worth doing is worth doing slowly.
MAE WEST

Spirals

A circle is the reflection of eternity. It has no beginning and it has no end – and if you put several circles over each other, then you get a spiral.
MAYNARD J. KEENAN Enigmatic lead singer of indie rock bands Tool and A Perfect Circle, sometime stand-up comedian and friend of Bill Hicks, now mostly a recluse holed up at his Arizona vineyards, (one of which glories in the name Merkin).

The human mind always makes progress, but it is progress in spirals.
MADAME DE STAËL

This seems to be the law of progress in everything we do; it moves along a spiral rather than a perpendicular; we seem to be actually going out of the way, and yet it turns out that we were really moving upward all the time.
FRANCES E. WILLARD

Growth is a spiral process, doubling back on itself, reassessing and regrouping.
JULIA MARGARET CAMERON

The desires of the heart are as crooked as corkscrews.
W. H. AUDEN

Sports

There are only three real sports: bull-fighting, car racing and mountain climbing. All the others are mere games.
ERNEST HEMINGWAY

No one who has been brought up on the works of Beatrice Potter can understand, much less appreciate, a bull-fight.
H. V. MORTON

All I know most surely about morality and obligations, I owe to football.
ALBERT CAMUS

Baseball is like church. Many attend, few understand.
LEO DUROCHER

Hockey is a sport for white men. Basketball is a sport for black men. Golf is a sport for white men dressed like black pimps.
TIGER WOODS

It is impossible to imagine Goethe or Beethoven being good at billiards or golf.
H. L. MENCKEN

There are six million shots in the game of pool.
ALBERT EINSTEIN

I thought tennis had had enough of manners.
JOHN McENROE

It always pays to get your retaliation in first.
WILLIE JOHN McBRIDE

Deerstalking would be a very fine sport if only the deer had guns.
W. S. GILBERT

Football combines the worst features of American life. It is violence punctuated by committee meetings.
GEORGE WILL

Serious sport has nothing to do with fair play. It is bound up with hatred, jealousy, boastfulness, disregard of all rules and sadistic

pleasure in witnessing violence: in other words it is war minus the shooting.
GEORGE ORWELL

A Chicago alderman once confessed he needed physical exercise but didn't like jogging, because in that sport you couldn't hit anyone.
ANDREW H. MALCOLM

It's not the winning that counts, nor the taking part; it's making fun of the little fat kid who always comes in last.
MATTHEW HANSEN

Stars

The stars are majestic laboratories, gigantic crucibles, such as no chemist could dream.
HENRI POINCARÉ Enigmatic mathematician who believed intuition was more important to his work than logic. He paved the way for Einstein's work on relativity but also had a practical side, working as a mining engineer and helping to introduce the international system of time zones.

It may be that the stars of heaven appear fair and pure simply because they are so far away from us, and we know nothing of their private life.
HEINRICH HEINE

Set your course by the stars, not by the lights of every passing ship.
GENERAL OMAR BRADLEY

When it is darkest, men see the stars.
RALPH WALDO EMERSON

Stories

There are only two or three human stories, and they go on repeating themselves as fiercely as if they had never happened before; like the larks in this country, that have been singing the same five notes over for thousands of years.
WILLA CATHER

A tale, fictitious or otherwise, illuminates truth.
RUMI

Everything is held together with stories. That is all that is holding us together, stories and compassion.
BARRY LOPEZ

The universe is made of stories, not of atoms.
MURIEL RUKEYSER Radical teacher, political activist and bisexual, her most
famous work, *The Book of the Dead,* was a sequence inspired by West Virginian
miners suffering from silicosis. She was a mentor to novelist Alice Walker and über-
feminist Andrea Dworkin worked as her assistant.

It's precisely the disappointing stories, which have no proper ending
and therefore no proper meaning, that sound true to life.
MAX FRISCH

Strangeness

We have found a strange footprint on the shores of the unknown. We
have devised profound theories, one after another, to account for its
origin. At last we have succeeded in reconstructing the creature that
made the footprint. And lo! It is our own.
SIR ARTHUR EDDINGTON

I know that queer things happen in this world. It's one of the few things
I've really learnt in my life.
LUDWIG WITTGENSTEIN

Though a good deal is too strange to be believed, nothing is too
strange to have happened.
THOMAS HARDY

Congratulate yourselves if you have done something strange and
extravagant and broken the monotony of a decorous age.
RALPH WALDO EMERSON

I am not strange, I am just not normal.
SALVADOR DALÍ

Statistics

I abhor averages. I like the individual case. A man may have six meals
one day and none the next, making an average of three meals per day,
but that is not a good way to live.
LOUIS D. BRANDEIS

I always find that statistics are hard to swallow and impossible to
digest. The only one I can ever remember is that if all the people who
go to sleep in church were laid end to end they would be a lot more
comfortable.
MRS ROBERT A. TAFT

Statistics are like bikinis. What they reveal is suggestive, but what they conceal is vital.
AARON LEVENSTEIN

Statistics are like prisoners under torture: with the proper tweaking you can get them to confess to anything.
JOHN ROTHCHILD

While the individual man is an insoluble puzzle, in the aggregate he becomes a mathematical certainty. You can, for example, never foretell what any one man will be up to, but you can say with precision what an average number will be up to. Individuals vary, but percentages remain constant. So says the statistician.
SIR ARTHUR CONAN DOYLE

Before the curse of statistics fell upon mankind we lived a happy, innocent life, full of merriment and go and informed by fairly good judgment.
HILAIRE BELLOC

I could prove God statistically. Take the human body alone – the chances that all the functions of an individual would just happen is a statistical monstrosity.
GEORGE GALLUP

. . . gentlemen who use MSS as drunkards use lamp-posts – not to light them on their way but to dissimulate their instability.
A. E. HOUSMAN This is the original quote from the acerbic introduction to his 1903 translation of a minor first-century Roman poet, Marcus Manilius. A very similar version is attributed to the folklorist Andrew Lang, with the slightly snappier substitution of 'more for support than illumination' as the final pay-off. It's possible Lang adopted it from Housman, but it has, anyway, become 'the' statistics quote, adapted by H. L. Mencken and David Ogilvy, the advertising guru, and pretty much anyone else who wants to sound smart on the subject.

Do not put your faith in what statistics say until you have carefully considered what they do not say.
WILLIAM W. WATT

Stupidity

The two most abundant things in the universe are hydrogen and stupidity.
HARLAN ELLISON

There is more stupidity than hydrogen in the universe, and it has a longer shelf life.
FRANK ZAPPA

The fine flower of stupidity blossoms in the attempt to appear less stupid.
GEOFFREY MADAN Among quote-junkies, his urbane, ironic, endlessly surprising *Notebooks* are a holy text. A brilliant Etonian classicist and Balliol man, he survived the First World War, but the world his collection evokes did not. Which is a huge part of its melancholic charm.

Flaubert discovered stupidity. I daresay this is the greatest discovery of a century so proud of its scientific thought . . . more important for the future of the world than the most startling ideas of Marx or Freud. For we can imagine the world without the class struggle or psychoanalysis, but not without the irresistible flood of received ideas that – programmed into computers, propagated by the mass media – threaten soon to become a force that will crush all original and individual thought.
MILAN KUNDERA

There is no idea so stupid that you can't get some professor to believe it.
H. L. MENCKEN

Only two things are infinite – the universe and human stupidity, and I'm not sure about the universe.
ALBERT EINSTEIN

We are all born ignorant, but one must work hard to remain stupid.
BENJAMIN FRANKLIN

The greatest lesson in life is to know that even fools are right sometimes.
WINSTON CHURCHILL

He may look like an idiot and talk like an idiot but don't let that fool you. He really is an idiot.
GROUCHO MARX

Style

Style that shows is only decorating.
SIDNEY LUMET

Style is a natural thing and has nothing to do with taste.
DAVID BAILEY

Many intelligent people, when about to write books, force on their minds a certain notion about style, just as they screw up their faces when they sit for their portraits.
G. C. LICHTENBERG

Style is the way in which a man *can*, by taking thought, add to his stature. It is the only way.
QUENTIN CRISP

Success

Success is 99 per cent failure.
SOICHIRO HONDA

Success is the ability to go from one failure to another with no loss of enthusiasm.
WINSTON CHURCHILL

A long apprenticeship is the most logical way to success. The only alternative is overnight stardom, but I can't give you a formula for that.
CHET ATKINS

People in their handlings of affairs often fail when they are about to succeed. If one remains as careful at the end as he was at the beginning, there will be no failure.
LAOZI (LAO-TZU)

All you need in this life is ignorance and confidence; then success is sure.
MARK TWAIN

Let me tell you the secret that has led me to my goal. My strength lies solely in my tenacity.
LOUIS PASTEUR

The secret of success is constancy of purpose.
BENJAMIN DISRAELI

To know how to wait is the great secret of success.
JOSEPH MARIE DE MAISTRE

The secret of success is to know something nobody else knows.
ARISTOTLE ONASSIS

There's no secret about success. Did you ever know a successful man who didn't tell you about it?
FRANK 'KIN' HUBBARD

The penalty of success is to be bored by the people who used to snub you.
LADY ASTOR The first serving woman MP in Westminster. Anti-semitic, a committed Christian Scientist, she was frequently an embarrassment to the Tory party: her exchanges with Churchill are legendary. Referred to during World War II as the 'member for Berlin', she coined the term 'D-Day dodgers' for the British troops in Italy, later the title of a bitterly sarcastic song.

Success is a beast. And it actually puts the emphasis on the wrong thing. You get away with more instead of looking within.
BRAD PITT

The higher a monkey climbs, the more you see of its behind.
GENERAL JOSEPH W. STILWELL

It is only at the tree loaded with fruit that people throw stones.
FRENCH PROVERB

Success is how high you bounce when you hit bottom.
GENERAL GEORGE S.PATTON

Success is dangerous. One begins to copy oneself, and to copy oneself is more dangerous than to copy others. It leads to sterility.
PABLO PICASSO

Each success only buys an admission ticket to a more difficult problem.
HENRY KISSINGER

Many a man owes his success to his first wife and his second wife to his success.
JIM BACKUS

Three keys to success: read, read, read.
LENIN

Whom the gods wish to destroy, they first call promising.
CYRIL CONNOLLY

If at first you don't succeed, well, so much for skydiving.
VICTOR O'REILLY Tough Irish ex-Marine who has built up a reputation as an expert on counter-terrorism and author of violent, fast-paced action thrillers.

Everything you see, I owe to spaghetti.
SOPHIA LOREN

Success to me is having ten honeydew melons and eating only the top half of each one.
BARBRA STREISAND

I don't know the key to success, but the key to failure is trying to please everybody.
BILL COSBY

A man is a success if he gets up in the morning and gets to bed at night, and in between he does what he wants to do.
BOB DYLAN

The toughest thing about success is that you've got to keep on being a success.
IRVING BERLIN

The common idea that success spoils people by making them vain, egotistic and self-complacent is erroneous; on the contrary, it makes them for the most part humble, tolerant and kind. Failure makes people cruel and bitter.
W. SOMERSET MAUGHAM

Try not to become a man of success, but rather try to become a man of value.
ALBERT EINSTEIN

The logic of worldly success rests on a fallacy, the strange error that our perfection depends on the thoughts and opinions and applause of other men. A weird life it is to be living always in somebody else's imagination, as if that were the only place in which one could become real.
THOMAS MERTON

The road to success is always under construction.
ARNOLD PALMER

Success is simply a matter of luck. Ask any failure.
EARL WILSON

Our business in life is not to succeed, but to continue to fail in good spirits.
ROBERT LOUIS STEVENSON

The measure of success is not whether you have a tough problem to deal with, but whether it's the same problem you had last year.
JOHN FOSTER DULLES

Nothing recedes like success.
WALTER WINCHELL

There are moments when everything goes well; don't be frightened, it
won't last.
JULES RENARD

If at first you don't succeed, try again. Then quit. No sense being a
damn fool about it.
W. C. FIELDS

Is there anything in life so disenchanting as attainment?
ROBERT LOUIS STEVENSON

Suffering

Most people get a fair amount of fun out of their lives, but on balance
life is suffering, and only the very young or the very foolish imagine
otherwise.
GEORGE ORWELL

Although the world is full of suffering, it is also full of the overcoming
of suffering.
HELEN KELLER

A man will renounce any pleasures you like, but he will not give up his
suffering.
G. I. GURDJIEFF Charismatic mystic who believed meditation, self-denial and
study were inadequate as routes to self-knowledge and incorporated music and
dancing into his own practice. He also believed most people lived in trance, barely
alive, and that this could only be broken by – in a much abused phrase – 'doing work
on oneself'.

People themselves suffer, and they fight tooth and nail against
admitting this even to themselves, let alone others. They act – this is
the point of their disguises – as if they do not suffer.
KARL BARTH

You think your pains and heartbreaks are unprecedented in the history
of the world, but then you read. It was books that taught me that the
things that tormented me were the very things that connected me with
all the people who were alive, or who have ever been alive.
JAMES BALDWIN

Nothing can work me damage except myself; the harm that I sustain I carry about with me, and never am a real sufferer but by my own fault.
SAINT BERNARD OF CLAIRVAUX

Only through suffering can we find ourselves.
FYODOR DOSTOEVSKY

Nothing happens to anybody which they are not fitted by nature to bear.
MARCUS AURELIUS

I know God will not give me anything I can't handle. I just wish He didn't trust me so much.
MOTHER TERESA

Suicide

I am the founder of the Samaritans. I am the only man in the world who cannot commit suicide.
ROBERT SOUTHEY

If you think nobody cares if you're alive, try missing a couple of car payments.
EARL WILSON

The chief consolation for Nature's shortcomings in regard to man is that not even God can do all things. For he cannot, even should he so wish, commit suicide, which is the greatest advantage he has given man among all the great drawbacks of life.
PLINY THE ELDER

The Bible doesn't forbid suicide. It's Catholic directive, intended to slow down their loss of martyrs.
ELLEN BLACKSTONE

It is cowardly to commit suicide. The English often kill themselves. It is a malady caused by the humid climate.
NAPOLEON BONAPARTE

There are many who dare not kill themselves for fear of what the neighbours will say.
CYRIL CONNOLLY

Hemingway shot himself. I don't like a man that takes the short way home.
WILLIAM FAULKNER

He is a little man in every way, for whom there are many reasons for
departing from life.
EPICURUS

In spite of all one hears to the contrary, the act of suicide requires a
certain courage of conviction or despair of which few persons are
capable.
PEARL S. BUCK The first American woman to win the Nobel Prize for Literature,
Buck was born and raised in China to a missionary family, learning English as a
second language. Her epic 1931 novel of life in pre-revolutionary China, *The Good
Earth*, also won her the Pulitzer Prize and was recently back in the best-seller lists
after being plugged by Oprah Winfrey.

A suicide kills two people, Maggie, that's what it's for!
ARTHUR MILLER

The thought of suicide is a great consolation: with the help of it one
has got through many a bad night.
FRIEDRICH NIETZSCHE

A man's dying is more the survivor's affair than his own.
THOMAS MANN

Superstition

Depend on the rabbit's foot if you will, but remember: it didn't work for
the rabbit.
R. E. SHAY

Of course I don't believe in it. But I understand that it brings you luck
whether you believe in it or not.
NIELS BOHR On a horseshoe nailed to his wall.

Surprise

The first step is always to succeed in becoming surprised – to notice
that there is something funny going on.
DAVID GELERNTER

Statistically, the probability of any one of us being here is so small that
you'd think the mere fact of existing would keep us all in a contented
dazzlement of surprise.
LEWIS THOMAS

No surprise in the writer, no surprise in the reader.
ROBERT FROST

Explanation separates us from astonishment, which is the only gateway to the incomprehensible.
EUGENE IONESCO

The secret of humour is surprise.
ARISTOTLE

T

Taste

Taste is the feminine of genius.
EDWARD FITZGERALD

Truffles are globose, whatever that is – brown, black, sandy, and warty.
The taste of truffles has been likened variously to that of strawberries,
garlic, flannel, and unclassified.
WILL CUPPY

Those . . . from whom Nature has withheld the legacy of taste have
long faces, and long eyes and noses; whatever their height there is
something elongated in their proportions. Their hair is dark and
unglossy, and they are never plump; it was they who invented trousers.
JEAN-ANTHELME BRILLAT-SAVARIN The original gastronome, his endlessly
quotable *The Physiology of Taste* was written as he was dying in 1825. It is an epicurean
hymn to food and the virtues of a discriminating palate, stuffed with anecdotes,
aphorisms and culinary one-liners. The classic translation into English by M. F. K.
Fisher in 1949 brought him a huge new audience in the English-speaking world.

Taste is not only a part and index of morality, it is the only morality.
The first, and last, and closest trial question to any living creature is
'What do you like?' Tell me what you like, I'll tell you what you are.
JOHN RUSKIN

Tea

Tea is not like vodka, which you can drink a lot of.
RUSSIAN SAYING

Where there's tea there's hope.
SIR ARTHUR WING PINERO

I always fear that creation will expire before teatime.
SYDNEY SMITH

We had a kettle; we let it leak:
Our not repairing made it worse.

We haven't had any tea for a week . . .
The bottom is out of the Universe.
RUDYARD KIPLING

If a man has no tea in him, he is incapable of understanding truth and
beauty.
JAPANESE PROVERB

The perfect temperature for tea is two degrees hotter than just right.
TERRI GUILLEMETS Pen-name for the creator of 'The Quote Garden' website
(guillemets are angled quotation marks: << >>).

Nobody can teach you how to make the perfect cup of tea. It just
happens over time. Wearing cashmere helps, of course.
JILL DUPLEIX

Tea! Thou soft, thou sober, sage, and venerable liquid, thou innocent
pretence for bringing the wicked of both sexes together in a morning;
thou female tongue-running, smile-smoothing, heart-opening, wink-
tipping cordial, to whose glorious insipidity I owe the happiest
moment of my life, let me fall prostrate thus, and adore thee.
COLLEY CIBBER

The best quality tea must have creases like the leathern boot of Tartar
horsemen, curl like the dewlap of a mighty bullock, unfold like a mist
rising out of a ravine, gleam like a lake touched by a zephyr, and be wet
and soft like a fine earth newly swept by rain.
LU YU Born in what is now Hubei province in central China, Lu Yu, a former clown,
became known as the Sage of Tea for his book, *The Classic of Tea*, written between
AD 760 and 780. As well as being the first book written on tea, combining practical
hints on growing and preparation, it is also a semi-religious text meditation which
sees the beverage as a reflection of the essential harmony of the Universe.

The hot water is to remain upon it no longer than whiles you can say
the Miserere Psalm very leisurely.
SIR KENELM DIGBY *The Closet of Sir Kenelm Digby Opened* (1603) included this
recipe for tea with eggs. (Saying Psalm 50 aloud lasts two and a half to three minutes.)

Our trouble is that we drink too much tea. I see in this the slow revenge
of the Orient, which has diverted the Yellow River down our throats.
J. B. PRIESTLEY

Its proper use is to amuse the idle, and relax the studious, and dilute
the full meals of those who cannot use exercise, and will not use
abstinence.
SAMUEL JOHNSON

The old philosopher is still among us in the brown coat with the metal buttons and the shirt which ought to be at the wash, blinking, puffing, rolling his head, drumming with his fingers, tearing his meat like a tiger, and swallowing his tea in oceans.
THOMAS BABINGTON MACAULEY

I suppose no person ever enjoyed with more relish the infusion of that fragrant leaf than Johnson.
JAMES BOSWELL

Tea, though ridiculed by those who are naturally coarse in their nervous sensibilities will always be the favorite beverage of the intellectual.
THOMAS DE QUINCEY

Thank God for tea! What would the world do without tea? – how did it exist? I am glad I was not born before tea!
SYDNEY SMITH

Indeed, Madame, your ladyship is very sparing of your tea; I protest the last I took was no more than water bewitched.
JONATHAN SWIFT

Why do they always put mud into coffee on board steamers? Why does the tea generally taste of boiled boots?
WILLIAM MAKEPEACE THACKERAY

Is there no Latin word for Tea? Upon my soul, if I had known that I would have let the vulgar stuff alone.
HILAIRE BELLOC

Drink your tea slowly and reverently, as if it is the axis on which the world earth revolves – slowly, evenly, without rushing toward the future.
THICH NAT HAHN Founder in 1966 of the Order of Interbeing, and one of the most influential Buddhist teachers to operate in the West, he evolved the practice of 'Engaged Buddhism', which combines meditation and political action (all washed down with a nice cup of tea).

. . . it must be evident to every one that the practice of tea drinking must render the frame feeble, and unfit to encounter hard labour or severe weather . . . Hence succeeds a softness, an effeminacy, a seeking for the fireside, a lurking in the bed, and, in short, all the characteristics of idleness.
WILLIAM COBBETT

Meanwhile, let us have a sip of tea. The afternoon glow is brightening the bamboos, the fountains are bubbling with delight, the soughing of the pines is heard in our kettle. Let us dream of evanescence, and linger in the beautiful foolishness of things.
OKAKURA KAKUZO

Teachers

To be good is noble, but to teach others how to be good is nobler – and less trouble.
MARK TWAIN

The test of a good teacher is not how many questions he can ask his pupils that they will answer readily, but how many questions he inspires them to ask him which he finds it hard to answer.
ALICE WELLINGTON ROLLINS Mostly forgotten, she was a collector of aphorisms who lived in the elegant literary suburb of Bronxville. *Uncle Tom's Tenement* (1888) painted a shocking portrait of the poverty and hardship of life in New York, without the 'impracticable vaporing of Socialism'.

Any subject can be taught effectively in some intellectually honest way to any child at any stage of development.
JEROME BRUNER

Teaching is the process by which the notes of the professor become the notes of the student without passing through the mind of either.
ANONYMOUS Although often attributed to Woody Allen.

I taught Bill and Hillary Clinton when they were at Yale. Let me rephrase that. Bill and Hillary Clinton were in the room when I was teaching at Yale.
JUDGE ROBERT H. BORK

We teachers can only help the work going on, as servants wait upon a master.
MARIA MONTESSORI

A schoolmaster should have an atmosphere of awe, and walk wonderingly, as if he was amazed at being himself.
WALTER BAGEHOT

To teach is to learn twice.
JOSEPH JOUBERT

I am indebted to my father for living, but to my teacher for living well.
ALEXANDER THE GREAT

Math was always my bad subject. I couldn't convince my teachers that many of my answers were meant ironically.
CALVIN TRILLIN

A poor surgeon hurts one person at a time. A poor teacher hurts 130.
ERNEST BOYER

One looks back with appreciation to the brilliant teachers, but with gratitude to those who touched our human feelings. The curriculum is so much necessary raw material, but warmth is the vital element for the growing plant and for the soul of the child.
CARL JUNG

Technology

Technology is the knack of arranging the world so that we don't have to experience it.
MAX FRISCH

Where there is the necessary technical skill to move mountains, there is no need for the faith that moves mountains.
ERIC HOFFER

We live in a society exquisitely dependent on science and technology, in which hardly anyone knows anything about science and technology.
CARL SAGAN

For a list of all the ways technology has failed to improve the quality of life, please press three.
ALICE KAHN

It is a mistake to believe that any technological innovation has a one-sided effect. Every technology is both a burden and a blessing: neither either-or, but this-and-that.
NEIL POSTMAN

The technology of hay was unknown to the Roman Empire but was known to every village of medieval Europe. Like many other crucially important technologies, hay emerged anonymously during the so-called Dark Ages.
FREEMAN DYSON

The factory of the future will have only two employees, a man and a dog. The man will be there to feed the dog. The dog will be there to stop the man touching the equipment.
WARREN BENNIS Best known for inventing leadership studies as a major discipline and as a pioneer of the flatter, less hierarchical organisation.

Television

You have put something in my room which will never let me forget
how strange is this world – and how unknown.
RAMSAY MACDONALD To John Logie Baird after a demonstration of television at
10 Downing Street in 1930.

The television set in American homes is like the toaster. You press a
button and the same thing pops out almost every time.
ALFRED HITCHCOCK

Watching television is like taking black spray paint to your third eye.
BILL HICKS

In Russia, we had only two channels. Channel One was propaganda.
Channel Two consisted of a KGB officer telling you: 'Turn back at once
to Channel One.'
YAKOV SMIRNOFF

Television is the first truly democratic culture – the first culture
available to everybody and entirely governed by what the people want.
The most terrifying thing is what people do want.
CLIVE BARNES

I know exactly what the people want, and I'm damned if I'm going to
give it to them.
LORD REITH

Dealing with network executives is like being nibbled to death by ducks.
ERIC SEVAREID Originally a war correspondent working for the legendary Ed
Murrow of CBS, he became a roving reporter and master interviewer, at one point
finding himself on the wrong end of McCarthy's anti-communist witch-hunt. His
brief 'thinkpieces' on Walter Cronkite's CBS evening news broadcasts led to his
nickname, the 'Grey Eminence'.

Theories

We've formed many a theory and belief, but as we look about the
human world, it is clear that nobody actually knows what's going on.
Yet claims to Truth are being made at every hand, including the claim
that there is no Truth.
STEVE HAGEN

In theory, there is no difference between theory and practice. But, in
practice, there is.
JAN L. A. VAN DE SNEPSCHEUT

A theory is the more impressive the greater the simplicity of its premises, the more different kinds of things it relates, and the more extended its area of applicability.
ALBERT EINSTEIN

There are many examples of old, incorrect theories that stubbornly persisted, sustained only by the prestige of foolish but well-connected scientists. Many of these theories have been killed off only when some decisive experiment exposed their incorrectness. Thus the yeoman work in any science, and especially physics, is done by the experimentalist, who must keep the theoreticians honest.
MICHIO KAKU

It is also a good rule not to put overmuch confidence in the observational results that are put forward until they are confirmed by theory.
SIR ARTHUR EDDINGTON

There are only forty people in the world, and five of them are hamburgers.
CAPTAIN BEEFHEART

That theory is worthless. It isn't even wrong.
WOLFGANG PAULI Famous perfectionist, known by his colleagues as 'the conscience of physics' because of his rigour, this famous remark was prompted by a student paper. 'Not even wrong' is a very succinct statement of the key principle of 'falsifiability', which many consider to be the essential precondition of scientific truth (i.e., if you can't test a theory, you can't claim it as true).

Things

The aspects of things that are most important to us are hidden because of their simplicity and familiarity.
LUDWIG WITTGENSTEIN

Sometimes when I consider what tremendous consequences come from little things, I am tempted to think there are no little things.
BRUCE BARTON Ad man (he co-founded BBDO), Republican congressman, implacable opponent of the New Deal and best-selling self-help author, credited with naming both General Motors and General Electric.

The world is made up of facts, not things.
LUDWIG WITTGENSTEIN

There are no things, only processes.
DAVID BOHM

I don't paint things. I only paint the difference between things.
HENRI MATISSE

I do not believe in things. I believe only in their relationships.
GEORGES BRAQUE

Thinking

It is a profoundly erroneous truism, repeated by all copy books and by eminent people when they are making speeches, that we should cultivate the habit of thinking what we are doing. The precise opposite is the case. Civilisation advances by extending the number of important operations which we can perform without thinking about them.
A. N. WHITEHEAD

I think people have had too much to think and ought to flex their magic muscles.
CAPTAIN BEEFHEART

Don't think. Thinking is the enemy of creativity. It's self-conscious, and anything self-conscious is lousy. You can't try to do things. You simply must do things.
RAY BRADBURY

You don't think thoughts any more than you hear hearing or smell smelling.
ALAN WATTS

The trouble with most people is that they think with their hopes or fears or wishes rather than with their minds.
WILL DURANT

Isn't it strange that we talk least about the things we think about most?
CHARLES A. LINDBERGH

The highest stage in moral culture at which we can arrive is when we recognise that we ought to control our thoughts.
CHARLES DARWIN

Thought is only a flash between two long nights, but this flash is everything.
HENRI POINCARÉ

Thinking is the crest of deep physical turbulence rushing from a point

of original unity at the beginning of the universe. It is a product of the same motility and physical processes that created galaxies. When one thinks clearly about thinking, one is present at the first instant of time.
EDGAR ALLAN POE His prose poem 'Eureka' (1848) first expressed the idea that all matter had once been concentrated into a single particle which then expanded to fill space, a theory not accepted by science until 1931. 'Eureka' goes on to predict the general theory of relativity, parallel universes and the structure of the atom. Pretty good going for a poem that doesn't rhyme.

It has been said that we have approximately 187,000 thoughts a day, 98 per cent of which we had the day before, and the day before that.
ARIEL AND SHYA KANE

A great many people think they are thinking when they are merely rearranging their prejudices.
WILLIAM JAMES

Intellectual blemishes, like facial ones, grow more prominent with age.
LA ROCHEFOUCAULD

Our thinking should have a vigorous fragrance, like a wheat field on a summer's night.
FRIEDRICH NIETZSCHE

The vitality of thought is in adventure. Ideas won't keep. Something must be done about them.
A. N. WHITEHEAD

We are no more responsible for the evil thoughts which pass through our minds, than a scarecrow for the birds which fly over the seed-plot he has to guard; the sole responsibility in each case is to prevent them from settling.
JOHN CHURTON COLLINS Edwardian who had an eye for the choice epigram. He died – of accidental causes – in a ditch.

Our most important thoughts are those which contradict our emotions.
PAUL VALÉRY

We are all capable of evil thoughts, but only very rarely evil deeds: we can all do good deeds, but very few of us can think good thoughts.
CESARE PAVESE

People do not like to think. If one thinks, one must reach conclusions. Conclusions are not always pleasant.
HELEN KELLER

I think and think for months and years. Ninety-nine times, the conclusion is false. The hundredth time I am right.
ALBERT EINSTEIN

Time

What then is time? If no one asks me, I know what it is. If I wish to explain it to him who asks, I do not know.
SAINT AUGUSTINE

The past is solid, the future is liquid.
J. L. AUBERT Philosophically minded distinctive lead singer of Téléphone, the greatest French group of the late seventies and early eighties (according to their official website).

There are many different opinions concerning the essence of time.
BLAISE PASCAL

It's a question of whether we're going to go forward into the future or past to the back.
DAN QUAYLE

So little time, so little to do.
OSCAR LEVANT

Eat the present moment and break the dish.
EGYPTIAN PROVERB

Time is a great teacher. Unfortunately, it kills all its pupils.
HECTOR BERLIOZ

What is time and what is its nature? Is it a being? Is it a non-being? Does it imply space? Does it insist on change? And what is its origin?
ARISTOTLE

Only in the present do things happen.
JORGE LUIS BORGES

It is common error to infer that things which are consecutive in order of time have necessarily the relation of cause and effect.
JACOB BIGELOW

Time is more valuable than money. You can get more money but you can't get more time.
JIM ROHN

Without music to decorate it, time is just a bunch of boring production

deadlines or dates by which bills must be paid.
FRANK ZAPPA

Most of us spend too much time on the last twenty-four hours and too little on the last six thousand years.
WILL DURANT

Who cannot give an account to himself of 3,000 years may remain in darkness and inexperience and live but from day to day.
GOETHE

I'm a visionary; I'm ahead of my time. Trouble is, I'm only about an hour and a half ahead.
GEORGE CARLIN

Half our time is spent trying to find something to do with the time we have rushed through life trying to save.
WILL ROGERS

Love a girl with all your heart and kiss her on the mouth: then time will stop, and space will cease to exist.
ERWIN SCHRÖDINGER Nobel laureate in 1933, friend to Einstein and inventor of the most famous modern thought experiment, which demonstrated the strangeness of quantum processes inside the atom by comparing them to a cat inside a box, which, theoretically, could be both dead and alive simultaneously. His personal life was unconventional, too: he lived openly with two women for most of his adult life.

What we perceive as the present is nothing but the recent past tinged with a vivid fringe of anticipation.
A. N. WHITEHEAD

The world was made, not in time, but simultaneously with time. There was no time before the world.
SAINT AUGUSTINE

People like us, who believe in physics, know that the distinction between past, present and future is only a stubbornly persistent illusion.
ALBERT EINSTEIN

There exists only the present instant . . . a Now which always and without end is itself new. There is no yesterday nor any tomorrow, but only Now, as it was a thousand years ago and as it will be a thousand years hence.
MEISTER ECKHART

Time is not a road – it is a room.
JOHN FOWLES

Time is the meaning of life.
PAUL CLAUDEL

Now mark what I say. The Right Eye looketh forward in thee into Eternity. The Left Eye looketh backward into Time. If thou now sufferest thyself to be always looking into Nature and the Things of Time, it will be impossible for thee ever to arrive at the Unity which thou wishest for.
JAKOB BÖHME

For eternally and always there is only one now, one and the same now; the present is the only thing that has no end.
ERWIN SCHRÖDINGER

I went to a restaurant that serves 'breakfast at any time'. So I ordered French Toast during the Renaissance.
STEVEN WRIGHT

The time you enjoy wasting is not wasted time.
BERTRAND RUSSELL

Time is that which man is always trying to kill, but which ends in killing him.
HERBERT SPENCER

Tools

The finest workers in stone are not copper or steel tools, but the gentle touches of air and water working at their leisure with a liberal allowance of time.
HENRY DAVID THOREAU

The big artist . . . keeps an eye on nature and steals her tools.
THOMAS EAKINS

My own experience has been that the tools I need for my trade are paper, tobacco, food, and a little whisky.
WILLIAM FAULKNER

Towns

Aberdeen, a lazy town.
ROBERT BURNS

Bologna is celebrated for producing popes, painters, and sausage.
LORD BYRON

I wish I could think of just one nice thing I could tell you about Hull.
Oh yes . . . it's very nice and flat for cycling.
PHILIP LARKIN

Ipswich isn't twinned with anywhere, but it does have a suicide pact
with Grimsby.
KEN DODD

Venice is like eating an entire box of chocolate liqueurs at one go.
TRUMAN CAPOTE

I would like to live in Manchester, England. The transition between
Manchester and death would be unnoticeable.
MARK TWAIN

My cousin François and I are in perfect accord. He wants Milan, and so
do I.
CHARLES V, HOLY ROMAN EMPEROR François I, King of France, formed an
alliance with the Ottoman Turks against Charles to try and regain his former
possessions in Italy in 1536.

This day show that you are Boswell, a true soldier. Take your post.
Shake off sloth and spleen, and just proceed. Nobody knows your
conflicts. Be fixed as a Christian, and shun vice. Go not to Amsterdam.
JAMES BOSWELL

New York is a gothic Roquefort. San Francisco reminds me of a
romanesque Camembert.
SALVADOR DALÍ

If Amsterdam or Leningrad vie for the title of Venice of the North, then
Venice – what compliment is high enough? Venice, with all her
civilisation and ancient beauty, Venice with her addiction to curious
aquatic means of transport, yes, my friends, Venice is the Henley of the
South.
BORIS JOHNSON

Travel

Peculiar travel suggestions are dancing lessons from God.
KURT VONNEGUT

Travel makes a wise man better but a fool worse.
THOMAS FULLER

If you board the wrong train, it is no use running along the corridor in
the opposite direction.
DIETRICH BONHOEFFER One of the leaders of the Christian resistance to the
Nazis. In 1943 he was arrested for participating in an intelligence plot to kill Hitler.
He was tortured and brutally executed at Flossenbürg concentration camp in April
1945, just a fortnight before it was liberated.

Modern travelling is not travelling at all; it is merely being sent to a
place, and very little different from becoming a parcel.
JOHN RUSKIN

Sooner or later we must realize there is no station, no one place to
arrive at once and for all. The true joy of life is the trip.
ROBERT J. HASTINGS

Do not require a description of the countries to which you sail.
RALPH WALDO EMERSON

No travel writer I have ever known has written about the importance of
parking.
J. G. BALLARD

The further one travels, the less one knows.
LAOZI (LAO-TZU)

A sure cure for seasickness is to sit under a tree.
SPIKE MILLIGAN

Treachery

Betrayal is the only truth that sticks.
ARTHUR MILLER

Anyone who hasn't experienced the ecstasy of betrayal knows nothing
about ecstasy at all.
JEAN GENET

A woman's best love letters are always written to the man she is betraying.
LAWRENCE DURRELL

All men should have a drop of treason in their veins, if nations are not
to go soft like so many sleepy pears.
REBECCA WEST

If I had to choose between betraying my country and betraying my
friend, I hope I should have the guts to betray my country.
E. M. FORSTER

In politics, it is necessary either to betray one's country or the electorate. I prefer to betray the electorate.
GENERAL DE GAULLE

Corporations cannot commit treason, or be outlawed or excommunicated, for they have no souls.
EDWARD COKE

The best way to keep your friends is not to give them away.
WILSON MIZNER As well as writing, he was a restaurateur, thief, boxing promoter, opium addict and master of the witty one-liner. He is the original source for the old saw: 'Be nice to people on the way up because you'll meet the same people on the way down.'

Trees

Except during the nine months before he draws his first breath, no man manages his affairs as well as a tree does.
GEORGE BERNARD SHAW

The wonder is that we can see these trees and not wonder more.
RALPH WALDO EMERSON

The clearest way into the universe is through a forest wilderness.
JOHN MUIR

For in the true nature of things, if we rightly consider, every green tree is far more glorious than if it were made of gold or silver.
MARTIN LUTHER

As the poet said, 'Only God can make a tree' – probably because it's so hard to figure out how to get the bark on.
WOODY ALLEN

Trees are poems that earth writes upon the sky,
We fell them down and turn them into paper,
That we may record our emptiness.
KAHLIL GIBRAN Lebanese but he grew up in Boston. His 1923 classic of spiritual verse, *The Prophet*, became a counterculture sensation in the 1960s. It was the second best-selling book of the twentieth century in America, narrowly beaten by the Bible.

Trees are much like human beings and enjoy each other's company. Only a few love to be alone.
JENS JENSEN

Trees cause more pollution than automobiles.
RONALD REAGAN

The tree which moves some to tears of joy is in the eyes of others only a green thing which stands in the way. As a man is, so he sees.
WILLIAM BLAKE

The best time to plant a tree was twenty years ago, the second best time is now.
CHINESE PROVERB

The creation of a thousand forests is in one acorn.
RALPH WALDO EMERSON

The planting of trees is the least self-centered of all that we can do. It is a purer act of faith than the procreation of children.
THORTON WILDER

When eating a fruit, think of the person who planted the tree.
VIETNAMESE PROVERB

The axe forgets what the tree remembers.
AMERICAN PROVERB

No tree falls on the first stroke.
GERMAN PROVERB

When a tree is falling, everyone cries, down with it!
ITALIAN PROVERB

When the big tree falls, the goat eats its leaves.
AFRICAN PROVERB

From a fallen tree, all make kindling.
SPANISH PROVERB

When the axe came into the forest the trees all said, 'Well, at least the handle is one of us.'
TURKISH PROVERB

In a moment the ashes are made, but the forest is a long time growing.
SENECA

Suburbia is where the developer bulldozes out the trees, then names streets after them.
BILL VAUGHAN

I like trees because they seem more resigned to the way they have to live than other things do.
WILLA CATHER

Trouble

Nobody, as long as he moves about among the chaotic currents of life, is without trouble.

CARL JUNG

If you will call your troubles experiences, and remember that every experience develops some latent force within you, you will grow vigorous and happy, however adverse your circumstances may seem to be.

JOHN R. MILLER Appointed senior adviser to the State Department on human trafficking in 2003, and until 2007, US Ambassador-at-large on the issue of modern slavery.

She would take any amount of trouble to avoid trouble.

WILLA CATHER

If I had a formula for bypassing trouble, I wouldn't pass it around. Wouldn't be doing anybody a favor. Trouble creates a capacity to handle it. I don't say embrace trouble. That's as bad as treating it as an enemy. But I do say, meet it as a friend, for you'll see a lot of it and had better be on speaking terms with it.

OLIVER WENDELL HOLMES

That's what stoicism is: the avoidance of bother when bother's the other option.

JONATHAN MEADES

Trust

Few things help an individual more than to place responsibility upon him and to let him know that you trust him.

BOOKER T. WASHINGTON Born into slavery, the first African American invited into the White House and the leading campaigner for civil rights and education for Black Americans in the early twentieth century. His best-selling autobiography, *Up from Slavery* (1901), is still widely taught and read.

Put not your trust in money, but put your money in trust.

OLIVER WENDELL HOLMES

Never trust a man who speaks well of everybody.

JOHN CHURTON COLLINS

Never trust a man who, when left alone in a room with a tea-cosy, doesn't try it on.

BILLY CONNOLLY

Truth

Nothing is too wonderful to be true.
MICHAEL FARADAY

The Truth shall make you free.
JOHN 8: 32

For ye shall know the truth, and the truth shall set you free.
MOTTO OF THE CIA The full verse from John 8:31–2 is: 'If ye continue in my word, then are ye my disciples indeed; And ye shall know the truth, and the truth shall make you free.' In context, Jesus was trying to explain why he wasn't going to lead a revolution to 'free' the Jews from the Roman yoke. His freedom was an inner state of grace, not something most of us associate with the CIA.

Ye shall know the truth, and the truth shall make you mad.
ALDOUS HUXLEY

There is nothing more likely to drive a man mad than an obstinate, constitutional preference for the true to the agreeable.
FREIDRICH NIETZSCHE

There are very few human beings who receive the truth, complete and staggering, by instant illumination. Most of them acquire it fragment by fragment, on a small scale, by successive developments, cellularly, like a laborious mosaic.
ANAÏS NIN

Truth is for the minority.
BALTASAR GRACIÁN Author of *The Art of Worldly Wisdom* (1637), a witty and influential collection of maxims, praised by Schopenhauer, Nietzsche and Churchill. When re-released in 1992, it spent several weeks on the US non-fiction best-seller lists.

Never tell the truth to those unworthy of it.
MARK TWAIN

There are no whole truths; all truths are half-truths. It is trying to treat them as whole truths that plays the devil.
A. N. WHITEHEAD

Truth is eternal, knowledge is changeable. It is disastrous to confuse them.
MADELEINE L'ENGLE

One must explore deep and believe the incredible to find the new particles of truth floating in an ocean of insignificance.
JOSEPH CONRAD

As scarce as the truth is, the supply has always been in excess of the demand.
JOSH BILLINGS

The exact contrary of what is generally believed is often the truth.
JEAN DE LA BRUYÈRE His satirical portraits of his contemporaries, *Caractères* (1688), brought him, in his own words, 'many readers and many enemies'. As a writer of pithy maxims, he is (almost) the equal of his contemporary, La Rochefoucauld.

In war, Truth is the first casualty.
AESCHYLUS

Who ever undertakes to set himself up as a judge of Truth and Knowledge is shipwrecked by the laughter of the Gods.
ALBERT EINSTEIN

No man is likely to have arrived at complete and final truth on any subject whatsoever.
BERTRAND RUSSELL

Truth always originates in a minority of one, and every custom begins as a broken precedent.
WILL DURANT

The high-minded man must care more for the truth than for what people think.
ARISTOTLE

Truth is the daughter of search.
ARABIC PROVERB

Truth is a woman. One must not use force with her.
FRIEDRICH NIETZSCHE

The smallest atom of truth represents some man's bitter toil and agony. For every ponderable chunk of it there is a brave truth-seeker's grave upon some lonely ash-dump and a soul roasting in hell.
H. L. MENCKEN

No pleasure is comparable to the standing upon the vantage-ground of truth.
FRANCIS BACON

None attains to the Degree of Truth until a thousand honest people have testified that he is a heretic.
JUNAID OF BAGHDAD Sufi and former wrestler. Sufism is based on three principles: *islam* (submission – of the non-wrestling kind), *iman* (faith) and *ishan* (to act 'beautifully' through awareness of God).

Do not seek to follow in the footsteps of men of old; seek what they
sought.
BASHO

There is nothing so powerful as truth – and often nothing so strange.
DANIEL WEBSTER

Why shouldn't truth be stranger than fiction? Fiction, after all, has to
make sense.
MARK TWAIN

There is no *a priori* reason for supposing that the truth, when it is
discovered, will necessarily prove interesting.
ISAIAH BERLIN

Give me fruitful error any time, full of seeds, bursting with its own
corrections. You can keep your sterile truth for yourself.
VILFREDO PARETO

To arrive at the simplest truth, as Newton knew and practised, requires
years of contemplation. Not activity. Not reasoning. Not calculating.
Not busy behaviour of any kind. Not reading. Not talking. Not making
an effort. Not thinking. Simply *bearing in mind* what it is one needs to
know.
GEORGE SPENCER BROWN

All truth passes through three stages. First, it is ridiculed. Second, it is
violently opposed. Third, it is accepted as being self-evident.
ARTHUR SCHOPENHAUER

If falsehood, like truth, had but one face, we would be more on equal
terms. For we would consider the contrary of what the liar said to be
certain. But the opposite of truth has a hundred thousand faces and an
infinite field.
MICHEL DE MONTAIGNE

Truth is the daughter of time, not of authority.
FRANCIS BACON

The terrible thing about the quest for truth is that you find it.
RÉMY DE GOURMONT

Follow not truth too near the heels, lest it dash out thy teeth.
GEORGE HERBERT

U

Ugliness

Ugliness is in a way superior to beauty because it lasts.
SERGE GAINSBOURG

Ugliness is a point of view: an ulcer is wonderful to a pathologist.
AUSTIN O'MALLEY Bacteriologist-turned-English professor and keen correspondent with two Popes, who helped develop the diptheria antitoxin and wrote several books of homilies, many of which have survived in quote books. In 1902 his wife poisoned him and eloped with a younger man. He survived, left his professorship and started a third career as a distinguished opthalmologist.

I hate ugliness. You know I'm allergic to ugliness.
IMELDA MARCOS

I never saw an ugly thing in my life.
JOHN CONSTABLE

I do not feel I have wisdom enough yet to love what is ugly.
STENDHAL

There is no such thing as an ugly woman. However, there is such a thing as not enough vodka.
RUSSIAN PROVERB

Umbrellas

I am a lone monk walking the world with a leaky umbrella.
MAO ZEDONG (MAO TSE-TUNG)

All men are equal – all men, that is to say, who possess umbrellas.
E. M. FORSTER

He was so benevolent, so merciful a man that, in his mistaken passion, he would have held an umbrella over a duck in a shower of rain.
DOUGLAS JERROLD

Umbrellas are not allowed in the Vatican since the Pope's staff broke into bloom.
OSCAR WILDE

The rain it raineth every day,
Upon the just and unjust feller,
But chiefly on the just because
The unjust has the just's umbrella.
LORD JUSTICE BOWEN

Understanding

My goal is simple. It is a complete understanding of the universe, why it is as it is and why it exists at all.
STEPHEN HAWKING

The mind that does not understand is the Buddha. There is no other.
MAZU (MA-TSU)

There is one purpose to life and one only: to bear witness to and understand as much as possible of the complexity of the world - its beauty, its mysteries, its riddles. The more you understand, the more you look, the greater is your enjoyment of life and your sense of peace. That's all there is to it.
ANNE RICE

Everything that irritates us about others can lead us to an understanding of ourselves.
CARL JUNG

All those who do not understand will be damned.
SAINT ATHANASIUS

The hardest thing in the world to understand is the income tax.
ALBERT EINSTEIN

The hardest thing to understand is why we can understand anything at all.
ALBERT EINSTEIN

If one is master of one thing and understands one thing well, one has insight into and understanding of many things.
VINCENT VAN GOGH

When I have clarified and exhausted a subject, then I turn away from it, in order to go into darkness again.
ISIDORE OF SEVILLE Compiler of the *Etymologies*, the first, biggest and most influential encyclopaedia of the Middle Ages, preserving much classical knowledge – including that the world was round – that would otherwise have been lost.

Only one man ever understood me, and he didn't understand me.
G. W. F. HEGEL

Universe

In the beginning the Universe was created. This has made a lot of people very angry and been widely regarded as a bad move.
DOUGLAS ADAMS

If you want to make an apple pie from scratch, you must first create the universe.
CARL SAGAN

Why does the universe go to all the bother of existing?
STEPHEN HAWKING

The effort to understand the universe is one of the very few things that lifts human life a little above the level of farce, and gives it some of the grace of tragedy.
STEPHEN WEINBERG

Every grain of sand, every tip of a leaf, even an atom, contains the entire universe. Conversely, the universe can be perceived as the tip of a leaf.
GERHARD STAGUHN

Not I but the world says it: All is one.
HERACLITUS

The All is alive.
THALES

Man is a piece of the universe made alive.
RALPH WALDO EMERSON

There's only one corner of the universe you can be certain of improving, and that's your own self.
ALDOUS HUXLEY

The ultimate stuff of the universe is mind stuff.
SIR ARTHUR EDDINGTON

The universe displays no proof of an all-directing mind.
AUGUSTE COMTE

There is nothing uncultivated, nothing sterile, nothing dead in the universe; there is no chaos, no confusion except in appearance.
GOFFFRIED LEIBNIZ

Now, my suspicion is that the universe is not only queerer than we suppose, but queerer than we can suppose... I suspect there are more things in heaven and earth than are dreamed of, in any philosophy.
J. B. S. HALDANE

What is the universe? Is it a great 3D movie in which we are the unwilling actors? Is it a cosmic joke, a giant computer, a work of art by a Supreme Being, or simply an experiment? The problem in trying to understand the universe is that we have nothing to compare it with.
HEINZ R. PAGELS Physicist and human rights advocate who wrote engagingly on the science of complexity. He died in a climbing accident in Colorado in 1988. He once wrote: 'Science shows us that the visible world is neither matter nor spirit; the visible world is the invisible organization of energy.'

It is not impossible that to some infinitely superior being the whole of the universe may be as one plain, the distance between planet and planet being only the pores in a grain of sand, and the spaces between systems no greater than the intervals between one grain and the grain adjacent.
SAMUEL TAYLOR COLERIDGE

Considered in its concrete reality, the stuff of the universe cannot divide itself but, as a kind of gigantic atom, it forms in its totality the only real indivisible.
PIERRE TEILHARD DE CHARDIN

The universe is so vast in relation to the matter it contains that it can be compared with a building twenty miles long, twenty miles wide and twenty miles high that contains a single grain of sand.
ISAAC ASIMOV

The universe ought to be presumed too vast to have any character.
CHARLES SANDERS PEIRCE

It's embarrassing that 90 per cent of the Universe is unaccounted for.
SIR MARTIN REES The British Astronomer Royal and leading astrophysicist who specialises in black holes. He's since refined this percentage: it's actually made of '4 per cent atoms, about 25 per cent dark matter, and 71 per cent mysterious dark energy latent in empty space'.

The universe: a device contrived for the perpetual astonishment of astronomers.
ARTHUR C. CLARKE

All places are alike . . . in the universe.
ALBERT EINSTEIN

It is true that we emerged in the universe by chance, but the idea of chance is itself only a cover for our ignorance. I do not feel like an alien in this universe. The more I examine the universe and the details of its architecture, the more evidence I find that the universe in some sense must have known that we were coming.
FREEMAN DYSON

We do not really 'come into' the world ; we come *out* of it, as leaves from a tree. As the ocean 'waves', the universe 'peoples'.
ALAN WATTS

There is a theory which states that if ever anyone discovers exactly what the Universe is for and why it is here, it will instantly disappear and be replaced by something even more bizarre and inexplicable. There is another theory which states that this has already happened.
DOUGLAS ADAMS

That the universe was formed by a fortuitous concourse of atoms, I will no more believe than that the accidental jumbling of the alphabet would fall into a most ingenious treatise of philosophy.
JONATHAN SWIFT

I do not pretend to understand the universe. It is a great deal bigger than I am.
TOM STOPPARD

V

Vegetables

The only carrots that interest me are the number you get in a diamond.
MAE WEST

A cucumber should be well sliced, and dressed with pepper and vinegar, and then thrown out as good for nothing.
SAMUEL JOHNSON

On the subject of spinach: divide into little piles. Rearrange again into new piles. After five of six manoeuvers, sit back and say you are full.
DELIA EPHRON

Lettuce is divine, although I'm not sure it's really a food.
DIANA VREELAND

I have no truck with lettuce, cabbage, and similar chlorophyll. Any dietitian will tell you that a running foot of apple strudel contains four times the vitamins of a bushel of beans.
S. J. PERELMAN Key writer on the *New Yorker* during the golden age, Perelman is regarded by many as America's best comic writer, the US equivalent to P. G. Wodehouse. His two screenplays for the Marx brothers (*Horse Feathers* and *Monkey Business*) are classics and his short pieces, or *feuilletons*, were admired by T. S. Eliot and Somerset Maugham. Their style had a huge influence on the writing and stand-up routines of Woody Allen.

An onion can make people cry, but there has never been a vegetable invented to make them laugh.
WILL ROGERS

A world without tomatoes is like a string quartet without violins.
LAURIE COLWIN

If there is one vegetable which is God-given, it is the haricot bean.
JEAN HENRI FABRE

I confess that nothing frightens me more than the appearance of

mushrooms on the table, especially in a small provincial town.
ALEXANDRE DUMAS

Vegetarianism

A mind of the calibre of mine cannot derive its nutriment from cows.
GEORGE BERNARD SHAW

I won't eat anything that has intelligent life, but I'd gladly eat a network executive or a politician.
MARTY FELDMAN

A vegetarian is a person who won't eat anything that can have children.
DAVID BRENNER

You put a baby in a crib with an apple and a rabbit. If it eats the rabbit and plays with the apple, I'll buy you a new car.
HARVEY DIAMOND

Caesar's armies marched on vegetarian foods.
WILL DURANT

I was a vegetarian until I started leaning toward the sunlight.
RITA RUDNER

I am not a vegetarian because I love animals; I am a vegetarian because I hate plants.
A. WHITNEY BROWN

Vegetarians have wicked, shifty eyes, and laugh in a cold calculating manner. They pinch little children, steal stamps, drink water, favour beards.
J. B. MORTON Better known as 'Beachcomber', he was the Clarkson of his day, fulminating amusingly in his daily column about modern art, socialism, schools, new inventions and playing practical jokes on friends. From 1924, he wrote one piece a day for the *Daily Express* for the next fifty-one years. He spent his final years alone, living on bread and jam.

If we aren't supposed to eat animals, then why are they made out of meat?
JO BRAND

My situation is a solemn one. Life is offered to me on condition of eating beefsteaks. But death is better than cannibalism. My will contains directions for my funeral, which will be followed not by mourning coaches, but by oxen, sheep, flocks of poultry, and a small

travelling aquarium of live fish, all wearing white scarves in honour of the man who perished rather than eat his fellow creatures.
GEORGE BERNARD SHAW

Violence

I'm a student of violence because I'm a student of the human heart.
SAM PECKINPAH

Anyone who clings to the historically untrue – and thoroughly immoral – doctrine that violence never solves anything I would advise to conjure up the ghosts of Napoleon Bonaparte and the Duke of Wellington and let them debate it. The ghost of Hitler would referee. Violence, naked force, has settled more issues in history than has any other factor; and the contrary opinion is wishful thinking at its worst. Breeds that forget this basic truth have always paid for it with their lives and their freedoms.
ROBERT A. HEINLEIN

Even within the most beautiful landscape, in the trees, under the leaves the insects are eating each other; violence is a part of life.
FRANCIS BACON

Virtue

Always do right. That will gratify some of the people and astonish the rest.
MARK TWAIN

He that does good for good's sake seeks neither paradise nor reward, but he is sure of both in the end.
WILLIAM PENN

Virtue has its own reward, but no box-office.
MAE WEST

Search others for their virtue, and yourself for your vices.
R. BUCKMINSTER FULLER

I have found that the best way to get another to acquire a virtue, is to impute it to him.
WINSTON CHURCHILL

A healthy appetite for righteousness, kept in due control by good

manners, is an excellent thing; but to 'hunger and thirst' after it is often merely a symptom of spiritual diabetes.
C.D. BROAD

Nothing is more unpleasant than a virtuous person with a mean mind.
WALTER BAGEHOT

He who is too busy doing good finds no time to be good.
RABINDRANATH TAGORE

To be able under all circumstances to practise five things constitutes perfect virtue; these five things are gravity, generosity of soul, sincerity, earnestness and kindness.
CONFUCIUS

W

War

War is God's way of teaching Americans geography.
AMBROSE BIERCE

Our bombs are smarter than the average high school student. At least they can find Kuwait.
A. WHITNEY BROWN

No bastard ever won a war by dying for his country. He won it by making the other poor, dumb bastard die for his.
GENERAL GEORGE S. PATTON

War is cruelty. There's no use trying to reform it. The crueller it is the sooner it will be over.
WILLIAM T. SHERMAN

To a surprising extent the war-lords in shining armour, the apostles of martial virtues, tend not to die fighting when the time comes. History is full of ignominious getaways by the great and famous.
GEORGE ORWELL

One of the main reasons that it is so easy to march men off to war is that each of them feels sorry for the man next to him who will die.
ERNEST BECKER He believed that human culture evolved to enable individuals to hide from their terror of death. His refusal to specialise meant rejection by academia, but the posthumous award for the 1971 Pulitzer Prize for his key book, *The Denial of Death*, gained him a broad and enthusiastic readership.

I can picture in my mind a world without war, a world without hate. And I can picture us attacking that world, because they'd never expect it.
JACK HANDEY

War is not nice.
BARBARA BUSH

Dulce bellum inexpertis. War is delightful to those who have no experience of it.
ERASMUS

There are only three principles of warfare: audacity, audacity and AUDACITY.
GENERAL GEORGE S. PATTON

One who conquers himself is greater than another who conquers a thousand times a thousand on the battlefield.
BUDDHA

The world began with war and will end with war.
ARABIC PROVERB

The condition of man . . . is a condition of war of everyone against everyone.
THOMAS HOBBES

There has never been a kingdom given to so many civil wars as the Kingdom of God.
CHARLES DE MONTESQUIEU

The Lord is a man of war.
EXODUS 15:3

On the night that the Second World War was declared, there were crowds in the street. It was a summer's night and there was a blackout. On every side you heard people crying: 'Look at the moon!' The moon had been there every minute of their lives and they'd never seen it.
LAURENS VAN DER POST

It takes 15,000 casualties to train a major-general.
MARSHAL FERDINAND FOCH

Battles are sometimes won by generals; wars are nearly always won by sergeants and privates.
F. E. ADCOCK

Probably the battle of Waterloo was won on the playing-fields of Eton, but the opening battles of all subsequent wars have been lost there.
GEORGE ORWELL

My dear, the noise! And the people!
ERNEST THESIGER In a letter to his brother on life in the trenches.

No words could express the beauty of it. The dreary dismal mud was baked white and pure – dazzling white. White daisies, red poppies and a blue flower, great masses of them, stretched for miles and miles. The sky a pure, dark blue and the whole air, up to a height of about forty feet, thick with white butterflies: your clothes were covered with butterflies. It was like an enchanted land, but in the place of fairies were thousands of little white crosses, marked 'Unknown British Soldier' for the most part.

WILLIAM ORPEN The war artist describes the Somme six months after the famous battle in 1917.

There will never be a nuclear war; there's too much real estate involved.

FRANK ZAPPA

As long as war is regarded as wicked, it will always have its fascination. When it is looked upon as vulgar, it will cease to be popular.

OSCAR WILDE

To subdue the enemy without fighting is the acme of skill.

SUNZI (SUN TZU)

Being in the army is like being in the Boy Scouts, except that the Boy Scouts have adult supervision.

BLAKE CLARK

I don't know what weapons World War Three will be fought with, but World War Four will be fought with sticks and stones.

ALBERT EINSTEIN

Water

Water is H_2O, hydrogen two parts, oxygen one, but there is a third thing that makes it water and nobody knows what that is.

D. H. LAWRENCE

Thousands have lived without love, not one without water.

W. H. AUDEN

Water is the only drink for a wise man.

HENRY DAVID THOREAU

Ever wonder about those people who spend $2 apiece on those little bottles of Evian water? Try spelling Evian backward.

GEORGE CARLIN

You know when you put a stick in the water and it looks like it's bent but really isn't? That's why I don't take baths.

STEVEN WRIGHT

The grand leap of the whale up the Fall of Niagara is esteemed, by all who have seen it, as one of the finest spectacles in nature.
BENJAMIN FRANKLIN From a 1765 letter to a London newspaper mocking English ignorance of the American colonies.

It would be more impressive if it flowed the other way.
OSCAR WILDE Commenting on Niagara Falls.

Expect poison from the standing water.
WILLIAM BLAKE

I bought some powdered water but I don't know what to add.
STEVEN WRIGHT

Wealth

Wealth is like sea-water; the more we drink, the thirstier we become.
ARTHUR SCHOPENHAUER

There is no wealth but life.
JOHN RUSKIN

It is better to have a permanent income than to be fascinating.
OSCAR WILDE

Who is rich? He that is content. Who is that? Nobody.
BENJAMIN FRANKLIN

No one can earn a million dollars honestly.
WILLIAM JENNINGS BRYAN

It isn't necessary to be rich and famous to be happy. It's only necessary to be rich.
ALAN ALDA

I will tell you the secret to getting rich on Wall Street. You try to be greedy when others are fearful. And you try to be fearful when others are greedy.
WARREN BUFFET

It's years since I gave a mink coat to anyone except a member of my own family.
LORD THOMSON OF FLEET

To suppose, as we all suppose, that we could be rich and not behave as the rich behave, is like supposing that we could drink all day and keep absolutely sober.
LOGAN PEARSALL SMITH

There is a serious defect in the thinking of someone who wants more than anything else to become rich. As long as they don't have the money, it'll seem like a worthwhile goal. Once they do, they'll understand how important other things are – and have always been.
BENJAMIN JOWETT Legendary teacher, trenchant theologian, influential classicist and master of Balliol College in Oxford, turning it into one of the most influential educational institutions of the nineteenth century and producing a string of Prime Ministers. His surname rhymes with 'know it'.

At the back of every great fortune lies a great crime.
HONORÉ DE BALZAC

Never esteem men on account of their riches or their station. Respect goodness, find it where you may.
WILLIAM COBBETT

Riches appear to me not at all necessary; but competence, I think, is.
SIR HUMPHREY DAVY

One can see the respect God has for riches by the people he gives them to.
ALEXANDER POPE

Someday I want to be rich. Some people get so rich, they lose all respect for humanity. That's how rich I want to be.
RITA RUDNER

Weather

There are seven or eight categories of phenomena in the world worth talking about, and one of them is weather.
ANNIE DILLARD A writer who has assumed the Thoreau mantle. Her most famous book, *Pilgrim at Tinker Creek* (1975), followed a period of illness, and she spent a year filing twenty volumes of notes about her solitary life in rural Virginia. It won her the Pulitzer Prize. A convert to Roman Catholicism, she calls it a 'book of theology'.

To an outsider, the most striking thing about the English weather is that there is not very much of it.
BILL BRYSON

Sunshine is delicious, rain is refreshing, wind braces us up, snow is exhilarating; there is really no such thing as bad weather, only different kinds of good weather.
JOHN RUSKIN

There is no such thing as bad weather, only inappropriate clothing.
SIR RANULPH FIENNES

Don't knock the weather; nine-tenths of the people couldn't start a
conversation if it didn't change once in a while.
FRANK 'KIN' HUBBARD

Climate is what you expect, weather is what you get.
ROBERT A. HEINLEIN

No matter how rich you become, how famous or powerful, when you
die the size of your funeral will still pretty much depend on the
weather.
MICHAEL PRITCHARD

In Minnesota it's so cold some nights you have to wear two condoms.
BRUCE LANSKY

Weeds

What is a weed? A plant whose virtues have not yet been discovered.
RALPH WALDO EMERSON

They know, they just know where to grow, how to dupe you, and how
to camouflage themselves among the perfectly respectable plants, they
just know, and therefore, I've concluded weeds must have brains.
DIANNE BENSON

Make no mistake, the weeds will win, nature bats last.
ROBERT MICHAEL PYLE

Whisky

Whisky is liquid sunshine.
GEORGE BERNARD SHAW

My favourite drink is a cocktail of carrot juice and whisky. I am always
drunk but I can see for miles.
ROY 'CHUBBY' BROWN

No married man is genuinely happy if he has to drink worse whisky
than he used to drink when he was single.
H. L. MENCKEN

I love to sing, and I love to drink scotch. Most people would rather hear
me drink scotch.
GEORGE BURNS

I'm on a whisky diet. I've lost three days already!
TOMMY COOPER

Wind

The wind shows us how close to the edge we are.
JOAN DIDION

A man should learn to sail in all winds.
ITALIAN PROVERB

When everything seems to be going against you, remember that the
airplane takes off against the wind, not with it.
HENRY FORD

Kites rise highest against the wind, not with it.
WINSTON CHURCHILL

Good timber does not grow with ease; the stronger the wind the
stronger the trees.
DOUGLAS MALLOCH

Windows

Every time I close the door on reality it comes in through the windows.
JENNIFER UNLIMITED The nom de plume of Jennifer Yane, a fine artist from
Richmond, Virginia who specialises in using her designs on buttons (or badges as
they are known in the UK). This quote is from her website and has spread, virus-like,
across the web.

When God closes the door, He opens the window.
ITALIAN PROVERB

Our dream dashes itself against the great mystery like a wasp against a
window. Less merciful than man, God never opens the window.
JULES RENARD

Instead of a trap door, what about a trap window? The guy looks out of
it, and if he leans too far, he falls out. Wait. I guess that's like a regular
window.
JACK HANDEY

She was a blonde. The kind of blonde that would make a bishop
kick in a stained glass window.
RAYMOND CHANDLER

People are like stained-glass windows. They sparkle and shine when the sun is out, but when the darkness sets in, their true beauty is revealed only if there is a light from within.
ELIZABETH KÜBLER-ROSS

If God lived on earth, people would break his windows.
JEWISH PROVERB

Wine

Wine is sunlight, held together by water.
GALILEO GALILEI

Wine is bottled poetry.
ROBERT LOUIS STEVENSON

Why do people say it is so prosaic to be inspired by wine. Has it not been made by the sunlight and the sap?
WILLIAM MORRIS

Great people talk about ideas, average people talk about things, and small people talk about wine.
FRAN LEBOWITZ

A good general rule is to state that the bouquet is better than the taste, and vice versa.
STEPHEN POTTER

Burgundy makes you think of silly things; Bordeaux makes you talk about them, and Champagne makes you do them.
JEAN ANTHELME BRILLAT-SAVARIN

Before Noah, men having only water to drink, could not find the truth. Accordingly, they became abominably wicked, and they were justly exterminated by the water they loved to drink. This good man, Noah, having seen that all his contemporaries had perished by this un-pleasant drink, took a dislike to it; and God, to relieve his dryness, created the vine and revealed to him the art of making le vin. By the aid of this liquid he unveiled more and more truth.
BENJAMIN FRANKLIN

The best wine is the oldest, the best water the newest.
WILLIAM BLAKE

A man who was fond of wine was offered some grapes at dessert after dinner. 'Much obliged,' said he, pushing the plate aside; 'I am not

accustomed to take my wine in pills.'
JEAN ANTHELME BRILLAT-SAVARIN

Wisdom

Those who love wisdom must investigate many things.
HERACLITUS

There are many who know many things, yet are lacking in wisdom.
DEMOCRITUS

Wisdom comes by disillusionment.
GEORGE SANTAYANA

True wisdom is less presuming than folly. The wise man doubteth often, and changeth his mind; the fool is obstinate, and doubteth not; he knoweth all things but his own ignorance.
AKHENATEN Enigmatic husband to Nefertiti and father to Tutankhamen, he established Egypt's first monotheistic religion. He has been called the first 'individual' in history, as he is the first historical person whose actual ideas and beliefs we can evaluate. A theory, enthusiastically endorsed by Sigmund Freud, suggests that Moses founded Judaism having first served as priest in Akhenaten's faith.

Where fear is present, wisdom cannot be.
LACTANTIUS North African Christian apologist active in the fourth century AD and sometimes referred to as 'the Christian Cicero', perhaps because his style was rather more arresting than his ideas.

Wisdom comes from experience. Experience is often a result of lack of wisdom.
TERRY PRATCHETT

All wisdom can be stated in two lines:
What is done for you – allow it to be done.
What you must do for yourself – make sure you do it.
ALI AL-KHAWWAS

We don't receive wisdom; we must discover it for ourselves after a journey that no one can take for us or spare us.
MARCEL PROUST

Wisdom doesn't necessarily come with age. Sometimes age just shows up all by itself.
TOM WILSON

He swallowed a lot of wisdom, but it seemed as if all of it had gone down the wrong way.
G. C. LICHTENBERG

Though wisdom cannot be gotten with gold, still less can it be gotten without it.
SAMUEL BUTLER

Knowledge is proud that he has learned so much, wisdom is humble that he knows no more.
WILLIAM COWPER

It's so simple to be wise. Just think of something stupid to say, and then don't say it.
SAM LEVENSON

The wise are always at peace.
ARABIC PROVERB

The wise man can pick up a grain of sand and envision a whole universe. But the stupid man will just lay down on some seaweed and roll around until he's completely draped in it. Then he'll stand up and go, 'Hey, I'm Vine Man.'
JACK HANDEY

Ninety percent of all human wisdom is the ability to mind your own business.
ROBERT A. HEINLEIN

Keep me away from the wisdom which does not cry, the philosophy which does not laugh and the greatness which does not bow before children.
KAHLIL GIBRAN

Wit

Wit lies in recognising the resemblance among things which differ and the difference between things which are alike.
MADAME DE STAËL

Wit is the rarest quality to be met with among people of education, and the most common among the uneducated.
WILLIAM HAZLITT

A witty saying proves nothing.
VOLTAIRE

You can pretend to be serious; you can't pretend to be witty.
SACHA GUITRY

Women

I hate women because they always know where things are.
JAMES THURBER

Women rule the world. No man has ever done anything that a woman hasn't either allowed him to do, or encouraged him to do.
BOB DYLAN

I love those decadent wenches who do so trouble my dreams.
REMBRANDT

A woman, especially if she has the misfortune of knowing anything, should conceal it as well as she can.
JANE AUSTEN

Biologically speaking, if something bites you, it's more likely to be female.
DESMOND MORRIS

I think it's OK for a woman to have a fine cleavage and sleep around.
PAMELA HARRIMAN Influential socialite who married and divorced Churchill's son Randolph and whose subsequent liaisons with rich and powerful men gained her the reputation as 'the twentieth century's greatest courtesan'. President Clinton made her his ambassador to France in 1993 and she became the first female foreign diplomat to receive the Légion d'honneur.

I have lived and slept in the same bed with English countesses and Prussian farm women . . . no woman has excited passions among women more than I have.
FLORENCE NIGHTINGALE In fact, it seems likely the mother superior of modern nursing died a virgin. After her eighteen months in the Crimea she hardly got out of bed for the next fifty-three years, struck down by some form of 'nervous illness'. However, she continued to work hard and productively from her bed until her death, producing 200 publications and 13,000 letters.

I don't know whether you've ever had a woman eat an apple while you were doing it. Well, you can imagine how that affects you.
HENRY MILLER

A woman should never be seen eating or drinking, unless it be lobster, salad and champagne. The only true feminine and becoming viands.
LORD BYRON

Can you recall a woman who ever showed you with pride her library?
BENJAMIN DE CASSERES

The years that a woman subtracts from her age are not lost. They are added to other women's.
DIANE DE POITIERS

Even when they meet in the street, women look at each other like Guelphs and Ghibellines.
ARTHUR SCHOPENHAUER

A woman is like a tea bag. It's only when she's in hot water that you realize how strong she is.
NANCY REAGAN Sometimes also attributed to Eleanor Roosevelt.

One can, to an almost laughable degree, infer what a man's wife is like from his opinions about women in general.
JOHN STUART MILL

Most men who rail against women are railing at one woman only.
RÉMY DE GOURMONT

Women are like elephants to me; they're nice to look at but I wouldn't want to own one.
W. C. FIELDS

Next to the wound, what women make best is the bandage.
BARBEY D'AUREVILLY

All the books extolling the simple life are written by men.
WILLIAM FEATHER

To be a woman is something so strange, so confusing, and so complicated that only a woman could put up with it.
SØREN KIERKEGAARD

Words

Wishing to entice the blind,
The Buddha playfully let words escape from his golden mouth;
Heaven and earth are filled, ever since, with entangling briars.
DAI-O KOKUSHI

When ideas fail, words come in very handy.
GOETHE

Words are loaded pistols.
JEAN-PAUL SARTRE

Sticks and stones may break our bones, but words will break our hearts.
ROBERT FULGHUM

The trouble with words is that you never know whose mouths they've been in.
DENNIS POTTER

Words, like eyeglasses, blur everything that they do not make clearer.
JOSEPH JOUBERT

It is with words as with sunbeams: the more they are condensed, the deeper they burn.
ROBERT SOUTHEY

The coldest word was once a glowing new metaphor.
THOMAS CARLYLE

Short words are best and the old words when short are best of all.
WINSTON CHURCHILL

Always and never are two words you should always remember never to use.
WENDELL JOHNSON

The two most beautiful words in the English language are 'Cheque enclosed'.
DOROTHY PARKER

The three most beautiful words in the English language are 'It is benign'.
WOODY ALLEN

Lord, give us the wisdom to utter words that are gentle and tender, for tomorrow we may have to eat them.
SENATOR MORRIS UDALL Better known as Mo, an American politician and former basketball star, who narrowly missed out to Jimmy Carter in the Democratic Presidential nomination of 1976. He was noted for his quick wit; one columnist suggested at the time that he was 'too funny to be President'.

In the course of my life, I have often had to eat my words, and I must confess that I have always found it a wholesome diet.
WINSTON CHURCHILL

The right word may be effective, but no word was ever as effective as a rightly timed pause.
MARK TWAIN

Work

Work is the province of cattle.
DOROTHY PARKER

While none of the work we do is very important, it is important that we do a great deal of it.
JOSEPH HELLER

Personally, I have nothing against work, particularly when performed quietly and unobtrusively by someone else.
BARBARA EHRENREICH

I like work. It fascinates me. I can sit and look at it for hours.
JEROME K. JEROME

I never did a day's work in my life. It was all fun.
THOMAS EDISON

If a chap can't compose an epic poem while he is weaving a tapestry, he had better shut up.
WILLIAM MORRIS Poet, painter, engraver, weaver, dyer, designer, printer, retailer and revolutionary, when he died in 1896 his physician attributed his demise to 'his simply being William Morris, and having done more work than most ten men'.

They say hard work never hurt anybody, but I figure why take the chance.
RONALD REAGAN

Appealing workplaces are to be avoided. One wants a room with no view, so imagination can meet memory in the dark.
ANNIE DILLARD

No man who is concerned in doing a very difficult thing, and doing it well, ever loses his self-respect.
GEORGE BERNARD SHAW

One of the symptoms of an approaching nervous breakdown is the belief that one's work is terribly important.
BERTRAND RUSSELL

I was obliged to be industrious. Whoever is equally industrious will succeed equally well.
J. S. BACH

The reward for work well done is the opportunity to do more.
JONAS SALK He developed the polio vaccine in 1955 and refused to patent it.

My grandfather once told me that there are two kinds of people: those who do the work and those who take the credit. He told me to try to be in the first group; there was less competition there.
INDIRA GANDHI

In order that people may be happy in their work, these three things are needed: They must be fit for it. They must not do too much of it. And they must have a sense of success in it.
JOHN RUSKIN

Basically, I no longer work for anything but the sensation I have while working.
ALBERTO GIACOMETTI

When I work I relax. Doing nothing makes me tired.
PABLO PICASSO

Blessed is he who has found his work. Let him ask no other blessing.
THOMAS CARLYLE

Anyone can do any amount of work, provided it isn't the work he is supposed to be doing at the moment.
ROBERT BENCHLEY

The better work men do is always done under stress and at great personal cost.
WILLIAM CARLOS WILLIAMS

What you do instead of your work is your real work.
ROGER EBERT America's most influential film critic in print and on TV, the first to win a Pulitzer Prize for writing on film and the first to receive a star on the Hollywood Walk of Fame.

Well, we can't stand around here doing nothing, people will think we're workmen.
SPIKE MILLIGAN

Worry

A day of worry is more exhausting than a week of work.
JOHN LUBBOCK

It is not work that kills men; it is worry. Work is healthy; you can hardly put more on a man than he can bear. Worry is rust upon the blade. It is not the revolution that destroys the machinery, but the friction.
HENRY WARD BEECHER

Worry is a sustained form of fear caused by indecision.
BRIAN TRACY

We are, perhaps, uniquely among the earth's creatures, the worrying animal. We worry away our lives, fearing the future, discontent with the present, unable to take in the idea of dying, unable to sit still.
LEWIS THOMAS

We experience moments absolutely free of worry. These brief respites are called panic.
CULLEN HIGHTOWER

Writing

Of all the fatiguing, futile, empty trades, the worst, I suppose, is writing about writing.
HILAIRE BELLOC

Writing is the geometry of the soul.
PLATO

Bunyan spent a year in prison, Coleridge was a drug addict, Poe was an alcoholic, Marlowe was killed by a man he was trying to stab, Pope took a large sum of money to keep a woman's name out of a vicious satire and then wrote it so that she could be recognized anyway, Chatterton killed himself, Somerset Maugham was so unhappy in his final thirty years that he longed for death . . . do you still want to be a writer?
BENNETT CERF Known to children throughout the world as the author of *The Book of Riddles*, he was also one of the twentieth century's most important publishers, founding Random House in 1927 – 'We just said we were going to publish a few books on the side at random' – responsible for the first US publication of Joyce's *Ulysses* in 1934, and the discoveries of Dr Seuss, James Michener and Truman Capote.

Everywhere I go I'm asked if I think the university stifles writers. My opinion is that they don't stifle enough of them.
FLANNERY O'CONNOR

On the day when a young writer corrects his first proof sheets, he is as proud as a schoolboy who has just got his first dose of pox.
CHARLES BAUDELAIRE

Some editors are failed writers, but so are most writers.
T. S. ELIOT

Should not the Society of Indexers be known as Indexers, Society of, The?
KEITH WATERHOUSE

Writing is so difficult that I often feel that writers, having had their hell on earth, will escape all punishment hereafter.
JESSAMYN WEST

It took me fifteen years to discover that I had no talent for writing, but I couldn't give up because by that time I was too famous.
PETER BENCHLEY Son of the less famous, more talented Robert, his 1974 novel, *Jaws*, was a best-seller before Spielberg transformed it into one of the most influential movies ever made, the first summer blockbuster.

You can't help respecting anybody who can spell TUESDAY, even if he doesn't spell it right; but spelling isn't everything.
A. A. MILNE Rabbit about Owl in *Winnie the Pooh*.

I don't give a damn for a man that can only spell a word one way.
MARK TWAIN

How vain it is to sit down to write, when you have not stood up to live!
HENRY DAVID THOREAU

Great novels are always a little more intelligent than their authors.
MILAN KUNDERA

The best kind of writing, and the biggest thrill in writing, is to suddenly read a line from your typewriter that you didn't know was in you.
LARRY L. KING

Look in thy heart and write.
SIR PHILIP SIDNEY

A novel should cater for the fact that life is mostly confusion, that most people's inner sense is of not knowing, rather than knowing.
GRAHAM SWIFT

Two people writing a novel is like three people having a baby.
EVELYN WAUGH

Finishing a book is just like you took a child out in the back yard and shot it.
TRUMAN CAPOTE

He that writes to himself writes to an eternal public. That statement only is fit to be made public which you have come at in attempting to satisfy your own curiosity.
RALPH WALDO EMERSON

Close the door. Write with no one looking over your shoulder. Don't try to figure out what other people want to hear from you; figure out what you have to say. It's the one and only thing you have to offer.
BARBARA KINGSOLVER

If a writer has to rob his mother he will not hesitate; the *Ode on a Grecian Urn* is worth any number of old ladies.
WILLIAM FAULKNER

It is a delicious thing to write, to be no longer yourself but to move in an entire universe of your own creation. Today, for example, as man and woman, both lover and mistress, I rode in a forest on an autumn afternoon under the yellow leaves, and I was also the horses, the leaves, the wind, the words my people uttered, even the red sun that made them almost close their love-drowned eyes. When I brood over these marvellous pleasures I have enjoyed, I would be tempted to offer God a prayer of thanks if I knew he could hear me. Praised may he be for not creating me a cotton merchant, a vaudevillian, or a wit.
GUSTAVE FLAUBERT

When we encounter a natural style we are always surprised and delighted, for we thought to see an author and found a man.
BLAISE PASCAL

When I see a paragraph shrinking under my eyes like a strip of bacon in a skillet, I know I'm on the right track.
PETER DE VRIES

The language of truth is simple.
EURIPIDES

To write simply is as difficult as to be good.
W. SOMERSET MAUGHAM

If there is a book you want to read but it hasn't been written yet, then you must write it.
TONI MORRISON

Why do writers write? Because it isn't there.
THOMAS BERGER

I'm all in favor of keeping dangerous weapons out of the hands of fools. Let's start with typewriters.
FRANK LLOYD WRIGHT

I heard someone tried the monkeys-on-typewriters bit trying for the

plays of W. Shakespeare, but all they got was the collected works of Francis Bacon.
BILL HIRST

The difference between an author and a horse is that the horse doesn't understand the horse dealer's language.
MAX FRISCH Telling it how it is for authors and publishers.

A publisher who writes is like a cow in a milk bar.
ARTHUR KOESTLER

Who is more real? Homer or Ulysses? Shakespeare or Hamlet? Burroughs or Tarzan?
ROBERT A. HEINLEIN

Y

Yes and No

In Yes and No all things consist.
JAKOB BÖHME

I only have 'yes' men around me. Who needs 'no' men?
MAE WEST

Never allow a person to tell you no who doesn't have the power to say yes.
ELEANOR ROOSEVELT

The formula for my happiness: a Yes, a No, a straight line, a goal.
FRIEDRICH NIETZSCHE

The art of leadership is saying no, not saying yes. It is very easy to say yes.
TONY BLAIR

To say yes, you have to sweat and roll up your sleeves and plunge both hands into life up to the elbows. It is easy to say no, even if saying no means death.
JEAN ANOUILH

Go not to the elves for counsel, for they will say both no and yes.
J. R. R. TOLKIEN

Youth

The problem with the youth of today is that one is no longer part of it.
SALVADOR DALÍ

There's nothing worse than being an ageing young person.
RICHARD PRYOR

The cheerfulness and vivacity of youth are partly due to the fact that when we are ascending the hill of life, death is not visible; it lies down at the bottom of the other side.
ARTHUR SCHOPENHAUER

The secret of staying young is to live honestly, eat slowly, and lie about your age.
LUCILLE BALL

A museum . . . oftenest induces the feeling that nothing could ever have been young.
WALTER PATER

Z

Zen

Be soft in your practice. Think of the method as a fine silvery stream, not a raging waterfall. Follow the stream, have faith in its course. It will go its own way, meandering here, trickling there. It will find the grooves, the cracks, the crevices. Just follow it.
SHENG-YEN

Zen is not some kind of excitement, but concentration on our usual everyday routine.
ROSHI SUZUKI

Even to speak the word Buddha is dragging in the mud soaking wet. Even to say the word Zen is a total embarrassment.
THE BLUE CLIFF RECORD A collection of Buddhist koans compiled in China in 1125. Koans are the main currency of Buddhist teaching: enigmatic phrases, questions or fragments of story that contain a truth that may not be immediately obvious, and may (or may not) require a response.

The only Zen you find on the tops of mountains is the Zen you bring up there.
ROBERT M. PIRSIG

I'd like to offer something to help you but in the Zen school we don't have a single thing!
IKKYU Zen Buddhist famed for his eccentricity. He was a great calligrapher, helped to invent the formal tea ceremony and believed consorting with prostitutes was a legitimate route to enlightenment.

In the midst of this pageant of personality, this hail of epigrams, who will hear the bang or the whimper when it comes?

Who will care?

QUENTIN CRISP How to Have a Lifestyle (1975)

Index

ff

Faber and Faber – a home for writers

Faber and Faber is one of the great independent publishing houses in London. We were established in 1929 by Geoffrey Faber and our first editor was T. S. Eliot. We are proud to publish prize-winning fiction and non-fiction, as well as an unrivalled list of modern poets and playwrights. Among our list of writers we have five Booker Prize winners and eleven Nobel Laureates, and we continue to seek out the most exciting and innovative writers at work today.

www.faber.co.uk – a home for readers

The Faber website is a place where you will find all the latest news on our writers and events. You can listen to podcasts, preview new books, read specially commissioned articles and access reading guides, as well as entering competitions and enjoying a whole range of offers and exclusives. You can also browse the list of Faber Finds, an exciting new project where reader recommendations are helping to bring a wealth of lost classics back into print using the latest on-demand technology.